Shared Roots

Shared Roots

Tales from the Indosphere

Curated by

Ratul Chakraborty

ink | OCCAM

ISBN: 978-93-92209-75-8

First published in India 2024
This edition published 2024

BluOne Ink Pvt. Ltd
A-76, 2nd Floor, Sector 136, Noida
Uttar Pradesh 201301
www.bluone.ink
publisher@bluone.ink

Printed and bound in India at Sanat Printers

ink | OCCAM

To the unrivalled chisel of the Hindu temple sculptor,
carving eternity out of stone

Contents

Curator's Note

This anthology is not an exercise in historical jingoism. Our intent is not to lay claim to any sort of cultural ancestry. It is important to state this clearly at the outset to avoid any misunderstandings.

I embarked on this journey a year and a half back, when Hari Kiran *garu*, the founder of Indic Academy, called me up one morning and proposed this idea. To be honest, I needed some time to fully warm up to the concept. If I were to commit to this, I needed to find an answer to a most fundamental question: Why does this book need to exist?

I opened my browser and typed 'Cambodia' on the search bar.

श्रीसिद्धि स्वस्ति जय नमः परमेस्वराय।
निष्कलाय स्वभावेन स्वेच्छया धृतमूर्तये॥
शिवाय परमेशाय नमोऽस्तु परमत्मने॥१॥
येनैकेनाप्यनेकेषु तिष्ठता युगपत् पृथक्।
आत्मापि क्रियते नित्यं तस्मै शूलभृते नमः॥२॥

Sri Siddhi Swasti Jai Namah Parameswaraya.
Selfless nature, voluntary idols.

Shivay Parmeshay Namostu Paramatmane||1||
Yenaikenapynekeshu tishthata yugapat abhyaya.
Atmapi kriyate nityam tasmai shulbhrite namah||2||[1]

This invocation to Lord Shiva is inscribed on a stele in the temple of Prah Ko in the Siem Reap District of Cambodia. It goes on to eulogise King Indravarman, lists out the gifts given by him on the occasion of establishing statues of Shiva and Devi—palanquins, golden shields, cows, buffalos, and artistes among other things—and ends with a warning to potential thieves and a salutation to loyal benefactors. Dated 801 CE, this Sanskrit inscription is but one among the countless memory capsules that serve to remind us that, for millennia, a unique bond connected the vast expanse between the Indus and the Mekong.

This civilisational link between India and Cambodia is perhaps one of the greatest examples of a robust non-colonial cultural exchange between two nations. Instead of power and profit, it was a shared sense of dharma that underpinned the magnificent tapestry of this civilisation, its glorious patterns woven by kings and adventurers, priests and traders, artisans and farmers, artists and philosophers, by *people* using the twin threads of commerce and culture.

The impact of this cultural unity is visible to us even today. The exquisite verses of the Reamker tell the eternal story of Preah Ream or Lord Rama. The gorgeous Lakhon Khol dance dramas recount the exploits of Hanuman. The awe-inspiring majesty of the Angkor Wat recreates the glory of Mount Meru itself. Even the quintessential morning greeting, *Arun Susdai*, has its roots in Sanskrit—the same Sanskrit used to inscribe the faith and the glory of Cambodian monarchs on the countless temples built by them.

The more I came across the evidence, the more I could visualise a magical land that scarcely felt real in the present context, a cultural continuum connected by Dharma, flowering with diversity.

The linguist James Matisoff named it the Indosphere.

You see, it was a real place. It is still a real place. Go to any old temple in the Indian subcontinent or in Southeast Asia, touch its walls, and close your eyes. Listen very closely, and you will feel its presence—perhaps faint, perhaps dying, but still living.

I had finally found my answer.

Shared Roots is a dream, maybe a silly, foolish dream. Nonetheless, it is a dream that burns so intensely it makes the heart ache. To show the world that a better way to engage with people was—no, *is* possible. To remind people that a culture founded on the principles of dharma has the strength to unite and assimilate generations in a manner that is global in thought but intensely local in form. To give our present-day readers the means to imagine what a truly diverse civilisation looks like.

Perhaps if we all remember the Indosphere, it will emerge again, brushing off the centuries of cobwebs and becoming more and more real to the naked eye. Preposterous perhaps, but certainly worth a try, don't you think?

Let this book be a tiny step towards that worthwhile goal. The Indosphere must be revitalised, if not in our lifetimes, then in our children's. The fate of this planet depends upon it.

It was my good fortune to be able to embark on this journey with some extraordinarily talented authors. I thank them for their patience throughout the long gestation period and beg their forgiveness for any frustration that may have risen during the intense creative process.

I thank Shri Michael Thorn for painstakingly editing this anthology.

I would like to thank Shri Otis Haschemyer for his valuable feedback to all the authors and Shri Abhinav Agarwal for helping to arrange the feedback sessions under the auspices of Indic Book Club.

I would like to thank Shri Hari Kiran Vadlamani for being a constant pillar of support throughout this endeavour.

Finally, I would like to thank our ancestors, the original citizens of the Indosphere, for leaving us the enduring cultural legacy that is now a beacon of light in a darkening world.

Like all things worth doing, our labours are a humble offering at the feet of Ma Saraswati. May she bless us all.

Ratul Chakraborty
Kolkata, October 2023

1

Strei[1]

Srivalli Rekha

Every carving is a story waiting to be told

1923, Angkor

She crept along the blackened walls of the *wat* (temple), hiding amongst the thick vegetation that no one cared to clear. The first star of the night shone in the twilight sky, a guiding sign for her to follow. Sreymau skipped up the broken steps and disappeared into a dark opening. Removing the tattered *krama*[2] covering her head and shoulders, she thought it was strange to find a French soldier guarding the entrance.

The temple was in ruins and had been left to rot by the French protectorate. The secret meeting place was the only clean part of the ancient, abandoned temple compound, courtesy of her lover. Sreymau slipped inside from the other entrance but could not stop thinking about the sudden appearance of the guard. She leant back on the walls with a soft sigh. Sorya had said he would be late to meet her. They had grown more corn on the farm where he worked, and things had been busier than ever. At least, people would have enough to eat.

'Moon!' Sorya called out, announcing his entry. Sreymau smiled into the night. It always amazed Sreymau that he called her his moon when she was dark as a new moon night. Even her name reflected her skin tone. Yet to him, she was brighter than a full moon.

He sat down beside her with a deep sigh and rested his head on her shoulder. Sreymau ruffled his hair. The coarse texture was a result of slaving in open farms to serve the French masters.

'Did you see the guard?' she whispered.

'I almost came upon him when I saw a shadow and turned back.'

'Do you know why he's here?'

'Maybe they want to use this place,' Sorya said, a heartbeat later.

Sreymau sat up straight and glared. 'For what? Isn't it enough that they stole our land?'

'I don't know, Moon.' He shrugged and hugged her close. 'If they can find a way to provide more food for the hungry bellies, I don't mind. Father can't work anymore, and we don't have enough to pay the taxes for the year. This place doesn't help anyone … except us.'

'But I like it. I come here early sometimes to see the carvings. I … they make me feel safe and happy … like you do,' Sreymau protested.

'Let's not worry yet.'

A sudden sound startled them. Sreymau pressed a hand to her mouth to stop a yelp from escaping. Sorya gestured for her to stay put and crawled out of the opening to investigate. She followed behind to see a blurry yellow light a few metres away.

'That's the new Frenchman,' Sorya whispered.

'Oliver … something. Mother said he was snooping around,' Sreymau responded.

They stared as the new Frenchman—the one with an elite designation and strange expression—dug and poked around as if searching for something in the soil. It annoyed Sreymau. Wasn't it enough that he was messing about all day? Why did he have to come in the dark too?

Then it struck her. He must have posted the guard. But *why*?

She saw that Oliver had picked up four exquisite *devata*s (idols of gods and goddesses) from the earth. He dusted them with a cloth and tucked them into a bag. Sreymau noticed the grin on his face when the lantern swung from his arm. It was the expression of superiority she loathed, the kind found only on their pale white and red faces. He whistled to himself and walked away, carrying the treasures that belonged to none but the land.

'Thief!' Sreymau hissed.

'What if he has permission? That guard, you know—' Sorya tried to calm her.

'I don't care. He and them … all these French people are thieves. I'm tired of them stealing from us.'

'Me too, Moon. But you know we can't get involved in this. Let's go now. I have to start before dawn tomorrow, and you look hungry.'

Sreymau nodded, not wanting to argue with him. She knew he was trying to make light of the situation, but it didn't help her mood. The sudden unease confused and scared her. She didn't realise when the restless urge to fight began to claw her insides. Sreymau had been submissive for all the eighteen years of her life. The constant oppression was suffocating her now, and she wanted to break free. She didn't know how yet.

'Damn you, nasty Frenchmen. I'll find a way to make you pay for what you did.'

967 CE, Angkor

Davuth could never get enough of the marvellous architecture in his kingdom. He stared at the carving of a lion on the court pillar as people jostled around him. He held his cloth bag to his chest to protect his tools. Someone knocked him into the hard pillar and murmured an apology before moving away. Davuth didn't bother to acknowledge it. He liked the feel of the carving pressed against his face. The rock was smooth with the outline of the lion highlighted in precise strokes. Davuth was confident that his sculptures would also be praised by future generations. He had been learning and carving for most of his twenty years on earth.

The overflowing crowd made it hard to stay close to the pillar for long. The murmurings got louder as people arranged themselves in the gaps.

Someone whispered behind him, 'Will our king, Rajendravarman II, grace the throne today?'

'I don't know. I hope we can see him. He has been on the battlefield for a long time now.'

Davuth recalled his grandmother's words about the king: He was a diamond in body, thought, and mind—a warrior who knew how to win. That was why Davuth had sculpted a four-inch figurine of the king and taken it with him to the fort. Artists were respected and encouraged to display their talents. The king or the ministers wouldn't stop him. But Davuth didn't want to show the figurine when the king was not on the throne. It wouldn't be the same, after all.

He turned to them and said, 'I also hope he is back at the fort. Let's go to the front.'

The trio pushed their way forward just in time to see the minister Yajnavaraha appear on the dais. The throne was empty. Davuth's shoulder sagged in disappointment. He would have to wait longer.

Six feet tall, Yajnavaraha cut an imposing figure. He wasn't as commanding as the king but had the persona to control his audience. The minister was a friend to the good and a foe to the bad, much like the king. Rajendravarman II made the decisions, and the minister ensured that they were implemented. Yajnavaraha clapped twice, and the hall fell silent.

'Our beloved king is fighting the enemies to keep us safe. Rest assured, we will safeguard the Khmer Empire from greedy hands. However, our gathering today is for another reason. The king sent a message, asking us to take up a divine cause. He wants us to build a wat for Shiva to bless our land with prosperity and happiness.'

The crowd roared with delight. Davuth cheered up, making plans right away. He would work in this wat, sculpt the devatas, and etch the tales of his favourite text, the Ramayana, on the walls. He could already see the wat in his mind and knew that the minister would give them full freedom to design it as they wished. He would be hailed for sculpting life-like devatas on the walls.

Davuth had to pause his daydreaming when the minister raised his hand and continued with the announcement. 'We will call it Tribhuvanamahesvara Wat, and it will be constructed in Isvarapura. The head sculptors from our kingdom have finalised the basic details. This announcement is also an invitation for all sculptors to step forward and join the pious mission.'

The minister let his message sink in before continuing. 'Many of you know of our good relations with the great Chola empire across the sea. Their king, Sundara Chola, is the grandson of the notable king Parantaka I who ordered the building of temples like Shivayoginathar Temple. The trade relations between the kingdoms have prospered into friendship and trust that makes the Cholas good allies and supporters of the Khmer Empire. As you already know, we have priests from the Chola land taking care of Shiva in our temples and mentoring our young minds.

'To continue the gesture of goodwill, King Sundara Chola sent his best wishes and families of sculptors to help our artists in constructing the Tribhuvanamahesvara Wat. The boats reached our shores a few days ago. Let us welcome our guests of honour and show them the beauty of the Khmer kingdom and its kind-hearted subjects.'

Deafening cheers erupted in the court as a group of well-dressed men and women entered through the wide arched doorway. The crowd parted, clapping and smiling at the guests. Davuth clapped too, his eyes eagerly scanning the newcomers. He approved the sturdy build of the men in contrast to their slender yet rough fingers. The hands of a sculptor told everything one needed to know. He was also impressed by the soft shine of the clothes they wore.

The group bowed to the minister and the crowd with their palms together to say *namaskaram*. Appraising their colourful *dhovati*s[3] and sarees, Davuth's eyes landed on a young woman in a pale green saree. Davuth took in the young woman's thick hair, braided down to her waist, and her skin, which was the colour of damp earth. Her fingers were calloused, and Davuth wondered if she could sculpt. He knew a couple of girls who learnt alongside him, though they were nowhere near being close to his talent.

The young woman looked at Davuth and smiled. His breath caught in his chest. Her onyx-coloured eyes gleamed, dimming the glitter of her jewellery. Davuth had never seen anyone as beautiful as her. He felt the word didn't do justice to the young woman. She was the brightest gem in the king's crown. Her features looked as if they were sculpted by an artist. Davuth was in love with her even without knowing her name.

'Greetings from Thanjavur to the mighty king, the respectable ministers, and the good people of Khmer.'

A bulky man stepped forward from the group to make a speech.

'Our beloved king, Sundara Chola, has entrusted us with a momentous task, and we hope to live up to the expectations and worthiness of the love you have shown us. Let us bring Shiva from Kailasa to Isvarapura. Om Namah Shivaya!'

The chants reverberated in the packed court. The minister looked pleased, and the crowd cheered for the guests. Davuth continued to stare at the young woman, his mind racing ahead. He envisioned himself at the construction site, becoming friends with the newcomers, talking to his lady love, and showcasing his sculpting expertise.

'The artists will travel to Isvarapura in seven days. May your preparations begin.' The minister ended his announcement with a wave of his hand. The crowd began to disperse. The group from Thanjavur were being escorted to their temporary homes by the guards. Davuth lingered until he lost sight of the young woman and walked back home with his mind full of thoughts and ideas.

1923, Angkor

Sreymau couldn't be still. Three days passed, blending into one another, each no different from the previous or the next. She thought of the devatas removed from their original place and glared at the weeds threatening the crops. The weeds were just like the French, seemingly inconspicuous in the beginning and then taking over the land. Sreymau pushed her trowel into the dry earth even as she wondered why the theft had so affected her when they had enough troubles.

There wasn't enough food for the natives. The yield was erratic, and the French protectorate demanded more taxes. A fellow farm worker told her that the Frenchmen wanted to grow rubber next season.

'Will we eat rubber now? Who will make them rich if they kill us all?' Her friend spat before crushing an insect with her bare hands.

'Then they can steal everything. No one will be there to stop them,' Sreymau replied, as she wiped the sweat from her forehead.

They continued to remove the weeds growing at the base of the corn plants. Hard labour hurt her shoulders, arms, and back, but she persisted like every other woman in the field. Determination was the only thing that kept them alive, and Sreymau knew she had to channel it to show the French thieves their place. She would go to one of those buildings and try to learn more about Oliver. It was risky, but she couldn't think of anything else.

A few hours later, the sun sank into the horizon, turning the sky into a strange shade of orange and gold. It signalled the end of the day's work at the farm. Sreymau washed herself at the well and listened to the other women exchange recipes for body pains and ailments. She redid her hair into a top knot and smoothened the sarong to appear presentable.

'You look good, Sreymau.' A woman smiled at her. 'Make the most of the precious time you have with Sorya. Who knows what Deva has in store for us?' She patted Sreymau's arm.

Sreymau bade them goodbye for the day and went to the main street. She would have to make a small detour before going to the ruins. The French thief, Oliver *someone*, would be somewhere around, talking to her people and asking questions. She decided to follow him to see where he stayed. The devatas would be where he was.

After twenty minutes, luck favoured her. She would be late to meet Sorya, but this was important. Spotting Oliver on horseback, she tried to follow him without making it apparent. Sreymau speed-walked and ran into a couple of workers.

'Careful!' one of them shouted.

'Sorry!' she shot back in passing and wove through the trees dotted on the street. She was surprised to see Oliver stop near a large building a few metres away. He got down, carrying a bag. Sreymau narrowed her eyes as Oliver refused to let the guard take his bag. She was sure the devatas were inside it.

Sreymau didn't know how long she stood under a tree as the sky turned dark. Sorya would be worried about her. But she wanted to see if Oliver would come out. She could deal with her man later.

'Sreymau, what are you doing here?' a familiar face asked.

'Umm .. nothing. Mother told me to buy something. I forgot what. Can't go home without it. You know how it is.' She shrugged with a forced smile.

The wiry man barked a laugh. 'You are just like your father! Was it *prahok*? Don't tell me you have money to buy meat.'

'Yes! We used the last batch of the fermented fish paste. Mother doesn't like to cook without it. As for meat, we haven't had it in ages,' Sreymau replied with an exaggerated sigh.

'There you go. Buy it, and rush home now. Do you want me to come with you?'

'No, no. I'll manage,' Sreymau responded. She almost missed Oliver when he stepped out of the building. Waving at her neighbour, she noticed that Oliver was empty-handed. He got onto his horse and rode away, leaving Sreymau coughing in the dust. She turned around and ran towards the ruins, a plan forming in her mind. She would go to the building to see the devatas. If she could enter it somehow, Sreymau was confident of finding a way out.

967 CE, Isvarapura

The April sun shone high in the sky as Davuth surveyed the land spread around him. The site was smaller than the land used for temples. The head sculptors had decided they would make the wat bigger and more ornate to make up for the size. Hundreds of sculptors and their families had set up tents in the area. The open space was being filled up from one side. They would live in the outer perimeter and work inwards to the centre of the land. The central shrine would take months, but Davuth could imagine its majestic beauty.

Different dialects and languages echoed around him. He could hear a soft strain of Sanskrit chants. The women had installed a Shiva *linga* (a symbol of Lord Shiva in Hinduism) on the east side of the land. There would be a *puja* once they settled down by evening. The work would start the next morning. It was their tradition to begin a new day and new task by praying to Shiva for guidance and blessings.

Davuth noted that the place was fast turning into a small village. He saw locals from the nearby villages set up makeshift shops outside the perimeter marked for the wat.

'This red sandstone is a gem, Davuth. Well done!' An older sculptor slapped Davuth on the back with a grin.

'Thank you. When the master said we need something special for the wat, I knew we had to use that rock,' he answered with a proud smile.

Davuth had been a part of the team formed to identify suitable rock for building the temple. His explorations had taken him to the Mahendraparvata. After one look at the red sandstone, Davuth decided it was what they were searching for. After his master approved the sample they brought back, the team extracted the rock from the base of the mountain range. The red sandstone glittered on the barren land, inviting him to chip and turn it into an exquisite piece of art. Tribhuvanamahesvara Wat had to stand the test of time and make him famous.

The master sculptor let out a long whistle, gesturing to all the artists to form a group. Davuth scanned the faces to find his lady love and strode over to stand with her. She was wearing a pink saree. Her diamond nose pin glinted in the sunlight.

Davuth greeted the group with his palms clasped and raised to his chest. 'I'm Davuth.'

'Adalarasu,' a man said and returned his greeting. He gestured to the young woman beside him. 'Kalai, my daughter, the most famous sculptor in Thanjavur.'

Davuth blinked, unsure of what to say. His guess seemed to be right. She had a sculptor's hands. But to be the most famous in the Chola empire at such a young age? He wasn't sure what to make of it. He wondered how to respond without letting his doubt show.

Kalai laughed at his expression and explained, 'My father likes to boast about me. I am a sculptor like many from my community. It's our speciality. We work on the finer details that a man's hand isn't capable of.'

Davuth felt his shoulders relax as he beamed at them. Of course, the woman he had fallen in love with had to be almost as good as him. How could he accept anything less?

'I'm honoured to work with you,' he said, trying to sound humble.

Kalai's eyes twinkled with mirth as she pressed her palms together and bowed her head.

'So, tell me about Thanjavur,' he asked.

'What do I say? It's home,' Kalai replied, her smile dimming.

Her father gave a more enthusiastic response. 'Thanjavur is a rich land. Despite the battles and changing rulers, our land hasn't lost its charm. Sundara Chola, our king, has brought many reforms. Just like in your kingdom, we artists are respected by royalty and public alike. We continue to carve sculptures, build temples, and bring devas to earth.'

Davuth nodded, happy to get a glimpse into their lives in an alien land. Life wasn't too different after all. He looked at Kalai, who appeared a little homesick.

'Don't worry. Khmer will also be your home one day. You are a part of this. We'll build a wat that people will praise forever,' he told Kalai, gesturing to the chaos around them, and added, 'You can talk to me anytime you feel lonely.'

'Thank you,' she replied with a nod. Davuth felt encouraged and ready to start his mission. Two missions, he amended. Sculpt breathtaking devatas, and impress Kalai. He hoped to be a married man by the time the wat was ready.

1923, Angkor

Two days had passed since Sreymau had found the devatas. She tried to convince Sorya to help her enter the building. He refused and forbade her to take risks. Sreymau wasn't giving up, though. She decided to approach the building and ask to meet Oliver. At worst, they would send her off with a few words.

'Are you coming?' a woman called as they gathered to head home at the end of the day.

Sreymau nodded. The women preferred to leave in batches for safety. A drunken French soldier had lesser chance of accosting them that way. But wasn't she walking into the lion's den like a silly goat to slaughter? Reputable women didn't go to meet Frenchmen. Her father would be furious if he knew. What would Sorya say if he found out?

As the women went their way, Sreymau's initial determination wavered. Her secret trysts with Sorya weren't a secret. The women knew and supported her. Would they continue to stand by her if she did something as stupid as entering a French office at twilight?

Her plan was to get a peek into the office. She had already decided to take back the devatas by sneaking in later. Stealing from a thief wasn't wrong when the devatas belonged to her people.

Sreymau tugged the krama to cover her head and half her face. She took a couple of steps forward, only to turn back again. She knew she could convince Sorya to do this for her. He would relent if she persisted. Yet her feet refused to move. She was on a noble mission, Sreymau told herself. She squared her shoulders and turned towards the office before she lost her nerve again.

The large building loomed overhead, its shadow swallowing her. Sreymau gulped and stepped into the compound when a burly soldier blocked her path. She had to tilt her head to look at him. Fear crawled on her skin. It was now or never.

'I … Monsieur Oliver … help …' The words came out strangled and raspy. She didn't even know his full name.

The soldier said nothing. Nor did he move. Sreymau repeated her request. 'Monsieur Oliver said he would help us. He asked to meet him.'

'Help?' He sneered at her and laughed.

She flinched.

'So, some poor little scum wants to meet Monsieur Oliver. Let me guess why.' He took a step towards her.

Sreymau inched back.

'Aww, don't be shy now. Monsieur is busy digging up dirt somewhere. He is crazier about statues of women than real ones.'

'No! Not this help.' Sreymau tried to glare at him but ended up whimpering.

'Tsk, Tsk. Look at me, girl. I'm handsome and young too. I pay more, so you'll get more *help* from me.' His crude laugh irked and frightened her. She knew what he meant and dodged his arm as he tried to grab her. He lunged for her.

Sreymau ran, but he was faster and stronger. He didn't have to toil under the hot sun on a half-empty stomach. He gripped her waist and dragged her backwards. She cried in pain and wrestled to free herself.

'Want to play, sweetheart? Good. I like feisty girls even if you are too dark for my taste.' He laughed again.

Sreymau twisted in his grip, clawing at his arms as he carried her into the compound. Tears filled her eyes. She blinked them away and continued to struggle. She would not be one of those abused women left for dead by the French and ignored by the natives.

She sucked in a deep breath, ready to yell, when he clamped his hand on her mouth. 'No, you won't, girl. Not that anyone will come to save you.'

Sreymau sobbed, knowing it was true. The natives knew they couldn't afford to stop the Frenchmen from hurting and raping their women. Sometimes, even family members wouldn't dare to save the poor girl.

The guard continued to murmur in her ear as he half-dragged and half-carried her into the shadows. 'Your men are weak. They don't have the strength to work our land, let alone satisfy women.'

She tried to kick him. He laughed again. 'Who feeds you, dark beauty? You've got some flesh and soft curves unlike some of those sticks.'

His words brought her mother's face into her mind. Sreymau remembered the lessons her mother had drilled in her since she was a child. The guard had almost reached the back of the building. She had to escape now.

'Let them think you are weak and strike when you get the first chance. Take a step back to move forward.'

Sreymau forced her body to go limp with defeat and sagged in his arms. She hunched her shoulders and bent her head forward.

He noticed her defeated stance and loosened his grip a bit. 'You see, it's easier when you cooperate.'

He set her down and tugged the door open to take her inside. Sreymau faked a faint with a soft cry. He tried to balance her body and eased her to the ground when she punched him in the face.

'Ouch! You bloody—'

Sreymau scrambled and ran. He was enraged at her trick. She ran, seeing nothing with her blurred vision. Instinct kept her going until she crashed into a man.

'Sorya!' Sreymau gasped. A part of her was grateful for his appearance, while another part wondered what he was doing at the French building.

He said nothing as he tugged at her hand to keep her running with him. They rushed out of the compound and into a dark lane on the opposite side of the road.

The guard was cursing in French, threatening to get his revenge if he saw her again.

They were silent in the lane, Sreymau leaning against the wall and trying to catch her breath, while Sorya stood with his arms crossed over his chest.

'I know. I'm sorry,' she said before he could lecture her.

Sorya shook his head. 'What were you thinking, Moon? You thought they'll respect you or any of us? You know what would have happened if you couldn't escape. You do, don't you?'

Sreymau nodded. Her heart was still racing double time. She continued to sob as she agreed with Sorya.

'I… only wanted to do something to save the devatas.'

'Moon, this is *not* how you do something. You cannot risk your life like this. They are brutes who care for no one. Who are we to save the devatas, anyway? Devas have to save us and themselves if they are so powerful. Come, I'll drop you home.' He wasn't the kind to get angry with her, but Sreymau could sense his frustration.

'My parents don't need to know,' she said, straightening her clothes and hair.

Sorya wrapped the krama around her shoulders. He stiffened when he saw a long, red scratch on her right arm. 'That pig. I wish I could kill him.'

'Getting the devatas back would be enough,' she whispered.

Sorya sighed. 'Let's go now. I'll stop at a distance from your home. And leave this to me.'

Sreymau wanted to protest but thought better of it. She would talk to him after he had cooled down. In the meantime, she would think of a better plan. The ordeal had shaken her, but Sreymau wasn't going to back down—not after experiencing such humiliation and fear first hand. Her people deserved to be respected.

967 CE, Isvarapura

The sandstone rocks were no longer shapeless as the months passed. Days seemed cooler but shorter, and they began working from first light. Davuth was sculpting on the eastern side. He envisioned Shiva in Kailasa, sitting with his beloved Uma on his lap. Kalai was working beside him that day, carving a scene from Ravana's palace in Lanka.

Working at the wat was better than Davuth's expectations. He had been adding finer details to his carvings. The hard rock had a wonderful texture that made the carvings stand out even more. The red sandstone had a slight glint when angled in direct sunlight. The only sour part was that Davuth got almost no time to interact with Kalai. He worked with her father, but that day was the first time he'd gotten close to her place of work.

Davuth observed her handiwork and realised that her father wasn't boasting. Everything about her was amazing—her grip, her focus, and her attention to detail. She was adding finishing touches to Ravana's ten heads. Anyone who saw it would feel as if the king of Lanka was breathing in the rock. Davuth felt a twinge of insecurity but brushed it away. He scrutinised her carving for a couple of minutes more and smiled. He knew how to approach her.

'It's breathtaking, Kalai,' Davuth told her when she paused to stretch her arms.

'Thank you.' She smiled and added, 'Go ahead. You want to suggest something, don't you?'

Davuth nodded with a chuckle. 'This curve here … you can smooth it a little more.'

He pointed to one of the ten heads of the demon king. He turned to Kalai, who tilted her head to one side, then another, and examined the carving.

She stepped back and agreed. 'You're right. Maybe I'll even add extra details to show his determination. After all, the mighty asura is trying to lift Kailasa.'

'Yes! It is crucial to get the minute details with precision. I like to spend more time on finer aspects like the features and the jewellery.'

'That's good to know. May I?' She gestured to his carving of Shiva.

'Of course. I'm eager to know what you think of it.'

Kalai took her time in studying the carving of Shiva and Uma. She traced her fingertips on the detailing and stood motionless for a few seconds. She let out a soft sigh and turned to look at him.

'Beautiful, isn't it?' he asked.

'No.'

Davuth stared at her. 'No?'

Kalai shook her head. 'No. Beauty doesn't come from etching correct lines. It comes from the heart. Your carving has no heart, no devotion, and no love. It's only a piece showcasing your skills with a chisel and hammer.'

'Well, isn't that what sculpting is about?'

'If that's what you think, you aren't even qualified to be on this pious site. Here we are, carving the temple of Shiva, and you think devotion is not necessary?'

Davuth glared at her. 'I didn't say that, woman. I am devoted. I pray to Shiva twice a day. I perform all rituals to please him.'

Kalai laughed. 'Oh great sculptor, I have nothing to say to you. Shiva doesn't want your puja or rituals. He desires your heart and soul. You must surrender to him. Let him guide you always.'

She waved her arm at his carving and continued, 'I can't see Shiva's love for Uma. I don't feel the warmth of her adoration for him. There is no deva here.'

Kalai walked back to her carving and picked up her chisel and hammer. Davuth huffed and snorted before stalking off to take a break. How dare she judge his skills and devotion? Didn't everyone say he was blessed by the devas to have such talent since childhood? Did he not dedicate his life to learn all that he could? He would prove that he was as devoted as her. He would make sure his carvings look more real.

1923, Angkor

Sreymau was in her room, sulking a little after a small fight with her mother. She still stiffened if anyone got close to her, but she was feeling more confident since the disastrous evening four days ago.

She rolled her shoulders to ease the pain while she spread the bedding on the floor. She loved the rules of the past kingdoms. The girl of the house would have a room for herself, while the boys slept in the living room or outside. Lack of space and income forced them to adjust in smaller homes. Only a few like her family continued to follow this arrangement despite the inconvenience. Her father was adamant about certain traditions, and Sreymau loved him for it, even if he was infuriating.

She tugged the blanket around her shoulders and stared at the ceiling. Her father brought home news that the French thief was hiring women to clear the wat. Sreymau asked her father to get her a position. The pay was more, but her mother didn't like it. She had made this more than clear during their discussion at dinner.

'Don't give away your work at the farm for a little extra money. What will you do when those ruins are cleaned?'

'I'll go back to the farms. They always need more natives to work in the mud and dirt,' Sreymau replied. Her father supported her decision, which angered Sreymau's mother.

'Don't go exploring the ruins. Clean the place and leave. I don't like that new Frenchman. He has a nasty eye. Remember my lessons,' her mother warned.

Sreymau agreed. She guessed that Oliver wanted to search for more devatas to steal. Clearing the place on his own was beneath him, so he wanted the natives to do it. This worked in her favour. If only she could gain the courage to challenge him face to face!

Sreymau kneaded her arms and flexed her fingers to ease the pain. Toiling on a farm from dawn to dusk wasn't easy. She was used to it by now, but her body still hurt. She was trading one form of slavery for another, except the work at the ruins had a greater purpose. Her mind raced, making plans to keep an eye on him and catch him red-handed. She could also hide the devatas she found to keep them safe. Either way, she *had* to work at the ruins. She also had to meet Sorya, which was easier as she could stay back at the site.

968 CE, Isvarapura

Living at Isvarapura was like being in a bubble. Davuth was on one of his breaks again. He walked around the third enclosure margins. The biggest and outermost wall would be built here with the second and first enclosures nestled inside it. The libraries and shrines would be inside the first enclosure, creating a layered pathway from the outside to reach the Shiva linga in the centre.

'What are you carving? The curves are smooth here and rough there,' Davuth asked one of the women from Thanjavur working on the third enclosure wall.

She smiled and explained, pointing at a half-carved skirt. 'She is Tilottama, the *apsara*. These two rough markings will be Sunda and Upasunda, the demons. They lusted after her beauty and wanted to possess her. She is tricking them to escape.'

'It is from the Mahabharata, isn't it?'

She nodded. 'I like the Mahabharata. Kalai likes the Ramayana.'

Davuth looked at Kalai's handiwork in carving the Panchawati ashram with Sita and Ravana. It was the scene where Ravana kidnaps Sita. The ferocity of Ravana's features had more than a hint of his evil intentions. As always, Davuth couldn't take his eyes off Kalai. She was in her own world, her focus intent only on the rock and the tools in her hand.

He let out a soft sigh and thought back through the events of the previous days. Davuth had worked on dozens of sculptures during the last few months, but Kalai had said nothing. Even as his fellow artists praised his work, she stood silent or walked away. She still thought his work lacked devotion. It infuriated him for a long time. However, a serious discussion with his master three days earlier had made him reconsider everything he knew.

'Guru[A]ji, you said I was one of the best sculptors in the Khmer Empire,' Davuth had said to his master.

Two weary yet alert eyes assessed him. 'I said you have the talent to become one.'

'Yes, yes. I'm working hard to learn. I don't say no to advice.'

'What's troubling you, Davuth?'

'Kalai, that woman from Thanjavur, said my carvings don't have life. She said I am not devoted to or don't love Shiva. You know it's not true.' Davuth didn't care that his voice sounded whiny. He could share his concerns with his master. He always did.

'Ah!'

The master said nothing for a few minutes. Davuth waited, shifting from one foot to another. Tiny tendrils of doubt crept into his mind. Was Kalai somehow right in her assessment? But how?

'Davuth, remember what I told you when you showed me the figurine of our king?'

Davuth nodded. 'You said it was my finest carving ever and that it has life in it.'

'Do you know why?'

'I spent several hours on it. I chose a rock with a skin tone similar to King Rajendravarman II. I observed him until I could see every line of his face and body with my eyes closed. Then, I started carving the figurine,' Davuth replied, feeling proud of his work. He carried the little thing with him as a good luck charm.

The master smiled. 'And why did you do all this?'

'Because I love our king. He is my inspiration. He keeps the Khmer Empire safe.'

'Yes. You answered your question, Davuth.'

'I don't understand, Guruji.'

'Your figurine of the king is so like him because you put your heart and soul into it. Your admiration for the king can be seen in it. But when you carve these walls here, you are more focused on what you want others to think about your work.'

'But—'

'Davuth, when Kalai carves the rock, she doesn't see the rock. She doesn't think about who will praise her work. She sees her deva. Her chisel cuts into the hard stone and chips away the excess when her eyes are closed. She sees the deva with her mind and heart, like you saw our king when you made the idol.'

'Why didn't you tell me this before, Guruji?'

'There's a time for everything. Shiva wants you to see now. Ask Shiva, and he'll tell you why.'

The master picked up his tools, touched them to his forehead with reverence and got back to work. Davuth sat on the earth as his master carved Shiva in Nataraja form. For the first time, Davuth looked at his master's face instead of his handiwork. He was stunned to see that his master looked as if he was in a trance. His eyes were half closed. He lips moved in a silent prayer.

How had he missed it before? How did he not realise that he lacked something so vital? Anger and hurt made him restless. He didn't touch his tools for two days afterwards.

The nudge from his master got him back to work that morning. He had to apologise to Kalai as well. Davuth hesitated before walking towards her.

'Kalai.'

She turned to him.

'I apologise for my behaviour the other day.'

She nodded.

'I … umm … can you teach me how to be like you?'

'Like me?' she asked with a slight frown.

'Yes.'

She thought for a second and said, 'No.'

Before he could protest, she raised her hand, gesturing for him to wait.

'Devotion cannot be taught. You either have it or you don't. You have to learn it on your own. Trust Shiva, and leave everything in his hands. He'll tell you what to do.'

Davuth nodded, though he didn't understand. His master had said the same, and he felt like a fool for struggling to know what it meant. He went into the east enclosure to think and maybe try and talk to Shiva. Would the god respond? Davuth decided he wouldn't know unless he tried.

1923, Angkor

Sreymau had joined the cleaning crew at the ruins two days ago. The wat had been left to rot for years and looked more like a home of ghosts and spirits than a temple where her ancestors had prayed. Sreymau wondered if restoring it would please the devas and move them to bless her people and get rid of the Frenchmen. She was almost successful in convincing Sorya to agree to her plans. Of course, he would, she thought with a smile. He loved her and would do anything for her. His anger was more about his own helplessness rather than at her impulsive act.

She rushed to the ruins early, hoping to find any devatas before Oliver. She would not let him steal anything else from her land. Sreymau bound her hair in a knot and began hacking the weeds near the first enclosure. It was deep inside the wat, close to the central *mandapa* (raised platform or pillared hall in a temple) where the shrines were built. Since others would be cleaning around the outer second and third enclosures, she could act on her plan without being noticed.

Sreymau stopped every few minutes to trace the carvings on the enclosure walls with her rough fingers. She found Kaala, the monstrous representation of time, on one of the guarding walls and shuddered. He was a personification of evil, and she didn't want to think of his presence on that site. The world had enough evil. Why carve more on the temple walls?

A sound startled her. Sreymau rushed inside the enclosure and peaked over a broken wall. She saw an older woman standing with her head bowed down. The frail woman gripped a few flowers in her hand. More were scattered on the small pedestal at the feet of a broken devata.

Oliver was yelling at her for damaging the property. 'You worthless heathen! Always worshipping the devil and Satan in idols. This is a place of art, you fool. People like you shouldn't ruin its beauty with your superstitions. Get out of here!'

The woman sobbed, while a couple of others looked helpless. Sreymau couldn't believe his audacity. It was their wat, their temple. It was their place of worship, and this white man wanted to claim it as his own. She was furious that no one spoke back to him, including her. They couldn't risk losing a chance of earning extra income. The money would go to the French protectorate as taxes, but it was something more than what they had.

Before she could think it through, Sreymau laid her scythe across the path and hid behind the bushes. She crouched low, using the thick vegetation to hide her presence.

Oliver stormed out, muttering about bloody pagans and devil worshippers. Just as she had hoped, he stepped on the scythe. The sharp edge dug into his foot despite the expensive boots.

'Oww!' He shrieked in pain and jumped, holding the injured foot. The scythe's handle hit him on the arm. Oliver tripped, shouting and cursing in pain. 'Which bloody native scum left this here?'

He crashed into a thorny overgrown bush and almost fell face first, but a guard rushed to save him at the last moment.

Sreymau fumed at the lank guard's frame as he helped Oliver.

The guard turned to the other workers and ordered, 'Get back to work. Anyone careless with the tools will be jailed for attacking your officers. Clear?'

One of the workers rushed forward to remove the scythe. She looked at them with tears in her eyes and mumbled, 'Sorry, monsieur, sorry. We mean no harm. Why would we want to hurt those who feed us?'

'Worthless idiots,' Oliver spat and limped outside the enclosure, leaning on the guard.

Sreymau stayed put behind the vegetation and stepped out when no one was around. Satisfied with her small revenge, she grabbed an axe to hack at the overgrown branches of a wayward tree.

A few hours later, Sreymau was tired and sweaty. She paused when her friend hollered for her to take a break for lunch. She nodded and turned to find a devata etched on the dirty wall beside her.

Oh, how she loved the demi-goddess with a sword in one hand and a flower in another! The detailing of the features, the slight smile, the sharp eyes, and the finesse of the layers of the dress mesmerised Sreymau. She never knew sculptures could appear so lifelike and retain the essence even after many years.

'Which pious hands made you, Devi?' she asked aloud.

'My great-grandmother said sculptors from Thanjavur came to the Khmer Empire to build this wat.'

Sreymau jumped at the reply. She turned to find the same old woman Oliver had insulted. The old woman smiled. 'Do you know where Thanjavur is?'

Sreymau shook her head. She had no education, and her grandparents had passed away when she was young.

The old woman sat on a slab nearby. Sreymau and other workers sat on the ground around her. They shared their meagre meal as the woman told them about the wat and its glory days before it had been abandoned to rot.

'Thanjavur is far away across the sea. We have to travel by boat for days and weeks. My great-grandmother said women from that land came to carve our devatas. And look at us!' She sighed and continued, 'The wat was a marvel in those days. They spent years bringing the sandstone rocks from nearby hills and carving them. Do you know what they used for the walls? It's brick and laterite.'

'The same as the fort walls?' someone asked.

The old woman nodded. 'Yes. These were used to build the forts and make them strong enough to survive attacks from enemies.'

'But this one didn't survive,' Sreymau whispered.

'It did. The wat is here, and so are we,' the woman replied. 'One day, Deva will decide we have suffered enough and erase all our troubles. But we must believe in him and ourselves.'

'All this won't feed the children. Back to work,' someone else scoffed.

The time for dreaming was over. Sreymau longed to see the wat in its past glory and experience the same rush of pride and reverence her ancestors felt when they built it. The people in those days worked on despite the tragedy in their lives. They were intent on bringing the rocks to life. Sreymau wondered where that determination vanished. How did her people give up and surrender their land and pride to men who valued them nil?

968 CE, Isvarapura

Davuth was sulking in the sanctuary in the eastern library. He had taken over the space, saying he would carve the entire section. However, he wasn't happy with his latest carvings. He had made mistakes and had had to start over again. He observed his mentor and Kalai for hours as they chipped and hammered at the rocks, turning them into artistic carvings. Davuth tried to empty his mind of all thoughts and focused only on his work. Somehow it still wasn't enough. Kalai gave him a light smile when he showed her his latest design.

He had carved an apsara with flowers in one hand and a weapon in another. He had created a transparent layer of frills in her skirt and given her Kalai's features. She wasn't impressed. The carving was not good enough for her, it seemed. Davuth didn't know what to do. It was affecting his mood and his progress. How could he carve the sanctuary this way?

Davuth gave a frustrated sigh and walked out of his hiding place. He found Kalai teaching a little girl how to hold the chisel and hammer. The girl was one of the native kids who camped on the site with her father and mother.

His lips curved into a smile when he heard their discussion.

'I'll become an artist like my father,' the little girl said, her eyes shining with excitement.

Kalai tugged the girl's pigtail with a smile. 'Not if you dance with the chisel instead of using it on the rock. Come now.' She pulled the girl onto her lap and took a small slab of rock from the side. She held the girl's hands in her own, guiding her in marking the stone and making the first crucial hit.

'Wow!' the little girl whispered at the tremor that shook her wiry frame when the hammer hit the chisel.

'Yes. Feel it in your heart, dear. Every hit should echo with your heartbeat.'

The little girl nodded. Davuth continued to watch them until Kalai ended the lesson and the girl ran off to show her first carving to her parents. He hesitated before slipping back into his hiding place. Davuth didn't want to talk to Kalai until he figured out where he was wrong.

However, Kalai seemed to have other plans as she followed him inside the library. 'Can I say something?' she asked, standing at the entrance.

'What else is left to say?' he replied and shook his head.

Kalai turned. Davuth half-panicked and blurted, 'Sorry. Don't go. Please, go ahead and say what you wanted to.'

He feared she wouldn't talk to him ever if he didn't take the chance she offered.

Kalai hesitated but nodded. She stepped inside and sat a few feet away from him. '*Bhakti* and ultimate surrender to Deva doesn't come in a day or two. It is *tapasya*, a process that takes an entire life for some people. Do you know how they get to that stage?'

'How?'

'By realizing that everything we are and have belongs to Deva and not us. You are proud of the apsara you carved, aren't you? Give away this pride to Deva. Realise that it is him that made you carve the figurine. Try it once, and you'll experience a sense of satisfaction like no other. You will never want anything less.'

Davuth considered her words as she walked away, leaving him alone as he wanted to be. He was indeed proud of his carvings. So, was that it? Could he change from thinking *he* was blessed to realising that he was *blessed*?

1923, Angkor

Sreymau went to clean the ruins as she had been doing for the past two weeks. She felt a strange sense of anticipation that morning. Oliver was getting agitated. He couldn't find any more devatas to steal, unless he planned to break the enclosure walls to take the carvings.

She enjoyed his restlessness and hid yet another small devata in the sanctum sanctorum of the shrines. She had saved around eight idols—broken and unbroken ones—and placed them behind the fallen columns. It was a little difficult to manoeuvre around the sharp rocks, but practice made it easier.

Sreymau jumped down from the mandapa and picked up her scythe when she heard voices nearby. The worker women had arrived. She listened to them talk while thinking about her missed chances of sneaking into the office on the main street. The same guard was around, and Sreymau didn't want to go anywhere near him.

'Deva! I should've known you won't give up. I'll find out where the devatas are inside the office. Alright?' Sorya said in a mock exasperated voice.

She grinned and hugged him. 'I knew you would understand.'

'What other option do I have, my stubborn Moon? On the day after tomorrow, I'll meet you with the news in the evening,' he teased.

Sreymau was excited for the day to end. Sorya would bring her the information, and together they would steal the devatas to bring them back to the wat. She couldn't help but look happy as she hummed her favourite lullaby. She moved towards the library on the east, hacking and tugging weeds, keeping her eyes open for more devatas.

She talked to the old woman a few times to ask for more details about the wat. She learnt that the place used to be called Isvarapura, named after Shiva. Somehow, the name and the significance of the wat had slipped into the nooks and corners of history.

'The temple is waiting. Deva will rise again,' the old woman said, strengthening Sreymau's determination.

She swung the scythe close to the ground, and it struck something hard. The sound echoed and made her jump. Sreymau dropped her tool and bent to part the thorny shrubs.

'Oh, my!' she gasped, her eyes widening in wonder. Right in front of her was a tiny sculpture the size of her hand. She picked it up, worried that the scythe had damaged it. Relief flowed through her when she saw it was dirty but undamaged.

Sreymau used the hem of her sarong to wipe away the grime and the moss. She cleaned the face of the figurine and peered at it. Astonished, she took in the details of a wide forehead, almond-shaped eyes, straight nose, and full mouth—all in a small sculpture. It was the figurine of a young woman, someone around her age, Sreymau guessed.

'You are beautiful! What's your name? Are you one of the women from across the sea? Who made you with so much love?'

Sreymau felt stupid for talking to a rock, but she couldn't stop the rush of questions in her head. She would take it home for the time being. Of course, Sorya had to see it too. She let out a soft laugh as a plan to tease her lover formed in her mind.

She looked around to ensure that no one was about and tucked the figurine into the folds of her top. She got back to hacking at the weeds with renewed enthusiasm. However, Sreymau couldn't stop staring at the carvings on the walls nearby. She kept tracing them with her fingers, hoping to learn something from stones that had seen it all.

'Don't touch those with your ugly hands. No money if you don't clear this in half an hour.'

The angry voice startled her. It was Oliver, looking at her as if she was an insect.

Sreymau curled her fingers into a fist and squared her shoulders. She wanted to call him a thief and kick him out of her land. He had no right to order her about. This was the chance she was searching for.

'We … are not … ugly. You … you are a—'

'Come, Sreymau. I'll help.' Her friend tugged her hand and dragged her away from an angry Oliver.

She freed herself and opened her mouth when her friend shushed her.

'Whatever has gotten into you? Why do you want to argue with those white men? He can do *anything,* and no one will come to help you. Do you understand, stupid girl?'

Sreymau said nothing. She seethed with anger and humiliation and cursed herself for being stupid enough to think she could confront a Frenchman head on. What chance did a native have with a coloniser? *None.*

The bitter truth filled her eyes with tears. She could no longer accept that the injustice and the hate was something they deserved. They came from a glorious civilisation, and they would have to win it back.

'Calm down now. We have work to do.'

Sreymau nodded. Yes, they had work to do. She would do it as soon as possible. Everything else be damned. The risk was worth it.

968 CE, Isvarapura

Dawn was Davuth's favourite time of the day. He loved watching the reddish-orange sun rise over the horizon to fill the world with light. Every sunrise was unique. Davuth felt it in his bones. A sense of peace spread through his body and his mind. He noticed a twinkle from the corner of his eye and turned to his right.

A fresh slab of red sandstone glinted as sunlight danced on its surface. Davuth stared at it for several moments, an idea forming in his mind. He rushed to remove his tools from the bag and went to kneel beside the rock. With gentle fingers, Davuth traced the smooth and firm lines on the sandstone. He rested his head against the rock, feeling the stone's temperature change from cold to warm. He could sense the change in it as the sun crawled higher up the sky.

Davuth opened his eyes and touched the tools to his forehead. He said a small prayer to Shiva and marked the rock at three places before aiming the chisel and hammer. It would yield him four pieces. Davuth didn't stop working until it got too dark for him to see. His fingers were cramped from holding the tools for hours. His body hurt from staying in a single position. But his heart felt lighter than it had in a long time.

The routine continued for a few more days. Davuth stayed in the sanctuary, working from dawn to dusk. Someone would bring him food and urge him to rest for a while. He would nod and say nothing. Davuth didn't think of anything or anyone. He wasn't excited to finish his masterpiece and show it to someone. Nothing mattered except the devatas he was carving. It was as if he was possessed by a strange power to complete the job.

'A messenger has arrived from the kingdom!' a young lad hollered.

The sculptors paused their work to listen to his announcement. The messenger arrived occasionally to gather information about the progress. This time, though, he wanted more than updates. He came with news—news that burst their bubble and snatched all that they held dear.

Davuth didn't hear the message until at the end of the day. He felt the ground shatter beneath his feet when a friend told him they would have to leave the next day. The king needed more men to protect the kingdom. Davuth had realised things were becoming serious when the stalls outside the temple premises began to reduce in number. However, he had decided to ignore the inflow of women and children camping on the site. What he didn't acknowledge didn't hurt him.

Now, Davuth could no longer avoid the truth that threatened to snatch away everything. He had to leave his family and his master. He had to say goodbye to Kalai just as they were getting closer. She had even made a positive comment on the half-column he had carved outside the east library's entrance.

Davuth's vision blurred with tears. He rubbed his face and let out a strangled cry of frustration.

'Why now? Why should a sculptor pick up a sword?' he said aloud, already knowing the answer. The king was desperate and losing. He needed his kingdom to support him in these worst of times. But that meant Davuth would have let go of all that he held dear. If it was meant to be, he would be back to complete the wat and marvel at Kalai's progress. He knew she would carve the main shrines and the mandapa to erect the Shiva linga.

The silence at the site was heavy and foreboding. No one spoke much. They didn't know what to say. The full moon shone in the inky sky as Davuth looked at the Shiva, Narayana, and Parvati devatas he had been crafting. His idea to add Devi Lakshmi to the collection would be unfulfilled. He picked up his tools and got to work, knowing he had only a few hours left. The moonlight was enough. It had to be. The king, his hero, had sent a command, and he needed to prove his loyalty. Davuth had to answer.

1923, Angkor

Sorya hesitated for less than a second before entering the office on the main street. According to Sreymau, Oliver kept the devatas there. He was relieved when the guard wasn't at the entrance and slipped inside the building. Each time Sorya saw the man, he wanted to beat him to a pulp and wring his neck. But he knew they would shoot him on sight if he even dared to raise his voice against a white man.

'Monsieur … good man, please help,' Sorya blabbered, hoping his act as a desperate man was convincing enough. He had streaked his face and arms with mud to hide his identity.

'What is it, man? Stop acting like a lunatic and tell us what happened.'

'Horse fall there. Accident, monsieur. My good officer. He fall and hurt. No one to help. He send me to you.'

'Oh Lord! Where did it happen?' one of the guards shook him.

Sorya coughed and gasped, 'The town entrance.'

'Are you sure? Is this a trick?' another guard asked, pointing a gun at Sorya's chest.

He gulped. 'No, no, monsieur. I no lie. I fear my deva.'

'Yeah, whatever.'

The guards spoke to each other in rapid French. A couple of them dashed outside. The other two readied a medical bag. Sorya took a few steps backwards without taking his eyes off them.

'You'll stay here until we're back,' the Frenchman ordered.

Sorya waved his arms and shook his head. A guard grabbed him and pushed him into the office. Sorya tried to look around but was thrown into a dark room before he could break free. He heard the lock click on the door and sank to the hard floor with a sigh. The lock would open only from outside. He was stuck inside until the Frenchmen came back.

He shuddered, thinking what they would do to him when they found out the truth. Would Sreymau sense something was wrong? Sorya knew she would rush to save him. He groaned louder, not knowing which was worse—being killed for a lie or not being able to save his girl.

'Please, please, Deva, you have to help us!' Sorya prayed, cursing himself for not being quick enough to escape.

968 CE, Khmer Kingdom

Blood stained the once beautiful land Davuth loved with all his heart. Droplets splattered on the leaves, shrubs, and boundary walls of the fort. The army commander stationed Davuth and other men with little or no experience in fighting, along with a few experienced soldiers, to protect the fortress and its valuables. The ministers were moving the remaining women and children underground, to a safe place built for such situations.

The commander's orders were to delay the troops for as long as they could. The king was busy on the battlefield, killing those who attacked his kingdom. Davuth looked at the sword and shield in his hands and sighed. As much as battles and victories had fascinated him from afar, he wasn't a soldier.

The situation became worse, and news arrived that the king was bleeding on the field with multiple wounds. Davuth couldn't think of Kalai losing her father and brothers. What would happen to his and Kalai's future if he didn't survive? The thoughts suffocated him, making him breathless. He had grown up thinking the king was invincible. How dare he get wounded? How could he lose the battle to his scheming and devious cousins?

Davuth realised that returning alive was now a remote dream. There may not be a life with Kalai. He would never hear her admonish him for being proud of his sculptures. He would never have another chance to learn from her or to tell Kalai that he understood what tapasya is, that he was learning and getting there, one step at a time.

Davuth found it ironic that Kalai had opened his eyes to bhakti, and his deva had snatched it away from him. He didn't mind that the wat was being constructed by the Thanjavur women. Maybe they were destined for it.

A resounding war cry startled Davuth. His heart thudded in his chest, syncing with the clattering of swords and weapons. The sounds were getting louder and closer with each breath.

'Attack!' the head soldier yelled.

Davuth and other men raised their swords in unison and moved towards the entrance. They would guard it with their lives no matter what. Time had no meaning when every fibre of his body focused on attacking and shielding. Davuth was aware of the men falling around him. Kalai's father and a couple of his friends were the first ones to suffer the same fate as others. He continued to fight, ducking and scrambling.

Even when the enemy's sword cut a chunk off his right calf, he staggered but didn't stop. But a sudden jolt of pain shocked him. He stared at a shiny metal sword tearing through his midriff. His vision swam. The shield slipped from his hands. Davuth fell to the hard ground, blood pooling around him on the stony path. He had no strength to hope. Images of his king, the old master, his parents, and Kalai flooded his mind. He had hidden the devatas when he left the site. Why? He didn't know. It was an impulsive decision to prevent Kalai from seeing his work when he wasn't around.

Now, struggling to breathe as the pain became unbearable, Davuth hoped Kalai would find his devatas. He turned his head to the side and noticed the faint image of a Shiva linga on the fort's inner wall. It was the last thing he saw.

1923, Angkor

When Sorya didn't meet her as promised, Sreymau knew he must be in trouble. It didn't take much to figure out something had gone wrong with their plan. She ran to the main street and didn't stop until she was a few metres away from the building.

She paused to catch her breath and gathered fists full of dry earth. Anything was a weapon in desperate times. The twilight sky was dark enough to throw shadows that shielded her actions. She hoped the creepy guard wasn't around and dashed inside the office.

'Sorya!' Sreymau called after entering the front room.

'Hey, you!'

She froze, recognizing the voice of her tormentor. The urge to run was overwhelming. Sreymau took a few steps back before forcing herself to face him.

'You think you can waltz in here without consequences, you bloody dark waif,' he spat, aiming his gun at her.

Sreymau didn't take her eyes off his face as she grabbed a handful of dirt from her krama and threw it onto his face.

'Argh!' The guard roared, dropping the gun.

Sreymau pushed him with all her might. As he tripped over onto the floor, she shoved a nearby chair and overturned it on his chest. Not sure if it would be enough to stop him, Sreymau looked around for more items. Finding nothing to use, Sreymau dumped the remaining mud on his face and bound his hands by tearing her krama into long strips.

He tried to claw at her hands, but she was fast. He continued to curse and threaten her, reverting to French. She stepped aside when he turned to grab her ankle with bound hands.

'Oww! You—'

She pulled a long hairpin from her bun and stabbed him hard. The French guard howled in pain. Blood began to seep through his arm.

'Don't you dare touch me or any other woman,' she yelled and kicked him twice in the gut.

Sreymau was aiming for her third when Sorya called her from the room they had locked him in.

'Moon! Moon! Is that you?' Sorya's distressed voice stopped her.

'I'm here. Where are you?' she shouted back.

'In the third room on your left. Are you hurt? What are those noises?'

'I'm safe. It's … nothing,' Sreymau replied as she reached the room's door.

'How do I open this lock?' she asked, her voice strained and nervous.

She looked at the French guard rolling on the floor. He was struggling, but for how long? He would break free soon.

Sreymau tugged the lock. 'This won't open!'

'Moon, remember, I taught you to weave dried stems without breaking them? You saw mc use it on the old rusty lock last year. Try it here with the pins in your hair.'

Her hairpin was stuck in the guard's flesh. She had no intention of getting closer to him again.

'I stabbed the guard with it,' she shouted back through the door.

'Oh Deva! See if you can find anything. Long and thin but sturdy,' Sorya replied.

'Yes, yes,' Sreymau said, turning in a circle to scan her surroundings. She saw nothing except potted plants.

She went to the pots and searched for anything that would help her. The leaves were fragile, and the stems were too weak to braid. Sreymau felt her heart thudding in her ears. She gulped in panic.

What should she do? As she pushed her unruly hair behind her ears, it struck her.

Sreymau removed her bronze earring and straightened it. The earring was a simple piece of metal bent into a U-shaped curve. The thin metal was worn out from years of use and took the shape she gave it.

'Got it. Tell me what to do,' she hissed, bending over the lock and sliding the earring into the keyhole.

'Listen for the click sound and don't twist it too much. Ease it, little by little,' Sorya continued to instruct her. After a minute that lasted forever, the lock clicked.

Sorya pushed the door open and stepped out. Sreymau decided she would practise picking locks. Some skills came in handy in emergencies. She hugged him in relief and whispered, 'We need to find the devatas fast!'

The office had spacious rooms and corridors filled with ornate furniture. Sreymau wondered what all the Frenchmen hid in their offices.

'Moon, come here.'

Sorya called from a room further on down the corridor. Sreymau half ran to find him pushing a wooden box to the side. The lid was open, and inside it were the four devatas Oliver had stolen from the wat. The idols were wrapped in cloth but were easy to identify.

'He stuffed our devas into a box!' Sreymau huffed.

Sorya nodded as he handed her two idols. Together, they could carry the devatas and run. They hoped to do it before the officers arrived.

Sreymau felt the weight of the idols straining her arms as she walked behind Sorya. They decided to exit through the back door.

A sudden commotion startled them.

'Hurry, Moon,' Sorya urged.

Sreymau nodded. They had taken less than a few steps when a guard hollered. 'Hey! You dirty scoundrels!'

A shot rang out as Sorya ducked to the floor. Sreymau screamed.

968–969 CE, Isvarapura

The sounds of rocks being chipped filled the air. Kalai and other women who had arrived from Thanjavur continued to work on the site. Most of the men had left to take up arms and fight the battle. Only the older male sculptors were still at Isvarapura because of their age. They were torn and restless, conflicted by their emotions.

Kalai and a few of her friends spent many hours talking to them, asking for guidance and opinions. That kept the old men immersed in their art even when their hearts longed to see their children home safe from the battle.

'It's the same everywhere. There will always be someone who wants another kingdom. The Chola kingdom lost countless lives in battles.' A middle-aged woman sighed and leant on the rock she was carving.

Others nodded. The families of local sculptors moved to the site to assist the women. It was a welcome decision from both sides. They needed each other's company.

'Our king, Rajendravarman II, is a very good man. He's strict, but that's how a king has to be. He had been trying to unite smaller kingdoms through friendship. But those greedy cousins of his are brutes. They know they can't continue their ways when the kingdoms unite,' a frail old woman explained.

'What will happen if things go wrong?' another asked.

They avoided saying the exact words aloud, afraid that expressing their fears would manifest them.

'The heir is just ten years old, but that's not new either. Our ministers will train him and continue to manage the kingdom until he is of age. As for others … you already know.'

'Widows, no fathers, dead sons, and more deaths due to heartbreak. At least, we have this wat to keep us going.'

'But why didn't Shiva stop the battle? Why can't he make our king win and save our men?' a young girl demanded, hands on her hips.

Kalai and the other women gave her a rueful smile.

'Won't the people of other kingdoms also be asking Shiva the same thing?' the old master replied as he sank to the ground with a painful sigh. 'Shiva didn't start the battle. People did—and we have to pay the price for it. Don't go blaming Shiva for man's ego and greed.'

'But … he can still bring back my father, can't he?' The girl was in tears now.

Her mother pulled her into a hug as the girl sobbed. 'I miss him too, dear. Remember one thing. If you start to question Shiva for our actions, you will never find peace or happiness. No matter what happens, trust him. Do you understand?'

The girl hiccupped and nodded.

Kalai sat by the old master. She took his hands in hers to massage the crooked fingers. He was growing weaker with each passing day. She wondered what would happen if her father and relatives didn't come back from the war. What if Davuth didn't make it? Faith was a strange thing. It threatened to desert you when you needed it the most. She shook her head to clear it of thoughts. She wouldn't give in. Whatever Shiva had planned for her, Kalai would be ready to accept it.

'I hate battles,' a young boy whispered.

'We hate them too, child.'

'We are carving the Mahabharata and the Ramayana on the walls. If Rama and Krishna had to fight wars, who are we to escape?' the old master murmured.

'Good will triumph over evil, even if it takes lives. It is the price we have to pay,' another woman said, cradling a three-month-old baby in her arms.

'Messenger!' a kid shouted.

They looked at each other and waited as a dusty and fatigued man and beast rode into the centre. The stink of death was hard to ignore. He got down from the horse and removed his helmet.

'I apologise for the news I bring, mothers. We have lost many men during the last two days. Our dear king has attained *sadgati*, and his *aatma* has travelled to the other world. Minister Yajnavaraha has taken control of the situation. Our soldiers are wounded but undefeated. The kingdom will be safe. We will fight and suppress the attacks in a week.'

Isvarapura stood still as the women and the children processed his words. The messenger didn't move an inch. He bowed his head, hands clasped in a silent prayer, asking for the strength to share the news he had come to deliver.

'My father ...?' the little girl asked, desperate for something to hold on to.

'My apologies, mothers. The men had an honourable death and will be treated with the greatest respect.'

He listed the names of the dead men, bowed once again, got back on the horse, and rode off, leaving the women and the old men to deal with their grief.

1923, Angkor

'Sorya!' Sreymau screamed again when the second shot echoed in the building.

She didn't know what to do as the furious guard came closer. He wasn't the one she had dealt with earlier. Before Sreymau could react, Sorya flung the devatas at the guard.

The first one knocked the French guard's gun and hit his arm. He cried in pain when Sorya used the other idol to hit him on the head.

Sreymau stood still, holding the devatas close to her body. She didn't want to use them as a weapon. Sorya had no such reservations. He carried on hitting until the Frenchman collapsed. This brought the other nasty guard to the corridor. He was limping and cradling his hands.

'We'll kill you for this,' he shouted in frustration.

Sorya picked up the devatas. They rushed out of the building with the guard limping behind. Sreymau sighed in relief when she spotted the back door. They would be free at last. No sooner had the thought struck her than Sreymau heard more angry voices and sounds.

'They came back,' Sorya said, stepping out of the office as the shouts grew louder.

They still had to exit the compound. Time was running out.

968–969 CE, Isvarapura

No one at the temple site worked for the next fortnight. The dead deserved to be mourned. Kalai walked through the half-constructed libraries, tracing the carvings with her fingers. The pious site had seen its share of deaths as the women had predicted.

Cries of heartbreak and pain filled the atmosphere. Some found solace in prayer, while others huddled in their tents, refusing to come out. A few older women sat near the Shiva linga they had installed when they first arrived. They chanted his name from morning to night and into the next morning. The days blended into a blur of sunrises and sunsets.

Kalai didn't know whom to console. Her mother and her aunts mourned their husbands and sons. She had lost her father, uncles, cousins, and even the old master sculptor.

The master had asked one last thing from her.

'Davuth was my favourite student despite his attitude. I hoped he would realise the true meaning of sculpting and devotion one day. But never did I imagine he would go to Shiva in the process.'

He gripped Kalai's hands and whispered. 'Please find the devatas he carved before he left for the war. He hid them somewhere. I know you can find them. You were the reason for the change I wanted in him.'

It was the fourth day after the master's death. Kalai was tired of being strong and caring for others. It was time for her to grieve. She entered the sanctuary in the east library. It had been Davuth's hideout. The place and memories brought tears to her eyes. He was a warm and happy person, always making someone laugh.

Kalai hadn't intended to find love when she sailed across the sea from her home to a new kingdom. However, Davuth had caught her attention. She knew his pride in his talent wasn't even an issue. Not every sculptor worked for the god. Many artists considered it was in their blood and were proud of inheriting the skills. They enjoyed praise as much as they enjoyed the personal satisfaction of turning a shapeless rock into a lifelike statue.

She inspected the space, now filled with a layer of dust, and noticed a disturbed corner. Grabbing a trowel from the tools nearby, she sat on the ground to ease the mud aside. Kalai thought back to the time she had riled Davuth. She had wanted him to realise that his worth wasn't in his carvings but in his heart. The only way she knew to do it was to push him to discover his true self, to open his emotions and soul, and to embrace God. It had been her way of helping him think beyond materialistic life.

The trowel hit something hard. A clanging sound rang out, forcing Kalai to pay attention to the task at hand. She dropped the tool and used her fingers to claw the mud aside. Nestled in the earth were three exquisite idols of Shiva, Narayana, and Parvati. She lifted them out, mesmerised by the pulsating life she could feel from the devatas.

Kalai placed them on the ground, cleaning the mud and dirt with the corner of her saree. Tears streaked her cheeks, and she made no attempt to control them. This was what she had wanted Davuth to understand. The devatas glowed in the golden sunlight. It was as if they had flown down from Kailasa and Vaikuntam (Lord Vishnu and Goddess Lakshmi's abode) to stand in front of her.

'Why couldn't you do this earlier? Why did you have to go and get killed, you stupid man?'

Davuth wasn't around to answer her questions. Kalai felt the weight of his absence on her soul. She stared at the devatas until it struck her that Vishnu's consort was missing.

Kalai searched and searched but could not find any other idol. However, she found a semi-prepared rock that fit the size of the existing devatas. The markings on the rock told her what to do. She turned to Vishnu's idol and said, 'I'll bring Lakshmi Maa to your side, Deva. You don't have to miss her for long.'

She also decided to complete the library. The devatas would adorn the entrance as Davuth planned. She would carve the remaining base columns for installation. Kalai cried her heart out until she felt she no longer had tears left in her. She stood up to leave when she saw something glittering. The sun dipped low towards the horizon, and the rays lit up the area behind a huge rock. She bent for a closer look and gasped.

There were two small figurines. One was of the king, and another was of her. She had often seen the king's figurine in Davuth's hand. Now she was stunned to see a figurine that was her replica. Fresh tears filled her eyes. Pain overwhelmed her. She sank to the ground, clutching the figure as if it was her lifeline. In a way, it was. She would give the king's figurine a proper burial. One day, she would do the same to her own. But first, she had to complete the job Davuth had left for her. She wouldn't think about what could have happened. She would take one day at a time and trust Deva to guide her.

One thing Kalai knew for sure was that the Khmer Empire was her home. She now belonged to the land of the man she loved.

1923, Angkor

'Let's leave the devatas here and run,' Sorya suggested.

Sreymau stared at him. 'No!'

'It's too risky, Moon. We can't stand here arguing.'

Sreymau understood his impatience, but she wasn't giving up and running away when she was so close to her goal. She shook her head. 'I have an idea. Distract them.'

'Moon, no! Wait!'

She didn't give him a chance to stop her. Placing the idols in the nearby bushes, she rushed to the other side of the building. She had noticed a large open window while searching the office for the devatas. It was all she needed. Sreymau prayed they wouldn't shoot Sorya. She could hear random sounds, which meant Sorya was doing as she had asked.

Sreymau hitched her sarong up to her knees and jumped to sit on the windowsill. The room was dark. She noted that the door on the other side was closed before slipping inside. She groped around, thinking back to remember where she had seen a large can of kerosene.

She fumbled around, hurting her knee by knocking it against a broken chair. She almost tripped too but, at last, got hold of the can. Taking a deep breath, Sreymau went to the door that opened into the office. She eased it open an inch to peek through.

Luck seemed to be on her side—at least for the time being. The corridor was empty. The men were outside the building. She hauled the can and doused the office with the kerosene. The smell grew stronger as she let the blue flammable liquid spread over the flooring, the furniture, and the walls. Once done, she made enough noise to alert the Frenchmen.

Sreymau continued to shove and damage the furniture as she ran towards the entrance. The guards and the officers rushed inside. She could hear them wonder about the smell. She had to act before they realised.

She grabbed the oil lamp hanging at the main door and flung it into the room with all her might. There was a resounding crash, followed by an explosion of fire. The flames lapped at the kerosene-soaked interiors. They crawled up the walls to the roof. Sreymau tugged the main door closed to bolt it from outside. She hoped Sorya was safe and tried to search for him.

The Frenchmen shouted inside the office. She could hear their concerned and frightened voices over the angry hiss of the red-orange flames. The fire engulfed the building, the heat pushing Sreymau away from the structure. She didn't move.

'Sorya! Sorya! Where are you?' she yelled. He couldn't be inside, not unless the Frenchmen had somehow dragged him back in with them. 'Oh Deva, no!'

Sreymau dashed to the back door yet again. The smoke blinded her eyes and filled her lungs. She coughed and panted. Not finding Sorya anywhere, she decided to run into the flaming office.

'Moon!'

She turned to find him climbing over the wall and ran to hug him. 'You are safe. I couldn't … find you and thought—'

He pulled her close. 'I had to jump over when they shot at me. But what were you thinking, Moon!?' Sorya looked at her with tears in his eyes. 'I could have lost you.'

Sreymau shook her head. 'You won't lose me. I'm here. And we did it! We saved the devatas.'

'Sorry, Moon,' Sorya whispered. 'I couldn't save the devatas. They found them. The devatas are …'

Sreymau turned to the burning building, aghast. Tears streamed down her face. She had failed.

'Other Frenchmen are here. We should leave before they see us.'

Sreymau said nothing as Sorya helped her climb the wall. She didn't notice that only a couple of natives came to help the Frenchmen. They tried to contain the fire in vain. Unable to do much, they drenched the nearby building in water to prevent the fire from spreading.

Sreymau and Sorya were covered in dirt. She sobbed into his chest as they sat in a small hut behind the wall.

'We tried. You did your best, Moon. You put your life at risk for the devatas. They will protect themselves now if they want to,' Sorya murmured into her hair.

They sat for hours, not bothering about the frantic activities around them. Sreymau stared at the dark night through the hole in the thatched roof. It was a miracle this hut didn't catch fire too.

Wouldn't have mattered if it did, she thought.

'Moon, the sun will be up soon. Wake up.'

Sreymau sighed and straightened her neck, wincing at the pain. She blinked her eyes open to see Sorya staring at her with a smile. He looked happy.

'Why are you smiling?' she demanded, taking the hand he offered to stand up and stretch.

'Come. You'll see why.'

She followed him out of the hut to see half the compound wall broken. Almost nothing of the office remained. The ground was filled with charred debris, with smoke still rising in thin streams.

'See there, to the right,' Sorya pointed.

Sreymau squinted until she found what he wanted to show her.

'Oh!' she gasped, her eyes filled with tears again. 'They … the devatas…'

There, on a small half-burnt wooden desk, were the four stolen idols. They were smudged with dark ash, but Sreymau could see who they were. Shiva and Parvati stood side by side with Vishnu and Lakshmi.

'The devas rose from the fire. They had to … for you, my Moon.'

Epilogue—1930s, Angkor

Years have passed since the ruins were rediscovered. Many researchers have been exploring the wat, trying to restore it to its previous state. Sreymau understood nothing except that they were going to revive the temple ruins and protect the site using the materials of the existing structure itself to restore it.

She continued to spy on them. She didn't want them stealing more devatas. Sreymau stood near the inner entrance of the ruins. The place was given a new name, Banteay Srei.

'It's the citadel of the women indeed. Such glorious handiwork on the rocks!'

'I agree. I don't think a man could have carved something this intricate.'

'Well, isn't there a rumour that a local girl burned down a building to save the idols stolen from here?'

'Good for her! Men have had their way for too long now.'

'And here we are, more women, working on bringing this place back to life.'

'Banteay Srei couldn't have a better name.'

Sreymau heard the researchers—women in pants and boots—discuss the carvings and construction as they toiled under the hot sun. She stood taller with pride when they mentioned her. She had had to deal with her angry parents, Sorya's parents, and other natives. But everyone had stood by her and created a fake story about the fire.

The Frenchmen tried their best to investigate. After all, four men had lost their lives, and three others were injured in the fire. However, they could do nothing when the natives stuck to their story.

She smiled at the memory. Even Oliver had had to leave their land post-haste after the incident. No other white man dared to enter the ruins again. The fire inspired many natives to learn more about their heritage and gain confidence to revolt against the French protectorate.

Sreymau turned to look at the carving of a beautiful woman with a lotus in one hand and her skirts dancing around her legs as if she was in motion. The woman's face on the carving resembled the figurine she had found in the ruins years ago. Sreymau knew she eventually had to return it to the wat, but she had kept it with her as a good luck charm. The figurine of an unknown woman from the past somehow gave her peace and strength. She felt renewed energy surge through her each time she held it in her hands.

'Moon, time to go home,' Sorya said from behind her, his hand around her shoulder. She nodded, willing her feet to move. She would be back again soon.

Sreymau couldn't wait for the white men to get out of her land. Cambodia was changing, though not fast enough for her liking. Her people were learning to fight after being dormant for years. She and Sorya did their best to encourage and educate the next generation.

Nothing would be enough if the natives didn't reignite the fire in them to fight for their rights. The way to freedom was to be aware of their history.

Stories start with a tiny spark, and so do revolutions.

Author's Note

Cambodia gained independence from France on 9 November 1953, though it wasn't the last of their battles.

The story of Kalai and Davuth—and Sreymau and Sorya—isn't only about the country's heritage or its undeniable connection with Bharat. It is about women and men across the generations who strove to spread the glory of their heritage.

'Strei' arose from the speculation that women might have built Banteay Srei because of the finesse of its carvings. It led to thinking about how the Cambodians were being ruled by the French during the same time Bharat was fighting for her freedom.

What if a young woman with very little knowledge about her country's history was taught about the rich heritage of the land? What if a woman from Thanjavur became an inspiration for a man to seek the true meaning of art and bhakti?

This story is inspired, in part, by the true story of an infamous Frenchman, Andre Malraux, stealing idols from the temple ruins.[5] My other sources have included various articles, blogs, and news pieces from the internet.[6] It's possible that some of the information doesn't match the exact timeline or has another version of which I'm unaware.

2

A Siem Reap Saunter

Kavita Krishna Meegama

Sri gurubhyo namaha!
Salutations to the teacher!

Traipsing alone in the Phnom Kulen Mountains and its forests in 2018 without a guide, little did Amma (at seventy-two) and I (at forty-six) foresee the more dangerous future in store for us. The next year, COVID-19 would strike, and the world would forever be a changed place. Our yearly temple travels would be impossible until 2022, and we would not be able to see each other for years, separated by the Atlantic Ocean as well as a vast ocean of travel rules and restrictions that would force us to be physically apart. In those trying years, what kept me going was the memory of this wondrous trip that we had made together against all odds.

I was between semesters, doing my master's degree at George Washington University (GWU), Washington DC. Amma was always in demand at home and in the neighbourhood, with friends and family depending on her for everything—from cooking daily meals to looking after a sick relative and from accompanying a friend to the hospital to making pickles together in summer. It was tough to convince her to travel abroad and carve out time for herself. Travelling as a mother–daughter duo was not new for us. We are notorious for taking off to places on a whim but always for a short stint and never outside the borders of Bharatavarsha. Jetting off to a foreign country together was a novel experience for both of us. The Indian subcontinent is our safe haven. We know it and its peoples well. We know how to deal with most situations here and how to react and respond. Our typical instincts were not of much use outside these confines. We were tested many times, and the exhilarating part is that we emerged safe and victorious.

It is the summer of 2020, and I look out of the balcony of my apartment in Rockville Pike, United States of America—far, far away from anything remotely exotic, ancient, or brimming with Hindu culture and history. My time is well spent reminiscing about the hectic week I spent traversing in and around Siem Reap in Cambodia with Amma.

When Covid struck, the memory of our trip to Cambodia kept me going. People cooked, baked, prayed, walked, and did yoga and numerous other things while being homebound. I, on the other hand, had only to pull out from my memory the day-to-day incidents of what transpired in a faraway land and smile. The tree that overlooks my balcony, as though hugging me in understanding and comfort, is no match for the ones in Ta Prohm or Beng Mealea, but it has its own majesty. Old, craggy, and branching out with open arms, subconsciously, it takes me back to its Cambodian cousins. Perhaps it is friends with its Kampuchean sisters and is shaking hands with them underground as we speak. Nature is the greatest mystery of all, which I acknowledge humbly and bow to this grand old oak in reverence. We establish a connection. With this act, I realise I am imitating my mother and that I am closer to her than I think. In her own quiet way, without protesting too much, she has shown me in our days spent together how to be in command—of oneself and of one's situation.

The first thing to do when we travel is to choose the destination. Then comes the choice of one's travel companion. In this case, the decision about where we were going in the summer of 2018 was made easy for us by the fact that an e-visa was issued for a small fee to all Indian citizens arriving in Cambodia, and the process could not be simpler. What was also attractive was that the Indian rupee (brought in by Amma) or a few American dollars (that I had saved diligently over the span of a year with this destination in mind) would go a long way and make our six-day trip something to remember in tough times.

Asking my mother to join me in this adventure was a given. I get my adventurous spirit; the ability to appreciate new cultures, peoples, and mores; the forbearance needed for traveling in areas that might not be running at a pace most of us are used to these days, and the love of humanity and planet Earth in all its glory from her. Whenever my father was posted to a new town in India, it was she who could immediately converse with the locals, make our lives more than comfortable, teach us to respect the alien surroundings, and goad us to learn from them. I remember her sitting up late at night to watch foreign movies on Doordarshan state television and talking to us about them excitedly the next morning. Yes, travelling with Amma was a no-brainer.

To Cambodia then and with my mother! It also helped that Amma mostly (actually, always) gives in to my decisions and does not pose a threat to my authority. I could rely on her to work as a team and to not protest too much if things went wrong.

Emily, my classmate from GWU, had visited Cambodia a few months before on a study abroad programme, and I had been thrilled by her stories. 'Beng Mealea, Beng Mealea,' she had kept repeating. It was out of the world! She had liked that temple more than Angkor Wat. I could hardly wait to see both and decide for myself. Amma and I had our own mental idea of the place, based on an aerial shot of the Angkor complex on the front page of the *National Geographic* magazine from aeons ago. It had beckoned to us ever since. What better way to celebrate Amma's seventy-second birthday than in this manner? Onwards to the kingdom of Kampuchea!

Between 1986 and 1993—a time when peace was yet to be restored in Cambodia after the collapse of the Khmer Rouge regime—the Indian government, responding to an *appeal by Phnom Penh, undertook the conservation of the Angkor Wat temple at a cost of US$4 million.*

It was not merely a tourist's curiosity, though. Lurking in the back of my mind was the knowledge of the gory history that one does not talk about openly. The subject is brushed away politely to avoid upsetting anyone. Pol Pot was a known name even to us kids growing up in pre-Google 1980s India. But all we had heard consisted of mere names and the suggestion, from the elders, of something hush hush. I came to the United States in 2000. The then busy Borders bookstores were stocked floor to ceiling with *First They Killed My Father*, a memoir by the author Loung Ung, who grew up during the Khmer Rouge regime. It was a horrific read, and I remember crying for days on end, unable to come to terms with the tyrannic cruelty inherent in humans. How could a culture and people who could produce the finest art and architecture resort to such despicable acts in the name of revolution and communism? So, Cambodia had always intrigued me, and it did not disappoint. Keeping my mother in mind—or dare I admit, my own queasiness—I decided to stay away completely from the holocaust museums in Phnom Penh and concentrate only on the ruined heritage of the Hindus in the north-west of the country.

One good thing about an Indian travelling to east Asia is that there is so much shared history. There is the underlying common culture, the familiar customs, and the fact that our currency goes a long way, making any trip that much sweeter. Since Amma also wanted to contribute, I let her, and she was thrilled with the currency exchange we made at the airport. 'I can do this holiday again,' she blurted out happily, and I nodded understandingly. Plus, it is so safe and charming. Despite being full of tourists, Siem Reap is an outpost straight from the pen of Graham Greene, had he chosen to write about it as he did about Vietnam or Cuba.

Today, Cambodia celebrates its heritage better than India. Perhaps it is easier, being a small monarchy, or perhaps it just got lucky, given its French colonial past. The French expect one to honour one's history and art without guilt. This idea is made clear in a previous French colony, Pondicherry (Puducherry) in southern India, which also rises to such expectations in a grand manner. Either way, Cambodia's rich legacy is celebrated in every corner.

After landing at the small and narrow airstrip in Siem Reap, which reminded me of Kumbhirgram in Assam, an eastern Indian town where we lived in the 1980s, we walked to the immigration stall. It was flanked by giant *naga* (snake or mythic water being) torsos and faces of Buddha *bayon* (Buddha-like figures). At the end of the trip, when we flew out, we were bidden goodbye by exquisite figurines of Hanuman, Rama, and Lakshmana from the epic Ramayana, displayed in glass cases with studio mood lighting. The country's past pedigree is overtly celebrated there, which makes Hindus come alive and dig deep into their roots. The justifiable pride that comes from admiring the world's largest Hindu temple complex, with wall after wall of etchings from the Ramayana and the Mahabharata, along with numerous *apsara*s (celestial dancers) beckoning us to participate in this grandeur, is offset by the pain of finding no mention of its rich Hindu tradition in most history books. It is also seen in the lack of practising Hindus, *vaidika*s (those who follow the Vedas), or research scholars traversing these paths for a far deeper engagement. On the contrary, only mere tourists can be found there, wanting to update social media at the earliest possible time—we, too, being no different.

Thankfully, for both Amma and me, once in these ruins, with dilapidation and destruction all around, curiosity about what might have occurred in history and the mystery surrounding it all pulled us into each site with renewed vigour. Our shared roots got entangled beyond recognition. This is my account of how we got completely sucked in.

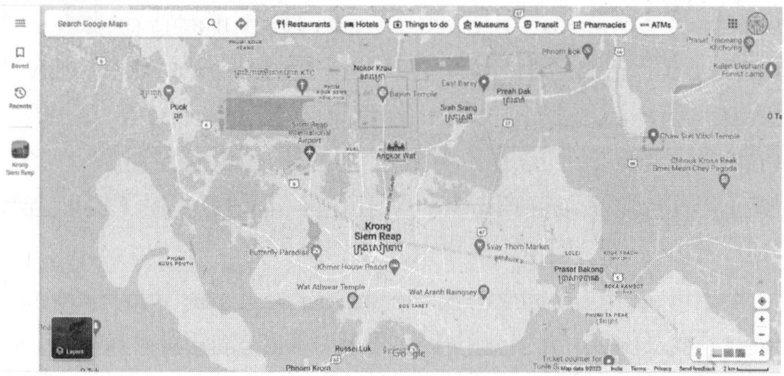

Day 1: Airport, Residence Wat Damnak, Angkor Panorama Museum, Massage Parlour, Wild Restaurant

I sat on my balcony in Rockville, sipping tea and staring at the giant oak that stood there with such dignity. It was neither bored nor upset. Wind, hail, snow, heat—it took them all without a grimace. Its broad trunk smiled back at me reassuringly. This, too, shall pass, it whispered. The trunk morphed into faces I was familiar with, perfectly chiselled faces from across the sea. The few gnarled roots that were above ground started making a move towards me. Where had I seen this all before? During the global Covid quarantine, especially in its first phase before the vaccines came out, the world was fearful and on edge. I fared no better. My parents were so far away, and travel bans were in place. With nowhere to go and no one to visit, what was I to do with so much time on my hands? Memories took over in the evenings—of Bayon, Ta Prohm but, above all, Angkor Wat.

In the summer of 2018, we stayed near the Wat Damnak area downtown at Residence Wat Damnak. The hotel was furnished in teak wood with lace curtains, large lush palms, red oxide flooring, and red doors, reminding us so much of Sri Lanka. Tropical, of course. Right next door, there was an eclectic French café, Wild, run by expatriates making a living off of a cosy food joint catering to their kind. Amma's birthday had been on 1 June, and we were there a week after that. Nevertheless, this was her birthday trip, and I wanted to make it special. The hotel help had devised swans and other birds with towels and arranged confetti saying 'Happy Birthday to the Bestest Mom' on the twin beds. However, I also wanted to have an evening about town—

well, next door. Unlike in Sri Lanka, where a mere mention that it was Amma's birthday brought out bouquets, cakes, and free snacks with waiters singing, the friendly French owners there, despite my explicitly mentioning that we were here to celebrate a birthday, did nothing more than wish her and light a candle. As good Hindus, we did not blow out the candle but simply let it die out on its own. The food was très delicious: a vegetable platter of hummus, wild potatoes, spring rolls, and more. The ambience was even better. That evening had the fragrance of nostalgia even while we were living it.

We sat there that first evening, breathing in the cool Cambodian air, far away from all that was familiar—just Amma and me, exhilarated at what we had managed to pull off. What might seem oh-so-normal was not so. It had not been easy to convince her that we could do this. She had been plagued by fear and worry. Would the funds suffice? What if? Also, how could she leave the household in Hyderabad for so long? How would my father manage alone? What if? What if? Was it alright for two women to fly away just like that? What would our relatives say? Was it necessary at her age to go gallivanting like this for pleasure? What if? No, it had not been easy to convince her, especially remotely by phone from across the seas, from the United States, while she was in India. Meanwhile, I had my own demons to handle: my pending schoolwork, office work, papers to submit, and files to document, not to mention the whole logistics of applying for the e-visa and finding a safe space for our stay. I also had to make sure that I was saving enough for the both of us.

At that moment in time though, sipping on an icy lime drink on the green lawns of Wild, gazing at the twinkling lights that adorned the palms, listening to French songs, and knowing that our hotel was next door with clean sheets awaiting us, we let go. I saw Amma smile at her birthday candle, satisfied. I, too, was content. Goddess Lakshmi was blessing us. I mentally bowed in gratitude and wished Amma a great year ahead. We toasted our soft drinks to 'Many more such adventures!' This one had only just begun.

Right after landing, our tuk-tuk man for the next five days found us (we simply said yes to the first cheerful one outside the airport standing next to a clean three-wheeler who offered his services). He took us to our villa, promising to come back to pick us up in an hour. We had to rush to the Angkor Panorama Museum to buy the three-day passes to the Angkor Wat complex, before settling in after our flight from Bangkok. At the entrance of our hotel, we were enthralled by the ancestral shrines that are ubiquitous all over Thailand too. Here, though, we found some Chinese deities too, a telling insight into who influences the nation. After a complimentary welcome treat of sweet potato chips, tamarind juice, and cold towels, we cooled our heels for quite some time in the oppressive June heat by the pool, while the room was being decorated appropriately to surprise Amma. The tuk-tuk driver, Vaesna, showed up as promised and sped us across town to the ticket counter before it closed at 5 p.m. for the day. The complex offers much more than mere entry passes. There are rows and rows of shops offering massages, tours, and merchandise. We indulged immediately in some easy-to-wear yoga pants for all the walking that lay in store and fell for the sales pitch for the no-oil Khmer massage by one of the vendors.

Vaesna dropped us off at the door of the massage place, saying he would be back in an hour (his payment was per day or half a day). In the muted light, we were greeted by the proprietor, who gave us warm towels and led us to our parlour. What the Khmers can do with the body without lubrication is amazing. After being pulled, squeezed, and trampled upon in myriad ways, we were treated to some jasmine tea and sent off with a cheerful namaste and *arkun* (thank you). It was not a bad start to our first day.

Averaging around seven to eight hours of walking, climbing, hiking daily and Amma being seventy-two years old and all, the ubiquitous Khmer massages were such a blessing. This type of massage ought to be de rigueur in every UNESCO World Heritage Site. They are cheap, a mere $7–14 for an hour. They use no oil, and they pound you well to thrash the tiredness out of your body so that you may walk more the next day. We got a massage almost daily. It was that good and necessary. Although we wanted to explore Pub Street, the night market, and the old market, which were but a short walk away, Amma and I decided to unpack, stay put, and take in the beauty of the place we were in. Most of the time, as tourists, we tend to spend so much money on lovely hotels but end up just sleeping in them. So, we told Vaesna, 'Take us home'.

The lazy atmosphere in the town of Siem Reap can be explained away by the humidity we encountered in the month of June, as hot and humid as in Chennai or Silchar. We were sweating away at 9 a.m. No wonder all our tours were set to start at 4 a.m., requiring us to leave the hotel by 3.30 a.m. The rickshaws or tuk-tuks that take you to the monuments in the Angkor Wat complex wait for you until you are done four or five hours later.

Meanwhile, there are hammocks beckoning you to lie in them and giant coconuts to sip on. It made me a tad bit envious that I had to be in this frenzy of trying to tick off every site I wanted to visit while the locals were taking it easy.

Food, though, was a serious issue. Although Siem Reap has tons of tourists and many eateries catering to all kinds of palates, Indian-style vegetarian food has not caught on in these parts. The hotel we stayed in had not heard of lentils, and without dal, it is tough for vegetarians to keep up their energy level and spirits. Finally, on our third night, we found an Indian restaurant that was heavily recommended and walked over for some much-needed sambar. The food was authentic, and the *agarbatti* (incense) and flowers gracing a large Ganesha statue at the entrance felt familiar. A living culture in the midst of all the dead and decaying. I wonder why there are not more Indian joints there, considering what a draw that could be. I also wonder why there are so few Indian tourists, although they, unlike me, might have checked on the weather before booking their tickets.

At the end of every day's tour, after hours and hours of walking, climbing up and down, and finally dropping down exhausted to a drink of coconut water, there was always one more temple to be visited as per the itinerary. I had made these detailed plans while simultaneously working on my schoolwork, all of which had been extremely strenuous. So now I had to stick to it. There is so much to see in Siem Reap that even a week is not sufficient. I was already rueing not staying for a few days more when I read how much there was to do. However, our tickets back to Bangkok were already booked and from there onwards to Delhi by Jet Airways and finally to Hyderabad. With so many connections to make and commitments to keep, changing our plans at the last minute was not an option. But how I wished!

How do the French and the others who come here as tourists manage to take so much time off from work, study, and family? How do people find time to just chill? I have grown to respect routine and discipline, without which lives can go haywire and meaningless, even though it sounds boring. I had slogged at my job teaching language and culture to Foreign Service Officers, who wanted nothing more than to pass the language test so that they could get on with their careers. I had wanted nothing more than the salary that I was given in return for bearing their entitled behaviour in the classroom so that I could travel the world, learn, and grow. It takes hard work, diligent saving, advance planning, and organisation to be able to pull off a trip like this. Most people have families, bank balances, connections, psychological support, or a large network for conducting their international travel. All Amma and I had was only passion for travel and people, but lots of that.

So, as much as I wanted to, I could not change the plans and itinerary at the last minute. I had a job to return to, which would essentially pay for my next trip. But that day, I wanted to forget all that, and I didn't want Amma to get a whiff of my concerns. We wanted to bask in our small victory. We were here after all, were we not?

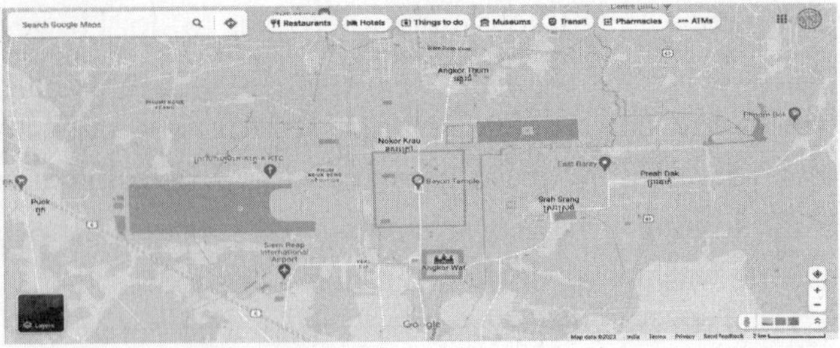

Day 2: Angkor Wat, Bayon, Baphuon, Phimeanakas, Terrace of Elephants, Terrace of Leper King, Ta Prohm, Bamboo Shoots at Molop Wat Damnak

'Let me drive the Luna back to Hyderabad. It will be such an adventure!' Amma pleaded. However, my father, my sister, and I had protested at such an unthinkable idea and squashed her spirit quickly. We were at a paying guest accommodation in Bidar, Karnataka (1995), which is about 300 km from Hyderabad. We were shifting base to the big city, and the ladies' vehicle in question, a two-wheeler bike, was about to be packed by the movers. Just then, Amma had excitedly blurted out this idea before they took it away. I remember with a twinge of guilt how disappointed she had been with us. She had thought it all out. 'I will follow the Gypsy, the four-wheeler you are in. If there is a problem, you will all be there to help me, no?' However, we had not given in. I wonder why. Was it her role as a mother that we did not want to ruffle with such unseemly doings? Was it because we lacked what she had—gumption and guts? Was it because she was a middle-aged woman, and women in the 1990s from small-town India did not aspire to such untoward desires?

All the trips we have made since as a mother–daughter duo have been my humble effort to make up for that one 'no'. I am not sure if I can ever match up to that spirit of Amma's from the 1990s, but there are days when I am very satisfied with how the holiday has gone. This day was one such. I can only hope that it went as wonderfully for Amma too.

Our second day was the most memorable of our trip. Although each day surpassed the previous and we were constantly being surprised, challenged, and tested, that day on the grounds of the Angkor Wat, we pushed our own boundaries and experienced a thrill like never before. We were free to explore with no time limit. We were headed nowhere but here. We were cut off from our daily duties. All we had was time and this gigantic complex to wander in. We met many kind-hearted people on this day, who made our trip so much sweeter.

Amma wore her sleeveless kurta to beat the heat, which was not acceptable by the local standards, especially in sacred spaces. Unfortunately, we were not aware of this. Despite pleading with the moral police, a stern lady in starched khakis, she did not let Amma climb up to the main shrine at Angkor *Bakan* to offer prayers. Whilst engaged in a fracas, I desperately tried to think of what to do.

'We have come all the way from India, ma'am. We are not here as tourists like most others. We are devotees, and this means a lot to us.'

Almost in tears, I urged the woman with a stiff chin to take heed and let up. She did not, but someone else did. A young Canadian couple were next in line and, on witnessing our strained interaction, appeared as Vishnu's attendants and offered Amma an oversized jacket.

'Hope this will do to cover up.'

Of course, it will, thank you, thank you, thank you!

Dressed in her borrowed black windcheater, Amma slowly climbed the almost vertical staircase to the heavens. At seventy-two, she was doing fine, much better than I was, frankly. At the top were shrines with fresh fruits, flowers, incense, Bodhi[1] tree replicas in gold and green, monks offering blessings, and the view. The view was enhanced by the wind god Vayu's presence, which cooled us down further—both our tempers and our growing hunger. A sea of green lay below us with apsaras in elaborate headgear, each different from the other, swimming in it. We were at the zenith of art, architecture, culture, and civilisation. This felt as exhilarating as when Amma had climbed Sigiriya in Sri Lanka last year (in block heels no less) and better. There is only one Angkor Wat, and we were at the top in spite of the hurdles. I looked at her in awe. I hope to be as fit when I am her age and as enthusiastic. Despite our daily back-and-forths, our *nok-jhok,* she is the only one I want to emulate as I grow older.

What Amma and I had expected from Angkor Wat is what we remembered from a *National Geographic* special on it from many moons ago. The photograph was an aerial shot, and the massive temple complex seemed far from reach, something to aspire to in the future but a place where we did not expect to land up someday. So, on the morning of our second day in Siem Reap, at 3.30 a.m. to be precise, we were loath to get up from our comfortable beds and let go of the air conditioning that had run all night. We had to take cold showers before the much-promised 'long day ahead'. The hotel receptionist who had helped us with local clues and such, the tuk-tuk driver Vaesna who we booked for this trip, the ticket counter lady who gave us a map with the $65 receipts—all of them had warned us to hydrate well, wear caps, rest in intervals, and carry some food. Most hotels prepare a sandwich pack and send you off at *brahmamuhurta,* so that guests can catch the sun god Surya peeking from behind the four famous *wat* towers (wat is temple in Khmer, from the Sanskrit *vata* or enclosure) and capture him for their Insta stories and Twitter threads. Whether it is Chichen Itza, Teotihuacan, Modhera, or Martand, architecturally, they are all built to show off the sun on the spring equinox rising behind their main towers or sunlight falling straight at the feet of the Surya *murti*[2] inside. This was no different, although it was not the spring equinox and was more like the summer solstice.

I was all agog, and the ride to the entrance in the wee hours with the Cambodian breeze caressing my hair turned out to be a long, competitive joyride of one tuk-tuk outdoing the other. Almost everyone from all the hotels and B&Bs were headed to the same destination. We had to make it to the park entrance in time before they stopped people and controlled the crowds going in. It hit me that this would not be a solitary quiet exploration of our ancient heritage across the seas. Instead, this would be another of those 'fighting the public to get a decent photo' scenarios. We had encountered the same scenario in the Wat Arun in Bangkok and in the royal palaces there. So Amma and I were already dreading it.

Then we saw the water twinkling in the moonlight. It went on and on, parallel to the road we were on. Was it a river? An irrigation canal? Whatever it was, it added to the mystery of what we would find at the end of this ride. The driver stopped and prepared to rest for the next six hours, saying, 'Come back here by 10.30 or 11. I will be under this tree.' We thought his English was weak or his mathematics. Was it not just about 4.30 a.m.? The 5 km ride to the Angkor Wat park entrance had not taken that long, but when we walked across the never-ending outer moat to reach a spot to view the spires rising 65 ft above ground (as per online research), we were thoroughly disappointed. It seemed nothing like the photos we had seen. There were a few intricate towers, shorter than expected, nothing grand or magnificent in size or shape from where we were standing. Dejected, we waited along with others for a disappointment.

There were hundreds of tourists just like us, though very few Indians from the looks of it. There was no shade whatsoever, just a vast expanse with people sitting on the floor and waiting for the arrival of Surya *bhagavan* (sun god). Some had taken refuge in a few ruins, sitting on steps at a higher elevation to get a better shot. Ahead of us was a pool of water with palm trees flanking it. The reflection of the temple towers and spires in the pool was probably more beautiful than the sunrise that day. Unfortunately for all of us, it turned out to be cloudy. The morning sunlight was hidden away, and only a few rays reached us, enough to get us trudging along for the next few hours. On the other hand, you could say it was fortunate that it was cloudy. The amount of walking and climbing we did would have been impossible if the rain god Indra had not intervened. After all, this temple was said to have been built on his orders, and he surely wanted us to have a good *darshan* (spiritual viewing) without getting fatigued.

Angkor Wat was built by Suryavarman II to represent Mount Meru. He dedicated the temple to Vishnu, the preserver of the world. Angkor Wat was the state temple of the Khmer Empire in the 12th century. It has Hindu and Buddhist iconography on its bas-reliefs. Just as in the Thai royal palace, here too, the walls of the outer perimeter are inscribed with tales from the Mahabharata and the Ramayana. The naga balustrades, a common feature in the architecture of these parts, made their grand appearance. We were immediately yanked into the world of apsaras, *devata*s (self-effulgent higher beings or deities), *garuda*s (celestial eagles), *gaja*s (elephants), and *simha*s (lions). What looked like rundown ruins slowly revealed their beauty to us, gallery by gallery. No space was without etchings or friezes. Artists had had a field day filling up the sandstone and laterite canvases with stories from Hindu literature. All roofs, columns, corners, corridors, and lintels—every available area—depicted the tales of our ancestors. All this glory came to naught when the Chams (from present-day Vietnam) invaded and destroyed the temple, which is when the successor, Jayavarman VII, moved the state temple to Bayon.

The second and the third gallery each consisted of four towers, marking the four directions, and each was higher than the preceding one. The innermost shrine of the holy section, called *Bakan,* was too steep to get to for many, who chose to sit it out. Since worship is carried out daily to the Buddha housed there, we were asked to be mindful of our clothing. There was policing at regular intervals to ensure that anyone not dressed appropriately could not enter. We had encountered this in Thailand too, where it is clearly stated at various tourist spots that no disrespect to the Buddha is permitted, especially in the clothes one wears. One tuk-tuk driver there had taken offence at the short top or kurta that I was wearing, which was printed with dancing heads, a raging fashion that year in Hyderabad. He was very upset until I showed him the head dot, the bindi[3], and convinced him that the pattern on my attire was of an Indian classical dancer and not Buddha.

Friends and family had wanted to join us on this journey, but we must do some things by ourselves, for ourselves. Not everyone we know can walk as fast or as slow as the situation demands. Not everyone who wants our company will take our orders to do this or that kindly. Not everyone who craves the same level of excitement and adventure has the same spirit to tolerate, accommodate, and endure. I have made many enemies in my friends' circle and family since I have started travelling alone. Most of them who want to join me in my sojourns would not last a day and could not rough it like I do. Only Amma qualifies, and hence, she was there with me.

Returning to the grounds from the high Bakan was not easy. Being at the top can get addictive, but there was so much more on our to-do list that we scrambled down in no time. We walked back to our tuk-tuk, satiated, after returning the black raiment to the lovely Canadians who had saved our day with their spontaneous, generous gesture.

Our stomachs reminded us that the jam and butter sandwich we had eaten had just been a snack and not a breakfast worthy of hard-nosed travellers who had trekked for six hours since daylight. It was almost 10.30 a.m. The morning sun was no infant but a full-blown adult claiming his rights, harsh and unrelenting. We were baked and grumpy by the time we headed back to our tuk-tuk guy. Finding him among the gazillion other fellows with their three-wheelers took some time, and soon, we were on our way back for the complimentary buffet at Residence Wat Damnak. Lots of locals, meanwhile, were enjoying their day in the country-made hammocks overlooking the moat and dozing off in the cool breeze under the shade of the trees. Not bitten by the bug of wanderlust, they were oblivious to our haste.

Brunch was more bread and fresh fruits with cornflakes, until we encountered the manager, the gracious Ms Vinny, who took it upon herself to make a quick spicy pulao for us. After this quick hearty meal had put enough carbs inside us, we headed back to where we came from to finish the rest of the circuit of Bayon, Baphuon, the Terrace of the Elephants, the Terrace of the Leper King, Chau Say Tevoda, Thommanon, and the famed Ta Prohm. The names became familiar with each passing day, but the places were one big jumble in the mind. Which temple was which, which statue was whose, and which was Hindu or Buddhist? It helped that we took tons of photos for reminiscing about this once-in-a-lifetime-excursion later.

Angkor is derived from the word *nokor,* which is Sanskrit for *nagara* (city). *Thom* in Khmer means 'big'. So Angkor Thom is 'Great City', with Bayon, the state temple, as its centre. When Vaesna stopped his tuk-tuk suddenly, we thought it was a mechanical issue—a flat tire perhaps. Maybe the chain had come off. After all, it was a motorcycle engine that was chugging us along. So, when the driver got off his seat, opened our rain coverings, the plastic sheet purdahs, and asked us to get off the vehicle, we were mentally prepared to wait by the roadside for a few hours. That is how long it takes in India when something like this happens. So imagine our absolute wonder when we step out. The seven-headed nagas at the end of the causeway into Bayon stared back at us. The massive heads of fifty-four celestial elevated beings, the devas, could be seen on one side pulling at the front. On the other side of Bayon, fifty-four celestial fallen beings, the asuras, tugged at the tail of the serpent, holding the naga body like a rope. The stone depiction of the *samudra manthan*[4] was as though the devas and the asuras were taking turns to churn the temple of Bayon itself.

Seeing the samudra manthan come alive in 3D in such massive proportions in stone made all the hours of walking and sweating worth it. The causeway on the moat surrounding Angkor Wat opened up a mythical world to us. Falling raindrops, creating moss on these warriors, as though in the sacred offering of *abhisheka*[5], would soon join the nearby Siem Reap River, which was already made holy by the thousand symbols of Shiva, the *sahasra linga*s[6], carved in its riverbed up north. The network of canals, moats, rivers, streams, and lakes spoke of a fabulously wealthy and highly refined civilisation adept at irrigation and engineering. Then we saw it.

At the far end of the bridge was the south tower, with four humongous faces depicting Brahma (while others say Buddha or Avalokiteshvara) held up by elephants on either side. This tower acts as a city gate and prepares you for what lies ahead. Traffic passes through it, and when we looked up, all we saw was a small circle letting in sunlight from *svarga*[7] on that rainy day. The enigmatic smiling faces, serene and all-knowing, refused to leave our side. Each face was composed of perfect squares, a jigsaw solved with precision.

Walking into the Bayon Temple, I saw many Shiva lingas broken or separated from their *panapatta*s (sacred bases). I felt a pang of regret and a deep sense of loss. My exhilaration turned to despondency, and I had to do something to ward off that feeling. We had walked almost eight or nine hours already, and our water supply was coming to an end, our small backpacks not being able to carry more than two large water bottles. I fished out the gurgling recycled plastic container and, with all the reverence I could muster in such a dire situation, managed to pour three drops on each of the lingas that were still intact with an inaudible 'Om Namaha Shivaya' and put some kumkum on them. Amma was taken aback as well on seeing them all abandoned like this. We were glad that our ancestors had taught us to drink water from the top and not off the bottle rim. The bottled water was, therefore, fit for a sacred offering in an emergency.

We found the courage to do what we did from the Cambodians themselves, who have incense, flowers, and candles at the feet of many a sacred statue in Angkor Wat. The security guards, stationed heavily at every structure, approved and encouraged such a show of devotion. The culture of the land and the people of Cambodia are not at odds with their monarchical government, unlike in secular India, where the management of many temples under the Archaeological Survey of India (ASI) would not be as compassionate towards a devout rural Indian wanting to express his or her *bhakti* towards an architectural wonder in their safekeeping.

Bayon has a mixture of Mahayana, Hindu, and Theravada influences due to the patronage of the kings that ruled and controlled these structures. Jayavarman VII followed Mahayana, and massive public works were undertaken in his reign, Bayon and the famed Ta Prohm among them. All of these works are very ornate, unlike the classical Angkor Wat. Bayon was called Jayagiri (city of victory) before the French took control. The 200-odd faces surrounding us on the terrace did indeed look victorious, but this victory was of the self. It was not a show of power against an invader, as was very evident from the contented smiles they sported. But for the rainy darkness enveloping the temple precincts, as it was soon to be evening, we would have wandered more in its alleys and various galleries. Amma, a typical *fauji* (defence personnel) wife, did not complain even once about the extensive climbing and walking that was needed to explore all these temples. So onwards we went to the next site on the checklist.

Baphuon, a Shiva temple, was spectacular. Gradual galleries and staircases lead to the top, which now houses only empty door frames. It has intricate and breathtaking carvings on its walls. Much of its shaky core has collapsed, and a large-scale undertaking to reconstruct it was abandoned when civil war broke out in 1970. Archaeologists and workers had labelled and numbered nearly three lakh pieces identifying the blocks but lost them all to the ensuing conflict and the Khmer Rouge. To put it back together, the largest jigsaw puzzle in the world, a second project was launched in 1996. The temple, finally complete after sixteen more years of hard work, was inaugurated in 2011 by the king of Cambodia, His Highness Norodom Sihamoni. My notes from that day say: 'Baphuon is a Shiva temple. modus operandi—long walk to temple, cross a moat, climb steep steps of 3–5 tiers, reach top, no idols, no murti, admire architecture, feel the pain of a civilisation in ruins, feel pride at the capacity, leave.' From there, it was a short walk to the Terraces through the thicket, and we saw many female guards employed by APSARA (Authority for the Protection of the Site and Management of the Region of Angkor) guarding the precincts along the way.

The two Terraces—Terrace of the Elephants and Terrace of the Leper King—mesmerised us with the sheer scale of *airavata*s (celestial elephants) and the maze of nagas. It was almost the end of the marathon we had walked since early morning, and we were exhausted. After viewing the Phimeanakas temple and the king's audience hall, where the royalty gathered for public ceremonies, Amma sat on the steps, asking me to go ahead. She indicated that she needed to rest, and since we still had to cover Ta Prohm, which I knew would need more energy, I let her be. She could see the god of death, Lord Yama, the leper king, from afar.

Locally, Lord Yama is called Dharmaraja[8], which is what he is in the Hindu pantheon too: the god who embodies dharma. A middle-aged Cambodian lady, dressed in the traditional attire of a pretty, puffy lace blouse and tight long A-line skirt, hair tied up in a bun decorated with a jasmine strand, was offering incense sticks and flowers to the deity. She moved around this deity of death with folded palms in deep reverence, bowing to him after every clockwise circumambulation. I followed her lead and did what she was doing, not knowing who the deity was at that time. Given the Bayon style of the sculpture, he looked more like a bodhisattva to me. After I was done, she and her friend called me aside to gift me a string of jasmine for my hair! I was so thrilled. I love *mallepuvvulu* (jasmine flowers), and these were strung very tight and very differently. It was touching to see them sharing so freely. I bowed again a bit more deeply and left to check on Amma. She was ready to explore more but was thirsty. So we walked to the nearest shack for a king coconut. It was extremely sweet and nutritious, filling our bellies up completely. Now we were ready for Ta Prohm.

For Amma and me, it was a matter of great pride to see the ASI noticeboards everywhere, in both English and

Hindi: 'Caution', 'Don't Touch', and 'This site is under construction by ASI'. Ta Prohm is a temple complex being devoured by giant strangler fig and silk cotton trees as we speak. *Tomb Raider*, the movie with Angelina Jolie, was filmed there. The trees are humongous, their roots intermingling with the stone of the various small enclosures within the temple structure and overpowering them. In many temples, the tree roots act like a flowing crown, as though blessing them from the top. The temple was built by Jayavarman VII in the Bayon style for his mother, and he called it Rajavihara. At its peak, it housed six hundred plus dancers and needed eighty thousand people to maintain its grounds.

There were many locals and tourists at the temple, but for the first time, we encountered hindrances in the form of heaps of stones and several people taking photos and selfies. There was a young newly married couple who had come for their photo shoot there. The bride was dressed in a mauve off-shoulder lace blouse and a silk skirt and had pretty plastic flowers in her hair. She looked beautiful and happy. Why would she want to start her life's journey, something auspicious, in these ruins, I wondered. I know the answer. Social media has not been kind to such ancient sites.

Ta Prohm was definitely a sight to behold—like an octopus eating its prey, spreading its tentacles to feel the victim before it engulfed everything in its path. This is a place to enjoy on an early morning with not many people around. A quiet, contemplative walk in its environs will certainly make humans ponder about the passage of time and how life takes over all else. It was definitely eerie too, as though these trees and their roots had a life of their own, going their way helter-skelter, not listening to what the elders said, and heading for the kill straightaway. We took pictures standing next to these tall trees that seemed to want to embrace everything. Amma refused to step on them and kept apologising, asking for *kshamapana* (act of forgiveness) from them. Then she went and hugged one of them, saluting it with a heartfelt *namaskara* (obeisance). We bade goodbye to Ta Prohm with a heavy heart. It was a very short sojourn. How I wish we had had more time to wander about there! How I wish we had gone in the morning and not at the end of the day when we were too enervated to walk further!

Exhausted, we returned to base. The food there is predominantly rice and coconut milk with a variety of meats and fish. Unfortunately for us, as vegetarians, we did not have any protein to fall back on, such as dal, beans, legumes, or tofu even. So we got tired easily with nothing to recharge our bodies. The rice grain though is amazing, and Amma bought a kilogram of local rice from the market just before leaving town on the way to the airport. The flooding of the plains by the Mekong and the Tonle Sap rivers helps in water-intensive rice cultivation. We also bought Amok spice, which is mainly lemongrass, galangal, and kaffir lime with black pepper. The markets had other delicacies such as live snails and insects on display on food carts, which we sidestepped while making our way to the rice stalls. Maggots, crickets, snakes, cockroaches, ants, grasshoppers, and locusts are street food here.

We had just about enough energy on our second night there to literally drag ourselves across the street to Molop Wat Damnak for a delicious dinner of papaya salad, veggie amok, and eggplant and bamboo shoots with rice. This place also offers cooking classes and is famous in the area. As luck would have it, the power went out as soon as we ordered our meal, and we ended up having an unexpected candle-lit dinner. It was quite an end to a fabulous day. We did not have the luxury of staying late in town as we had an early start the next day. So we came 'home' right after dinner.

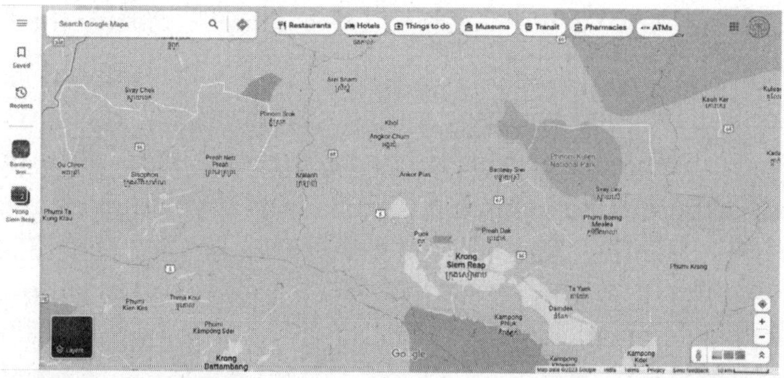

Day 3: Preah Khan, Neak Pean, Ta Som, Banteay Srei, East Mebon, Pre Rup, Banteay Kdei, Dosas at Dakshin

Here I am on my balcony on Rockville Pike. It is 2020, and I hear the metro train rumble past. The sounds of traffic reach my ears from the other end of the apartment. My tea is getting cold while I reminisce about the days gone by. Will I go on any more trips with Amma? This fear haunts me. I am insecure and fight off any depression that might set in with having to be confined to such a small space for God knows how long. We have been shopping online for food and groceries, not stepping out at all. We have been careful. But it has been two months already, and there is no sign of a Coronavirus vaccine or of the virus relenting. Reading the news is not helping. There is only death all around. Indians say it is worse in the United States, and Americans say India is going up in smoke. I am not sure what the truth is anymore. I rely on what has already happened to keep me going. I rely on the awed and contented look on my mother's face when she saw the miniature stone carvings at Banteay Srei and the way she walked ahead, alone and confident, towards Neak Pean. I jog my memory, rewinding to that day.

Preah Khan sounds like the name of a Bollywood actor, but that is far from the reality. Walking on the giant causeway lined with serpentine nagas carried by celestial devatas and asuras across the moat, just like in Bayon, a common motif all over Siem Reap it would seem, we were stunned to see the outer walls. One after another, there were statues of garudas holding the nagas upright. What a sight to behold! After days on end of walking and being constantly surprised and awed, we did not think that there was anything more to ooh and aah at. But there, right in front of us, was an example of what a human mind can conceive if given the freedom to create. There are fifty-two of these statues in total, one celestial eagle placed every few metres. Simply spectacular! Jayavarman VII dedicated this sacred temple to his father at the site of his victory over the Chams (after they had ransacked Angkor Wat). The temple houses Buddha as well as Shiva, Vishnu, Brahma, Krishna, and other Hindu deities in satellite shrines. After our regular rounds, as on the previous day, we got into our tuk-tuk, trusting Vaesna to help us cover the major sights in this area.

The highlight of this day for us was the walk in the pouring rain to Neak Pean. We had just completed Preah Khan, astounded by its beauty, and we were sure that nothing could surpass what we had just witnessed. However, we were proven wrong again and again. *Neak* is Khmer for the Sanskrit *naga*. Built as a hospital and a place to rest and rejuvenate, this temple sits on an island in the middle of a large pond. The pond is surrounded by four other small ponds on all four sides, representing earth, water, fire, and wind. Walking from the clean restroom at the entrance to this serene natural hospice, we expected yet another typical temple structure and were not prepared for the mystical combination of rainwater and light that shook us out of our complacency. We walked a long, narrow, muddy path with pond water on either side and a marsh of reeds and tall grasses guarding us (something like Thekkady in Kerala, visually speaking). Then we entered a copse of trees, which opened into the central pond. The pond had a tiny island with a small temple on it held by two giant nagas in stone: Nanda and Upananda. We had our yellow raincoats on (ones we had bought in Yosemite two years before), and with no place to sit, all we could do was go around this pond in a *pradakshina* (sacred clockwise circumambulation), admiring its beauty, praying for wellness of body and being, and hoping for miracles in this life and the next. Close by, to the east, was Ta Som, a miniature Ta Prohm but no less jaw-dropping. Ta Som was quieter, more peaceful and more eerie in the now pouring rain. The piece-de-resistance is the third eastern *gopura* (temple tower) being devoured by a sacred fig tree.

While the end of the second day of touring in Siem Reap was the triumphant Ta Prohm, at the end of the third day, the grand finale was the astounding carved red sandstone temple of Banteay Srei. The temple was not easy to get to. Most of these ancient sites are spread about in the hinterlands, and once you reach them, there is still a long walk before one gets to the actual ruins. In this case, the temple was another 30 km to the north-east of Siem Reap, near Phnom Dei Hill. This is not a ruin. This 'Citadel of Victory' or 'Citadel of Women', depending on who translates it, is indeed the 'the jewel of Khmer art', as it is called. Delicately carved bas-reliefs on its lintels are its claim to fame, and despite the surging crowds wanting to get a glimpse before it was closed to the public at the end of the day, Amma and I got to drop our jaws many times in admiration.

The architecture is from the 10th century and pays homage to Shiva. Commissioned by just a courtier, not even a king or emperor, it showcases the acme of the high culture of those times. Yajnavaraha was a scholar-philanthropist and counsellor in the reign of Rajendravarman II. He was a devout *bhakta* (devotee), judging by the elaborate decorative carvings of Indra, Kala, and Sita and scenes from the Mahabharata and the Ramayana of the Vali–Sugriva fight and the burning of the Khandava forest. It is a veritable feast for the eyes, an extempore quiz on our epics in stone. Like the Ranakpur or the Dilwara Jain Temple complex in Mt Abu, Rajasthan, which pays tribute to white marble, this compound is an ode to red sandstone by sculptors who were probably also goldsmiths in their artisanship, given their dexterity in miniature models. Doorways beckoned, and arches made our hearts soar. The fading red stood out against the green as a reminder of the old world, showcasing lost grandeur. The sight was indeed magical and mysterious at the same time, with many monkey-like *vanara*s from Sugriva's battalion kneeling in attention as *dwarapalaka*s (doorkeepers).

Should I stand still in silence and let the milling crowds continue to gasp around me? Should I walk around quickly to tick off all the must-do sights and get my money's worth? Should I capture this exquisite beauty on camera for posterity while adroitly avoiding others doing the same? Should I rue the fact that this painfully beautiful architecture will soon be reduced to dust in the sands of time despite all our efforts to contain it in our memories?

While I was ruminating thus, Amma had disappeared. I took it as a sign that I, too, should let myself wander and allow myself to be lost in this wonderland. She had been walking at least eight hours daily since the time we landed there and was not showing any signs of slowing down. Her ardour for travel and exploration, without complaints of heat or humidity, inspired me to ignore my sweaty and smelly clothes and bash on regardless. While I had a cap on, she refused to cover her head even with a dupatta (as it is not considered auspicious for married women to do so among Telugu Brahmins). There she was in her orange and green salwar suit, her outfit matching the environs, looking up at the apsaras in delight. I get my appreciation of art too from Amma. Growing up, I saw her paint a lot with India ink, sketch, draw, stitch, sew, knit, and crochet, basically indulging in every craft except sculpture. She is my benchmark on all things art, but here she was being exposed to something vastly superior and she could not be contained.

That day turned out to be very interesting. Despite the thoughts of being jaded by so many ruins and so much walking, we were taught to be a bit more humble by the gods. 'What, you think we can't better this?' they seemed to say. And, true to the lesson they were trying to teach us, here it was, one after another splendorous works of brick, laterite, and sandstone, showing us what was possible. East Mebon and Pre Rup, both dedicated to Shiva in the 10th century by Rajendravarman, had three or more tiers, with large life-like elephants and lions standing sentinel at the corners of each tier. Lintels with intricate carvings reminded us of Banteay Srei. At the top of these hill temples are towers, with the main shrine on a central square platform. This construction is typical of the times. East Mebon has brick shrines at the top and mysterious holes on its walls. There were also a few jasmine plants blooming at its doorways, and the scent wafted with the setting sun throwing gilded rays at us. This temple was once an island that could be approached only by boat. The very thought of it seemed so idyllic. So, we closed our eyes and let it all soak in before climbing down.

The 'Citadel of Monk's Cells' (Banteay Kdei) was also built by the great builder Jayavarman VII after he had defeated the Chams. This temple of Banteay Kdei was iconic because of the number of pillars it had supporting the roof and the many welcoming simhas and nagas at the entrance. To its east is the royal bathing pool of Srah Srang, where the king and his wives bathed, with a temple island in the centre of the pool for his royal highness to meditate. Today, many monks dot its banks, mingling with the commoners, reminding us gently of changing times and mores. What was royalty once has been wiped out. A different set takes over, and so on it goes. After a quick dekko, we walked a bit towards Pub Street to eat dosas and drown in the delicious sambar at Dakshin, of which I have spoken before.

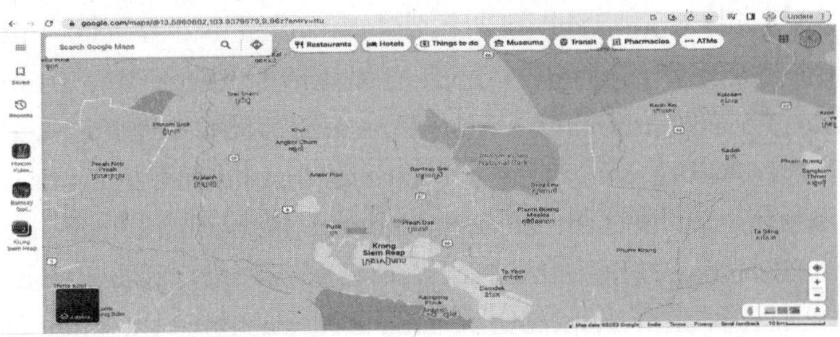

Day 4: Ta Reach, Phnom Kulen, Bakong, (Roluos Group) Preah Ko, Lolei, Vaesna's house on the way back, Dinner at Residence Wat Damnak

Every WhatsApp message, every news report, and every conversation with friends and family is about the dreaded Coronavirus these days. We tell one another to keep faith and hold tight, while worrying for loved ones who are far away and out of physical reach. I am on my balcony on Rockville Pike right on schedule for chai and snacks, but the pouring rain and impending storm prevent me from sitting and enjoying a quiet evening. The water-soaked balcony floor is slippery. The stream that flows behind us is overflowing and threatening to flood the banks. I look at it and wonder whether it hides any carved Shiva lingas in its bed. It is entirely possible. This area was once the ancient highway of Native Americans for thousands of years.

Before the white man made his move, natives traversed up and down this well-beaten route. Perhaps they might have given vent to their artistic genius by painting on rocks in the stream or carved deities from stone, like they did in Kbal Spean. I smile at my memory. I smile again to ward off the fear that is engulfing the world. I think of Amma often to get strength and confidence in these times.

Amma was always determined to be independent, but as a housewife in the 1960s, this posed a bit of a problem. She did not have an income of her own nor did she come from money. How then was independence to be achieved? She worked as a teacher after we girls grew up, saved some money, and bought herself a Luna moped with her savings, a moped that was to become all the rage in the 1990s. She was in her late forties and had never even been on a bicycle. We were in Jodhpur at that time (1990), a gorgeous princely town bordering the Thar Desert in western India, which was not known for its public transportation. How was she to go about the place without a vehicle at hand? My father had already moved to Hyderabad, and we would be following suit in two years, once I had completed graduation. So, next thing we know, she has roped in the neighbour didi to teach her to drive. Every morning, they would go to the Abhay Garh Parade Grounds and practise. In her handloom saris on a two-wheeler, she was quite a sight. I would like to think that what ultimately gave her the confidence to be on her own on the broad Rajasthani roads, where pearl-clad Rajput princesses raced past in Jeeps with heads covered by chiffon saris and eyes by foreign goggles, were my admonitions. Also, one time, I made her drive with me behind her, shouting at her like a drill sergeant on the main highway without helping her by word or deed. I simply shouted, 'Drive!' That did it. That is how we make a good team, I suppose. Just as she has always anticipated my needs and has more than fulfilled them, I know what she wants and make sure to give it before she asks for it. Our trip to Cambodia, too, was my fulfilling of one such unspoken desire of Amma's. She ended up surprising me here too, meeting every occasion head on without flinching.

Now, in our fascination with the place and the new surroundings and given my distaste for over-researching any spot for the fear of losing spontaneity, I had not really looked up online what to do at Angkor Wat. I had only made the basic arrangements for boarding and lodging and visas. I had wanted to simply go with the flow, but this time I had not paid attention to something precious.

After visiting Angkor Wat on the second day and completing the entire 'tourist' circuit on the third day, I thankfully went online to see if I had missed anything. For example, I had totally overlooked the fact that Kbal Spean was included in the $65 ticket, which I would not have known but for the kindness of a stranger, a fellow Indian, whom Amma and I ran into while exploring Banteay Kdei (the same person had also recommended that we eat at Dakshin as we were missing our daily quota of dal). During this cursory research, I panicked because it brought up Ta Reach, a giant murti of Vishnu, sixteen and half feet tall, housed in the entrance of the Angkor Wat complex. How had we missed this after making sure that we walked every inch of the place? Then I remembered that we had seen a crowd and lots of monkeys around this western entrance at Angkor Wat and had decided to go in later but had completely forgotten about it.

Today was the only day we could pay our respects and make offerings to Vishnu, given our tight schedule and impending departure. So we requested Vaesna to do a quick stop at the Angkor Wat on the way to Phnom Kulen National Park, which is where Kbal Spean is and where the holy stream flows deep inside the jungle.

We rushed into Angkor Wat early one last time to beat the crowds and were completely, totally, absolutely mesmerised. Ta Reach is such an imposing figure. We did our circumambulations under the shade of his large yellow parasol and eight arms in silence and prostrated in complete surrender. But for Vishnu's grace, we would have completely missed having this darshan. That Indian stranger had indeed appeared as a devata, giving us useful tips. People were making various offerings, and the guard stood smiling indulgently. He approved that the deities were being given due respect. He tacitly agreed that this was a live shrine. So what if it is a UNESCO monument? That does not mean that local sentiments ought to be disregarded. This was a very admirable Cambodian trait. We ran out, having made our salutations, and sat in the tuk-tuk panting, while Vaesna vroomed north towards the sacred stream.

What took me to Cambodia was not any tourist brochure or a Facebook post by some popular figure or my friends' vacation display pictures. Social media did inspire me but not something shared by the usual suspects. One day, while scrolling through Twitter, I chanced upon the surreal photo of thousands of Shiva representations, the sahasra lingas, submerged in a river called the Kbal Spean in the interiors of the jungles of the Kulen Mountains. You trekked uphill inside a great forest to be blessed with the sight of Brahma, Vishnu, Shiva, Uma, various devis and devatas, and assorted animals underwater, awaiting pilgrims like me to rescue them from being wet and hidden. Hermits had carved them during the reigns of Suryavarman I and Udayadityavarman II. One look at the waterfall in a lush green tropical setting completed the scenario with stories of a glorious Hindu past. It was enough to pull me towards it. Kbal Spean, not Angkor Wat, was the sole reason I had put Cambodia on my itinerary.

On the fourth day after landing in Siem Reap, when I asked if Vaesna would take us to Phnom Kulen National Park, he was not too keen to drive 25 km away from the city. After all, had he not driven us for hours on end the previous three days from very early morning to late at night? But we had the Angkor Wat admission ticket valid for another day at a hefty $65 apiece. So we coaxed him into it. It took him all of an hour. The roads were empty, but he had to drive against the wind. As he was miffed, he was not very helpful. Dropping us off at the entrance, he said, 'I wait here, long time, you go.' Ahead of me and Amma, who was dressed in a bell-bottomed skirt due to a packing mishap, was a narrow path entering the *aranya* (forest). The environs reminded me of where Lakshmana had accompanied pregnant Sita into the dark unknown of Valmiki's ashram from her rightful place at Rama's palace. We entered the path gingerly.

Amma and I walked in silence for fifteen minutes. Then she couldn't hold it in any longer: Come on … let us return. Come on. *Pada, tirigi veldaam … pada.* I know when she holds her chest tight and has a heavy air around her that she disapproves of what I am doing. She refrains from saying so outright to spare my feelings (or avoid being shouted at). I know what you are thinking. No, I had not Googled this place much, just enough to know how to get there, lest I lose the whole mystery and sense of adventure of travel in the bargain. I had no idea that this was a trek! A man at the entrance had offered his services to guide us through this thicket, but we had instinctively refused. Who wants a man to show us the way when we can manage by asking for directions? Except that there was literally no one to ask directions from.

I reassured Amma, 'Let us go till that shelter that we see from here, and if no one is there, we will turn back, okay? Promise'. My heart was beating heavy and fast. Oh God! Devuda (God), please help, I petitioned the gods mutely, and they responded instantly. In the shelter were seated a man, a woman, a girl, and a boy, who would be our Vietnamese co-hikers for the next three hours. We were so relieved to see them that Amma immediately started sharing all her secrets. We also shared the dates, some Indian snacks, nuts, chai, and sandwiches that the hotel had packed for us. All of us sat there as though one big happy joint family, picnicking and posing for photos. Then we proceeded with satiated hearts.

The young girl held Amma's hand tight, not letting it go. Her mother, a lady who spoke no English (and it was her birthday that day), kept dictating to her daughter on how to treat elders in Vietnamese. Both Amma and I could see how she was teaching her daughter and her son to be mindful, caring, and respectful even of strangers. The son tore away the twigs and thorns on our path while the daughter kept

Amma close with a strong grip so that she would not stumble over the stones and the outcrops of roots and fall into the plentiful ditches. We walked in silence with the father leading the way when it struck me that Shiva and Parvati had shown up just in time when I had prayed to make sure I got the darshan of the sahasra lingas.

We were sweating profusely by then. Cambodia is extremely humid in June. Did I mention that before? It was the wrong season to visit, albeit cheap—the only reason we chose to ignore the constant sweating. After a final stretch, we reached a clearing in the woods. Lo! A stream ran through it. The waters on one side were a bit shallower and more transparent, and we could clearly see various deities etched and carved into sandstone under the water. Simply spectacular and unforgettable! We stood there taking selfies and admiring the peace and quiet. There was no one else around. Thankfully, it has not turned into a tourist trap like other famous sights of Angkor, at least, not in the rainy month of June. After all, who would hike into the hills for peering at something underwater that may or may not be glimpsed?

It became a game of hide-and-seek, of trying to spot the rock reliefs. The Vietnamese had come here for adventure and to celebrate the lady's birthday, and we were here to connect with our heritage that had spread its dharma so far and wide. There were lots of squeals of happenstance and serendipitous sightings. 'I found one!' 'Who is this?' 'More lingas here.' We were all prancing about the edges of the stream, concentrating on what was beneath the flowing waters. It did not help that it was the monsoon season. The one local who was lounging in an indigenous hammock, who we had missed seeing, grunted aloud that it was the wrong time to visit. 'Else you would have spotted Hanuman too … right here,' he snorted, pointing vaguely to the muddy waters. We peered for another ten to fifteen minutes, but the eddies would not let up. We sighed in unison and decided to head back, leaving Hanuman to find us when he was ready.

It was fascinating to watch Amma through all this. Her easy acceptance of foreign cultures flowered in this jungle. To me, she seemed to be a teenager, all wide-eyed and agog with excitement, laughing and chatting away with strangers. Amma's face was clear of all worries and tensions as she was away from the burden of duties and responsibilities. She seemed to revel in this unexpected encounter with the Vietnamese, even going to the extent of whispering to me. 'Is there a visa on arrival for Indians in Vietnam?'

Our return was uneventful, except for the mandatory photos under the waterfall. We made sure that we stopped at the same gazebo on our return journey and polished off the remaining food and snacks. Our water was all gone, so the Vietnamese lent us some. We chatted some more, exchanged information, and promised to visit one another, all the while acknowledging silently that what we had done today, walking together as pilgrims, was something sanctified and special and not replicable in one's lifetime and that we may never meet again. We said our goodbyes and left our memories whispering on treetops inside that perimeter.

Our tuk-tuk guy was at the gate, waiting 'long time' as he had promised. It started raining right on cue once we sat inside the vehicle, and Vaesna stopped briefly on the highway to tuck us into the plastic sheets that he adroitly managed to curtain us with. Safe and ensconced, cold and shivering, Amma and I spent the next hour in a smiling quietude that comes from a mission accomplished. It was *a janma dhanya* (life-fulfilling) moment for me, while for Amma, running into the foreign family who seemed to have adopted her was a most happy unexpected turn of events. The stream that we had just seen, Kbal Spean (literally, the 'bridge head'), flows downstream as the Siem Reap and the Puok Rivers, passing through the Angkor Wat complex. We had partaken of such holy waters with a sip and dip. We had joined our palms in veneration and gratitude centuries later, thanking all those before us who had created such a natural wonderland. Udayadityavarman was said to have consecrated a golden linga deep in those hallowed groves. While I mentally pictured him doing so, I shivered some more. We were coming to the end of our Angkor journey with only one other section to complete.

There was a short stop on the way to Bakong when Vaesna veered to the left off the highway to introduce us to his school-going daughter who was a genius in Mandarin (a compulsory subject in schools in Siem Reap now). She was very shy yet greeted us amiably. His house was made of bamboo. There was a small garden outside and two dogs. There was also the mandatory shrine to the ancestors and the ever-present smile on the lips of everyone we encountered in Siem Reap. His friends, who hung about near the home-made hammocks, waved to us in a friendly gesture. We could see he was proud of what he had made of his life and wanted an audience to validate it. We were only too happy to oblige. His daughter spoke in English with us, phrases she had learnt at school, and he beamed happily on seeing that she could converse with us at ease. We shared some chocolate we had on us with her and said our goodbyes.

In Roluos, which was previously called Hariharalaya, we paid our respects at the many Shiva temples built in the 9th century by Indravarman. The Bakong Temple is patterned on the Borobudur Temple of Java. It is a temple mountain. Preah Ko is a group of stand-alone temples dedicated to Nandi. Lolei, meanwhile, is an island temple constructed to resemble Mount Meru. Honestly, at this point, we were in automaton mode: getting off the tuk-tuk; taking long, mid, and close-up shots; walking to the entrance; surveying the area; climbing the numerous stairs; reaching the top; looking down in awe; climbing down sideways gingerly; walking back to the three-wheeler and drinking all the water we could; and then onwards to the next destination. When we realised that the day's sightseeing had ended, we were absolutely thrilled and opted for an evening of well-deserved Khmer massage at the Khmer Wellness Spa nearby. For $10 per head, it was more than affordable, and it made all our aches and pains go away instantly.

Although Siem Reap has many cool cafes, hipster joints, and restaurants offering global fare like any other tourist towns, we were in no mood to walk all the way to some commercial space and be on our best behaviour. So, right after our massage, which made us hungry and dehydrated, we talked to the manager, Ms Vinny, who was most gracious and whipped up some wonderful dishes for us on the house, including amok pineapple rice, Khmer curry, and a fruit plate for dessert.

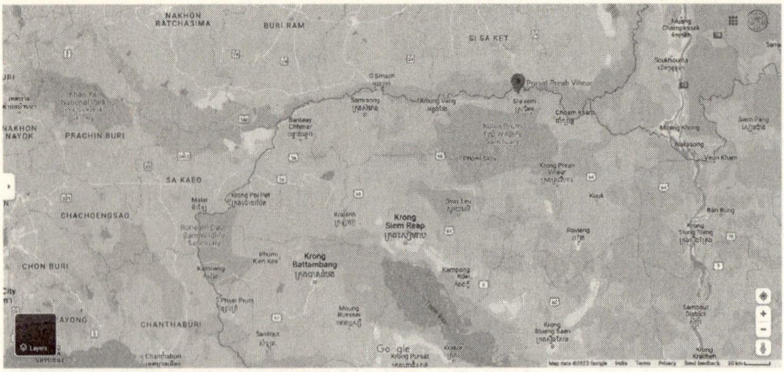

Day 5: Preah Vihear, Koh Ker, Beng Mealea, Spoons in Wat Damnak area, and Bamboo Street

Today I made Irani samosas (smaller, crispier, spicier than the regular ones and filled with onions, not potatoes) and *mirchi bajji*s (green chillies stuffed with special spices and fried in chickpea flour batter). YouTube is inundated with tempting recipes all of a sudden, and people everywhere, especially Indians, are making their lives liveable with such distractions. This is the year 2020, and God knows we all need something to take our mind away from the global pandemic at hand. Sipping my chai and taking a bite from the evening tiffin,[9] I try to jog my memory for 'my most memorable trip ever'—one of those quizzes that one cannot escape from if one is subscribed to any of the family WA groups.

If there is one day or trip that I will remember in my lifetime as mind-blowing, it is this, it is this, it is this. Well, I guess I have been saying this about every day in Siem Reap, but truly it was something out of this world.

I was on the lookout for visiting some more Hindu temples, given that we were in Cambodia for six days. Amma was sure I was wasting money unnecessarily. 'What will we do for six days there? You are simply crazy,' she said. '*Aarrojulu enchestaame nee picchi kaadukaani*.' But once we got there, we quickly realised that we could stay another week and then some without covering all that the region has to offer. We missed out on exploring Beng Mealea. Emily, my friend, had highly recommended it, preferring it to other temples. Alas! We only managed to reach the entrance at five in the evening, after doing Preah Vihear and Koh Ker, very close to closing time. It was scary with not a soul in sight, so we had to leave in a hurry. But first, we went to the 'Sacred Shrine', Preah Vihear, a World Heritage Site and the last place to fall to the Khmer Rouge.

If you read the news regularly, you would not have missed the altercation between Thailand and Cambodia over a temple in the mountains that both laid claims to. That it was dedicated to Shiva intrigued me, and ever since, I have been curious about the spot. Once the basic Angkor circuit was done, I inquired at the hotel reception regarding this temple. I also checked with our tuk-tuk guy, Vaesna, who promised to find a car and a driver known to him to take us there. It would take around three hours to get there by car, and perhaps on the way back, time permitting, we could see Koh Ker and Beng Mealea too. We did not want to trust an unknown cabbie for such a long journey, although Vaesna had been nothing but wonderful. So we asked the hotel to provide us with a car and their trusted driver, Samod. We would have to leave early as the temple was heavily guarded, and the journey required us to cross check posts. The International Court of Justice had ruled in their favour, but the Cambodians were not taking any chances with the Thais right across the border. This temple hangs off a cliff in the Dangrek Mountains and has been the bone of contention between the neighbouring countries for over a century. The conflict was supposedly resolved in 1962.

Although the construction was first begun in the 9th century, it continued under the reigns of Suryavarman I and Suryavarman II. When one reaches the top and sees the expanse, one can comprehend why it took so long to complete. There are gopuras after gopuras, staircases, naga balustrades, extremely intricate carvings a la Banteay Srei on the lintels and beams, colonnades with religious descriptions, avenues, stone-paved reservoirs, false windows, windows with many balusters, doorways leading to more doorways, galleries and alleys. There were heaps of rubble and rocks. Moss and lichens grew all over the grey and red sandstone and brick giving off a reddish green-grey hue, covered with the morning dew drops and emerging sunlight. The wood, worn smooth over the years, conferred an antique look to the temple complex, making it picture-perfect for photography.

It started to drizzle, and we had not carried our raincoats. So we simply let ourselves enjoy the elements. Everyone agreed that we were foolish to go to Preah Vihear. It is 2,000 ft high up on a mountain top, and even after we got there, we would have to trek a bit to get to the temple complex, which was nothing but ruins. There were many soldiers guarding it, and the Thais might cause cross-border trouble or firing or something. There were no stores, no bathrooms, and no facilities. How did we know that there were no landmines there? In short, it was dangerous for two women who clearly looked like tourists and did not speak Khmer. I had to go after hearing all this. It sounded downright adventurous and the right thing to do. It literally called my name and said, 'Come'! Amma did not dissuade me either. Over the past few days, I had started noticing how she was giving in to her innate spirit more and more. Without any restrictions placed on her station and her sex, she had started to soar. 'Let us do this,' she said! That was the only mantra I needed to decide.

The car whizzed past small towns and neat roads. We were going north to the border, and in long stretches, ours was the only car. Since it was daylight, both Amma and I were like *shernis* (lionesses). We passed many furniture stores with carpenters carving gorgeous pieces on wood. We were tempted to stop and buy some chairs or sofa sets and ship them off to Hyderabad but had to curb our instincts. The artisanship of these parts is colourful and skilled, passed down over generations. Mexican villages exude a similar feel, where people are extremely talented with their hands. The colours used in embroidery and local garments there also reminded me of my time south of the border.

We finally reached the bottom of the mountain. Our car was parked at the base, and Samod, our driver for the day, asked us to buy entrance tickets and wait for the government-issued four-wheel drive to take us up. No private vehicles are permitted on top, he said. He would wait here at the base. So we jumped into the one-tonner. Bodies of water whizzed past, banana plantations waved to us along with Buddhist flags, and dogs howled after us as we went up the steep incline. Amma squinched her eyes. We passed a few checkposts. The ride was terrifying. We held on to the railing of the truck for dear life, praying that the brakes of this vehicle were working fine. We are almost at a 70-degree incline. I can see why Samod shook his head in disbelief when I said, 'I bet you could drive your car up to the temple easily. Why do we need a special vehicle? It is all a scam to make us pay extra for their services.' The trip was turning out to be dangerous in more ways than one. Nice.

At the top, we passed a Buddhist monastery. I would have liked to explore that too, but time was of essence. There was the slight matter of the return journey too. We had not even begun. We reached another checkpost, and this time, the man in charge checked our tickets. He gestured for us to get down from the truck, and later to come back and hop into this same vehicle once we are done. We smiled our assent and hopped off. Two or three young girls ran after us with lotuses in their hands for offering at the shrine. We declined politely. We still had to trek another half an hour or more, so there was no point in having hands busy holding delicate flowers. I found the perfect walking stick in the bushes nearby to keep balance, meant for either Amma or me. We hung onto it until we reached Prang, where we left it by the iron railings before climbing up.

The narrow, wet, rocky path snakes upwards into the skies. We trudged along into the unknown with full faith that all would be well and that this was indeed worth the trouble we were taking. It was. Far ahead, we spotted the famed Khmer temple arches. Here we were. Had we run across the reeds, we would have arrived faster, but we strolled leisurely, exhausted from the past five days of walking and exploring. We carried food and water with us from the hotel—sandwiches, fruits, and juice. It was in our backpack along with some biscuits. We sat in the shade of the first temple ruins to take a bite and have a sip. We had finally managed to be true travellers, visiting this place that was off the beaten track and not on the regular tourist itinerary on a whim. I was doubly proud as I had trekked it in a saree! Frankly, our clothes choices on this trip were not the most practical.

The final enclosure of the five-temple lot houses a Ganesha. I was thrilled to see that puja was still being done for him. There was a monk and his helper inside the *garbha griha* (sanctum sanctorum) when we went in. The monk was having his meals in a separate corner. A lit lamp flickered in front of the murti, and incense was burning furiously, making up for the lack of pilgrims. Flowers in various vases, some plastic, sang an ode to the lord who removes all obstacles. All in all, having access to a 9th-century shrine where prayers are conducted even today is a great achievement for the Cambodians and for us. We came out with grateful hearts after making our mental offerings.

We were about to head back when we were called by a guard in uniform. He gesticulated frantically, pointing towards the opposite side, and said something. We took our time to decide whether to follow this guard to where he was pointing. We looked at him with suspicion. Why was he luring us away to a secluded spot? For what? There was no one else in sight. Should we shout back? What do we do? Right then, a young girl walked in and followed the guard and his instructions without any hesitation. I gave my mother the 'see?' look and followed the new entrant, head held high and trying to look fearless. Amma followed suit.

We emerged from the building walls to the outside, to the border, onto an escarpment that overlooked Thailand. We were truly on top of the world.

I had never felt so at one with the universe, myself, and Amma at any other place. This had to be the magic of these mountains and the Ganesha who resides here, blessing our first foreign trip. Sitting on that precarious rock, facing Thailand, posing for a photograph while the girl (she was Canadian-Indian, we came to know) captured Amma and me laughing away in abandon, I prayed fervently for many more such days in the future. Amma struck up a conversation with this young girl and was in awe of her travelling all alone in these parts. Inspired by such real-life examples, Amma told me she was not tired at all and would be happy to go forth to Koh Ker and Beng Mealea too. The driver shook his head in disbelief. It is too much for her at her age, he wanted to say, while I smiled to myself, happy.

When we reached the Koh Ker complex, we had had a full day at Preah Vihear, which was a very arduous journey and also a bit dangerous. It was remote, bordering Thailand, and as it was subject to intermittent attacks, teemed with security personnel and requiring permits. Despite the tiredness, we wanted to pack in all that we could. It was an unspoken understanding. We would probably never come back here to these parts, so we might as well complete the circuit. When one travels on a budget and when one is not living the life of leisure, when one works for a living and saves diligently for satiating wanderlust, it is normal to not visit the same place more than once, unless there is something more to that place that calls you. Cambodia thus far was one such place. I would love to go back and discover more and more, but given practical constraints, I knew that it might be a while before I get to do that. Amma was with me right here, and now at seventy-two … might as well … and she herself had said okay, so….

So Koh Ker it was, which had once been called Lingapura. The driver, Samod, was excited too. He wanted to show off his country's heritage as much as possible. So he zoomed ahead at full throttle. We landed in front of a very normal-looking, flat, broken-down structure. The area is vast, with one board announcing a whole complex of temples, the various Prasats (temple communes). Shiva linga after Shiva linga was housed amongst massive stones toppled by weather and quakes. The moss had crawled languorously over centuries, showing its might. The ancient trees kept vigil through their shady branches and paid obeisance via their humongous network of roots, which rose from the carcass of *kaala* (time). The black monoliths stood erect and ready to grant boons for the asking. Once I realised the sheer number of abandoned Shiva lingas abounding in the Siem Reap countryside, I had carried extra water bottles from day three for just such an opportunity. Pouring water over them, calming their energies, folding hands in worship, and seeking forgiveness seemed like the only option I had. Sometimes, even that was not simple. I had to climb over boulders and slippery rocks to reach wide pits that might house strange creatures and beings. Samod warned me against going into certain areas, saying that these parts had many snakes that guard the lingas and that I should be careful. Amma and I did our pradakshina to as many shrines as we could, and soon, we were ready to leave.

For some reason, I looked at the board on display again. The drawing on it had a pyramid, but what we saw ahead of us looked different. We went in and out two or three times. There seemed to be nothing like what was promised at the entrance: a huge pyramid-shaped building like that of the Mayans, Incas, or Aztecs. Given that we spoke no Khmer and that there were hardly any tourists here—no one but one or two guards—we did not know what to do. Then, like a *bhool bhulaiyya* (labyrinth) suddenly opening up and exposing the wonders of its secret interiors, there it was: a turn in the wall that looked like a dead end opened up into a vast swathe of land. Ahead of us was a tall, seven-storeyed skyscraper of ancient times, the Prang. Neglected and forgotten, hidden from public gaze, it is dying a slow, painful death in isolation.

At one point in time, a royal priest, *Brahmana,* of Jayavarman IV would climb all those stairs daily to perform puja and offer abhisheka to the Shiva linga on top of this superstructure. What a sight it must have been! Just to imagine it was mind-boggling. I was in a saree, and Amma had already climbed Preah Vihear. Would she want to climb? Yes! Yes, of course! When did I ever see Amma shy away from any adventure? 'Let us do it,' she said again with gusto.

Asking her to set aside the walking stick she had been carrying with her since morning, I told her to take it slow and not look down. These stairs were all metal, like the fire escape staircases of apartments in some of New York's boroughs, built for the convenience of those who might want to reach the top and gape at the hole that had once housed a 13 ft Shiva linga, the tallest there was at that time. 'Just look up and stop as many times as you want. I have water with me,' I told her. Given how hot and humid it was and that we were parched, there was hardly enough water for the two of us, post our Preah Vihear sojourn. There would also be a broken Shiva linga on top waiting for us. Thirsty too. It was as though history was goading us into the future. But we made it to the top and back without mishap, thanks to the gods watching over us. We had done it! At the top, we had waited just a few minutes to catch our breath and to peep into the crevice that once held the massive linga. We poured a little water there as an offering. Rubble and broken pieces, perhaps of the linga, were strewn about with weeds growing where they could. When we finally looked down from that vantage point, we knew then that this, too, would forever be one of our most memorable days of all times.

Once Samod had dropped us safely back at our hotel, we headed over to Spoons, a short walk away, to indulge in some local delicacies and spend the last evening here in style. Spoons is a very elegant open-air bamboo restaurant where local students are trained by the French parent company for future jobs in the restaurant business. We were too tired to make conversation with the students who served our food. They would have loved some feedback and tete-a-tete. But all we could think of was packing our bags and crashing on our beds, for the next day was to be our last in Siem Reap.

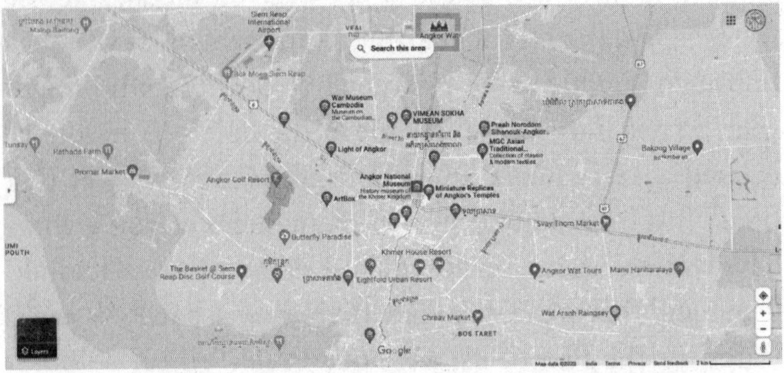

Day 6: Shopping! Fly out!

On the last day, we decided we had had enough of history and culture. We, or rather, I wanted to take it easy and try out the alternative and chic cafes and restaurants that abound there, while Amma wanted to shop for rice and local spices. So we walked towards the Narayana Circle (a roundabout with a statue of Narayana) and then onwards to Haven, a restaurant that offers a haven for disadvantaged youth and great fusion food. Not satisfied, I begged Amma to cross the river and try out some juice and dessert at Vibe, a plant-based eco-friendly cafe, and perhaps pack something for later too. We walked the streets of Siem Reap leisurely for the first time since we had arrived five days ago. Unfortunately, we missed going to the museum, which would need another day. It could be a sign that we must return to the city someday. Amma bought some food supplies and a few apsara figurines to give to her friends. I picked up a few Cambodian Buddha statues for my in-laws, and then I re-routed our walk towards Pub Street and towards the only bookstore I could spot for some reliable books on Cambodia, Angkor Wat, and the like. Nalin, my husband, always loved stationery from the places I travelled to. So I was on the lookout for something for him. Having found everything we needed and after making our purchases and carrying some fine packed lunches from Vibe, we headed back to Residence Wat Damnak for our final goodbyes and selfie sessions.

Seated on the plane, we looked out of the window after take-off, hoping for an aerial view of the Angkor Wat. However, the pilot veered away in a different direction.

Despite that small disappointment, I could see Amma smiling to herself at what we had pulled off. That, to me, was enough compared to all the sights of the world.

Now, in the summer of 2020, lounging on my balcony in the US., reminiscing about all that transpired in Siem Reap in the summer of 2018, I smile to myself too. The stream and the tree across from me smile back in genial agreement. I hear the phone ring. It is Amma on the line. She, too, has been browsing through our Cambodian chronicles from the sounds of it. 'How much we walked and climbed,' she laughs admiringly. I feel good that I could give her that memory to hold on to, especially now that she cannot hold me close and God alone knows how long this forced separation will last.

Amma and I don't always share a great camaraderie. We have our share of tiffs, our '*tu tu mai mai*[10]'. Typical mother–daughter duos go through similar hurdles, especially during the daughter's teenage years. While young blood wants to explore the world, heeding no advice, the mother is naturally worried for the safety and well-being of her daughter, admonishing her every act. My mother was no different, and I was more than a handful in the 1980s. It took me many years to recognise where our common interests lie, when is it that we enjoy each other's company, and when is it that we appreciate the other without getting in each other's way. How can we develop this aspect of our relationship without letting it fall apart? I pondered a lot on this question, and I found the answer after much introspection: when we travel together.

Travelling together to unknown lands may not be the solution for everyone and their problems but give it a try. You have nothing to lose but your fear of the unknown.

3

Mekong to Kaveri

Srinidhi Balasubramanian

At the start of the second millennium, powerful empires rose around the world, and simultaneously, there was a remarkable change in the structure of Asian maritime trade. The Chola empire, under Rajaraja and Rajendra, and the Kamboja empire, under Suryavarman I, were two such powers. Forging alliances, Rajendra Chola victoriously sent naval expeditions to Southeast Asia, and the victory over the rival kingdoms of Tambralinga and Sriivijaya was the climax of a period of intense competition. But was this the only aspect of a complex international and intra-civilisational interaction? Both the Kamboja rulers and the Chola rulers were known for their contribution to art and architecture. They were patrons of literature and scholarship, especially Shaivite works. This story is a fictional take on the interactions of these kingdoms in the early 11th century.

Prologue

Pratipa stood leaning against one of the many magnificent archways in the temple, gazing at nothing in particular. Moonlight filled the courtyard, and torches positioned at regular intervals caused the ripples of the pond to glimmer. Jahnavi, his mother, hummed a prayer while sorting out huge piles of *bilva* flowers.

'Mother, I was wondering if you could tell me something about Aryadesa?' he inquired.

Jahnavi looked up, surprised by her son's question. 'Even I don't know much. But I can tell you this. When I was younger than you, the kings and queens, the royals, and sometimes even rich merchants used to wear clothes made up of luxurious silk and cotton, woven with the finest threads. They say these clothes were from Aryadesa, a country far away,' she answered.

'Is it farther than Yawadwipa? ' Pratipa questioned, his eyes wide with curiosity.

'Alas, I don't know, my child. All I know is that it is very, very far away. Merchants left the town for long journeys to return only after months or years, sometimes never. Perhaps that's why people say it is a misfortune for a woman to be married to a trader who travels the seven seas.'

Pratipa's eyes followed the fumes of the nearly burnt incense stick, which was giving out the perfumed fragrance of sandalwood.

'Are they barbarians?'

His mother frowned at him. 'I do not think so. I have heard people say that it is where the *Kailasa* rests, the abode of Lord Shiva. It is the land watered by Ganga and fed by Annapoorna.'

Jahnavi glanced outside and noticed that people had long retired to their homes. Pratipa attempted to question her again, but she interrupted him. 'Enough questions now, son. It's dark, and we need some rest. After all, it's going to be a long day tomorrow.'

Pratipa nodded and walked away to put out the torches. His mother picked up the flower baskets and stacked them in one corner.

The incense stick burnt to its end, the last few fumes spiralling their way upwards.

~1018 CE, 940 of the Saka Era: Ancient Isvarapura, near modern Phnom Dei

People had already started assembling in the large courtyards of the temple, which were being decorated with auspicious designs and patterns. Rows of fresh and colourful garlands decorated the arches and doorways. The massive temple of Tribhuvaneswara towered over the crowd of people, looking resplendent in the rays of the early morning sun.

Pipers and drummers were lined up on both sides of the main road leading to the temple. A hundred young women, the traditional dancers attached to the temple, exquisitely dressed in rich *sampot*s and balancing elaborate and pointed crowns, were dancing gracefully to the music.

Inside the temple, the sacrificial altars were blazing, and the air reverberated with the chants of Vedic mantras.

'Today will perhaps be the most important day of my life,' thought Pratipa. His family was hosting a reception for their king, Suryavarman. The temple had been built by his uncle, Yajnavaraha. Following the law of succession, after his death, his sister Jahnavi's son, Pratipa, had taken the reins even though he was still in his teens. He proudly managed all the responsibilities of the temple. The temple formed the centre of the village. All economic, religious, cultural, and political activities were either directly or indirectly influenced by the temple's state of affairs. To be the head of a temple was, hence, an office of great power and responsibility.

Pratipa paced around, checking if everything was in place and hurriedly muttering instructions to his secretary, Visarada. He looked around to make sure everything was perfect.

'My *entire* reputation and the future of this temple depend on the king's visit today. So, look, if anything is out of place or something goes wrong, then you know what will happen,' Pratipa said, wringing his hands.

Visarada rolled his eyes. 'Will you stop being so hysterical? The temple looks magnificent. I have personally hired the best musicians, and the *prasada* is being made by the finest of chefs. Nothing can go wrong.'

'If you say so,' he muttered, eyes darting to the door every few minutes.

Soon, he was greeted by the servant who brought the most anticipated news. Bowing, the servant announced, 'His Highness, Raja Suryavarman, is arriving.' He bowed again and left.

The sound of the royal drums grew louder every second. Pratipa hurried to the doorstep of the temple with Visarada and other temple members to welcome the king.

Once at the gate, a commotion could be heard as people shuffled and tripped their way to the front to get a better look at the king.

Visarada hastily shooed the crowd away and commanded them to stand to the side. The king appeared around the corner of the street, seated atop an elephant, whose trunk was decorated with precious gems. Attendees waved cotton fans around him. Soldiers walked alongside the elephant with swords and spears, driving away commoners who came too close. Important ministers also followed in gold palanquins decorated with silk and handles studded with gems.

'Welcome to my humble temple, Your Highness.' Pratipa bowed to the king once he had arrived.

'Thank you.' The king looked around, impressed. 'This place looks well maintained. I suppose you're the head of this temple?' Without really waiting for an answer, he continued, 'I heard that your uncle, Yajnavaraha, served this temple under the late King Paramaviraloka excellently. I hope I can expect the same from you?' the king asked sharply.

'Indeed, you can, Sire,' Pratipa answered, bowing low.

While the king examined different sculptures and decorations, Visarada came up to Pratipa, unnoticed by anyone. Pretending to pick up a flower from the ground, he whispered urgently to Pratipa.

'The king has brought the finance minister, Dhananjaya, with him. Be careful. He will try to stir up some trouble. You know he hates your family.'

Pratipa immediately glanced around, and Dhananjaya was indeed standing near the king, also looking at the decorations, his face devoid of any trace of enthusiasm. Annoyance flickered inside Pratipa.

'I must not lose my patience.'

Mustering a smile, he approached the king.

'Will His Highness be interested to have a look around the temple? There is a marvellous story behind each and every charming sculpture here.'

Interested, the king followed him, listening to Pratipa with the utmost attention. They went around the temple, Pratipa narrating stories of the carvings of *Kamsa Vadha*, the burning of the Khandava forest, and the Kirata and Arjuna. 'When Arjuna realised that the Kirata was none other than Lord Siva, he was overwhelmed,' Pratipa said. As he narrated, bards sang the appropriate verses from the Mahabharata.

भवगद दर्शनाकाङ्क्षी पराप्तो ऽसमीमं महागिरिम
दयितं तव देवेश तापसालयम उत्तमम |
परसादये तवां भगवन सर्वभूतनमस्कृत
न मे सयाद अपराधो ऽयं महादेवातिसाहसात ||

> Thou art beyond the foremost of male beings, thou art the highest, thou art the subtlest, O Hara! O illustrious Sankara, it behoveth thee to pardon my fault. It was even to obtain a sight of thyself that I came to this great mountain, which is dear to thee and which is the excellent abode of ascetics. Thou art worshipped of all. (Translation by Kisari Mohan Ganguli)

Further inside the temple, Pratipa pointed out other intricate carvings and sculptures that narrated the stories of the three worlds.[1]

'This exquisite carving shows Ravana lifting the entire Kailasa mountain,' Pratipa said.

'That's an interesting story, isn't it, Dhananjaya?' the king commented.

Dhananjaya looked startled, for he hadn't been listening to a word Pratipa or the king had been saying.

'Huh? Yes, sir, it's a wonderful sculpture … of …' He squinted at the sculpture. 'Of … a man … lifting something? Yes, sir, it's a good sculpture,' Dhananjaya babbled, making no sense at all.

The king stared at him, raising his eyebrows. 'You *do* know what the sculpture depicts, right?'

Dhananjaya gaped at the sculpture, racking his brain. 'Um … is it Krishna lifting Govardhan mountain?'

The king gazed incredulously at him. 'Dhananjaya, how on *earth* can Krsna, as a child, lifting Govardhana Mountain, have *ten* heads and a moustache? And, as far as I know, Lord Siva was not sitting on Govardhana Mountain.'

Pratipa pressed his lips together, trying not to laugh. Nearby, Visarada also tried to conceal his laughter but failed.

'I can't believe you don't know about this story. Pratipa told it just a few moments ago. I have made it my priority that my ministers should be well versed in the Itihasas and Puranas. Maybe Pratipa here could give you lessons?' He turned around and gestured to both of them.

The smile slid off Pratipa's face. Both Dhananjaya and Pratipa now wore equally horrified looks.

Sensing the tension, Visarada cleverly slid in and showed the King the rest of the sculptures.

'Sir, have you seen this pristine statue of Durga Devi killing Mahisasura?' he said, hastily changing the subject.

The king was enjoying himself. He followed Pratipa around, exclaiming every now and then at a wonderful piece of carving.

'This, my lord, on the face of the third *gopura* and right in front of the main *griha,* is the engraving of Siva in the form of Nataraja.'

'Wait a minute, what is this?' King Suryavarman asked Pratipa, squinting at a small figure in the corner.

Pratipa froze, unable to remember anything related to that sculpture. He desperately racked his brain, trying to think, but as long as he had been in this temple, he had never *ever* seen that figure.

The king inquired, still waiting, 'Well? Doesn't this too have a marvellous story like the others?'

Pratipa desperately stared at Visarada, but he, too, had a panicked look. Clearly, nobody had any idea about this figure.

Eager to be in the king's good books, Dhananjaya drawled, 'Perhaps, Your Highness, it is a mistake of the temple. Doesn't look like it would have any backstory. It could be the work of a careless artist. But yes, it does make the temple … ugly, I suppose.'

Pratipa clenched his teeth, trying to prevent himself from punching Dhananjaya. Visarada murmured to him, 'The figure is half-hidden. That wretch hasn't said anything about the beautiful decorations, yet he manages to pick out all the faults.'

The king looked perplexed. 'Mistake? Why would anyone do that when the rest of the temple is filled with such wonders?'

Dhananjaya droned on, not wishing to let go of the opening. 'Let me be honest. Look at the figure, Your Majesty. It doesn't have any great beauty. The hair is spiky like a cactus, bones are jutting out from desiccated skin, and the clothes are torn and without any jewellery—'

'Sunken eyes and a woman looking like a ghost?' Pratipa interrupted before Dhananjaya could cause more damage. He continued, 'Why, my dear Dhananjaya, you just pointed out that the sculpture has so much detail.

This shows that the figure has been carved with utmost precision. I wouldn't say that it is a mistake at all. Also, isn't inner beauty more important? Maybe the ugliness has a hidden meaning to it.' Pratipa would not go down without a fight.

'And the hidden meaning is?' the king asked. He paused, apparently waiting for an answer. 'Do you know what this figure represents?'

Prickly silence followed his question. 'I see.' The king scanned the room, waiting for someone to answer. 'So, you're telling me that not *one* person here knows *anything* about this?' the king said, amazed.

'It could be a mis—' Dhananjaya tried to speak, but the king silenced him.

'Make an announcement,' the king commanded. 'Anyone who can give information about this sculpture in the next fortnight will receive five cows and two buffaloes as a reward from me.'

'Yes, sire.'

'Well, that went just amazingly,' Pratipa said sarcastically, scowling. 'Now *how* am I going to find out anything about that ugly statue?' He grumbled, crossing his arms over his chest and looking expectantly at Visarada.

'There is only one person who can help us now,' Visarada noted slyly.

'Not *him*!' Pratipa groaned.

Visarada grinned.

'We will need to visit the wine seller first.'

The next afternoon, Pratipa left for the king's palace with a frail old man who faintly reeked of revelry.

'I hope whatever you are going to say is true. You're not cooking up stuff, are you?' Pratipa asked sharply as they walked down to the palace.

'It hurts me that you think I am a lying drunk.'

Pratipa glared, remembering the smirk of the wine seller from last night. By now, the gossip would have reached his mother's ears.

'Of course, it is true! We, the great traders of the past, never lie—unlike you youngsters I meet nowadays!' the old man said, apparently shocked by the fact that someone could question him about such a thing.

'Hmph! Some great trader you are, always looking for the next cup.'

'You don't know how to have fun. Once you reach my age, young man, you will understand. But then again, you have not seen the world as I did. So maybe you will just become a cranky and boring old codger like everyone else.'

When they reached the king's quarters, a guard stopped them, saying, 'Halt! The king is in a very important meeting right now. Nobody goes into the king's private rooms without special permission.'

'Tell His Highness that I am Pratipa from Isvarapura and I have information about the statue in my temple.'

The guard nodded and went back inside. A few minutes later, he came back and said, 'You may go in.'

The king sat in his room, preoccupied with some work. Dhananjaya was standing just beside him. As they entered his room, the king looked up and said, 'Ah Pratipa! What do you have for me today? And who is this?' he asked, indicating the old man.

Bowing to the king, Pratipa said, 'I have excellent news about the statue we were discussing yesterday, sir. This is my uncle Kesava, a retired trader. He has been living in Isvarapura for more than eighty years and is here to tell us the story behind the sculpture.'

The king stared at Kesava, his brows furrowing.

There was an uncomfortable silence.

The old man swayed a bit, as if he would fall asleep standing.

The king sighed.

'So? What is the great mystery about this figure?'

Kesava cleared his throat and began. 'Many decades ago, sir, during the reign of your glorious ancestor, His Majesty the late Sivaloka, overseas trade flourished, and several colonies of foreign men existed in our country. The people of the Dravida country from Aryadesa earned a great reputation, not only for the luxury goods that they brought to the country but also for their contribution to local works such as the building of temples and ashramas. Unfortunately, many of them left the country during the famine, and those who stayed back and married Kamboja women died. But—'

'Where is the Dravidadesa?' the king interrupted.

'I do not know, sir, for I have never visited it myself. However, when I was young, I made frequent journeys to the country of Srivijaya. Merchants from all countries converge on the biggest port of Srivijaya—Kedah. Hundreds of prosperous merchants and other men from Aryadesa resided there. Going westward from Srivijaya for seven weeks, one can find the Dravida country,' Kesava said.

'Ok, continue,' said Suryavarman.

'The head of Isvarapura, during the reign of the late king Sivaloka, was Yajnavaraha. He was the one who built the temple, and he also had a lot of connections with the Dravida community. I was young when the temple was being built, and I remember the stories that the learned men used to tell. This sculpture that you have asked about is indeed very interesting.'

'Go on,' the king nodded as everyone in the room was now listening in rapt attention.

'Devotion to the Lord can be shown in many ways. Some dance to the celestial beats, and some others sing the Lord's praises. Stories of devotion are many, but in my entire life, I have never heard a more poignant story than this. Listen, Your Majesty, to the story of the revered mother of Karaikkal.

'Long, long ago, in the city of Karaikkal in the Dravida country was born Punitavati, a beautiful and virtuous woman. She married a rich merchant named Paramadatta and performed deeds of charity, living a pious life. One day, her husband sent her a pair of mangoes. When a devotee of Shiva knocked on their door, she dutifully served him food and also one of the mangoes. Later, when she was serving lunch to her husband, he asked her for the other mango, and Punitavati became petrified. Not knowing what to do, she prayed to Lord Shiva, and a fruit fell from heaven into her hands.

'The husband realised that the fruit was not ordinary and asked her for the truth. She immediately recounted how she had prayed and received the fruit. Being a materialistic person, he did not believe in miracles. However, the divine mother prayed to the lord again. Sure enough, a third mango fell into her hands. Paramadatta was beyond words, and considering her to be some superhuman being, he fled the house to seek his fortunes in a distant land.

'Many years passed, and his relatives took the fair lady to him, by which time he had remarried. They asked him to take his first wife back. To their astonishment, he fell at her feet and said that she was a goddess and not his wife. Aggrieved, she prayed to Lord Shiva to rid her of the beautiful body, which was a bane according to her. With bones bulging out of deadened skin, white hair sticking out like cactus spines, hollow stomach, and sunken eyes, she said, 'I've now become part of the *Bhuta Gana*s of Shiva.' She proceeded to Kailasa. Unwilling to step on the holy abode, she climbed the mountain with her head. When she fell at the feet of the lord, he himself addressed her as the mother. Thus is the story of the holy mother of Karaikkal, a most worthy subject to grace the walls of an abode of Shiva.'

'Beautiful! I'm moved beyond words.' The king was ecstatic. He stood up and took off his golden bracelet. 'Here, take this. Keep this as a reward.'

'Your Highness, after examining the archives, we found these,' Pratipa said, showing numerous old manuscripts, tattered at the edges due to termites but otherwise well maintained.

A month had passed since their last meeting, and Pratipa had toiled hard in the interim.

'What are these?' the king asked.

'I do not know, Sire, but Kesava says that the people from Aryadesa wrote in this script,' said Pratipa. 'Yajnavaraha had asked them to be translated, but it was never carried out apparently.'

'Is this how you waste our time?' Dhananjaya said snidely.

'Your Majesty, don't you think we should re-initiate trade and cultural connections with Aryadesa?' Pratipa said hopefully.

'Your Highness, may I remind you that our treasury is extremely weak and we cannot afford unnecessary expenses at the moment. When no one knows where this place is or the dangers of a journey, this would be like pouring gold into the sea.'

'But—'

The king raised his hand and waited until the bickering died down.

'When traders sail, they seek only gold. But what if scholars cross oceans? You must become a trader-scholar, Pratipa. Join up with the merchant guild and take to the seas. Go and find Aryadesa. Re-establish the trade routes to the forgotten lands. I will authorise you with a royal embassy. Set sail immediately.'

From the royal temple, the faint sounds of Vedic verses filtered in:

अपो सु मयक्ष वरुण भियसं मत सम्राळ रतावो.अनु मा गर्भाय |
दामेव वत्साद वि मुमुग्ध्यंहो नहि तवदारे निमिषश्चनेशे ||

Drive far, O Varuṇa, all perils. Receive me graciously, O King. Like a calf from its cords, undo me from the troubles that bind me. Without you, I am powerless even to open my eyes! (Translation by Raimundo Panikkar)

'Where's our first destination?' Pratipa asked, leaning on the taffrail of the ship.

'The port of Kedah. Hopefully, we will reach there by the end of next month,' replied Vanija Jnanakumara, head of the merchant guild, who had kindly agreed to sponsor his trip.

Pratipa gazed back at his city as the ship left its harbour. It grew smaller and smaller until it was a tiny speck under the glorious rising sun.

The pleasant winds of Aswini blew, guiding the ship away from perilous waters. Pratipa breathed in the salty sea air, admiring the beauty that surrounded him. The sun gleamed on the sea, and the ocean waves rippled around. After initially counting the days, he soon lost track of the time he spent on the ship. He watched the bright and clear-blue sky dim into a pitch-dark one, studded with stars, as days faded into nights and weeks blended into months.

One such uneventful evening suddenly changed into a busy one. Pratipa noticed people rushing about, talking swiftly, and moving things around.

'What is happening?' he asked Jnanakumara, who was rapidly giving instructions to a helper nearby.

Jnanakumara smiled and pointed westwards. 'We are less than an hour away from the port city of Kedah, my friend!'

Sure enough, as the predicted time edged nearer, he could see land and ports and noticed other ships moving in their direction.

Pratipa felt a rush of excitement as he gazed at a foreign land. Never in a million years would he have imagined travelling beyond his tiny village and capital city.

A little later, he could see the entire coast illuminated by a towering, elegant lighthouse. All along the coast, smaller lighthouses adorned the coastline. At least a hundred ships were docked in the harbour, which was busy with people vigorously loading and unloading cargo. Many tiny boats sailed around, ferrying local passengers.[2]

He disembarked, along with other members of the ship. Jnanakumara spread his hands wide and exclaimed, 'Welcome to the city of Kedah!'

Immediately, a person came forward, joining his hands to greet them. 'Namaskar! Good to see you again, Jnanakumara. Good to see you indeed.'

'Pleasure to see you too, Mayuri.' Jnanakumara smiled, indicating Pratipa. 'Pratipa, this is Mayuri, officer in charge of ships arriving at the port. Mayuri, this is Pratipa, a good friend of mine. He is here on scholarly work.'

Evidently, Mayuri was a person with great influence. Traders passing them waved to him, and many even came to give him gifts from distant lands. He had other Srivijayan officials with him, but he commanded the respect of a leader.

'Here are the records, seals, and all documents required,' Jnanakumara said, handing over copper plates and seals. Mayuri glanced at them and passed it all to his assistants.

'Alright, Mayuri, it's a busy visit this time. We have a lot of things to be sold and purchased in the city. So … when can we get all our goods unloaded from the ship?'

'Let's see. There are three large ships from Arabia, then seven from Tambralinga and…'

Mayuri muttered, apparently calculating. He looked up and said, 'We can unload your ship in a week.'

'That long? Can't it be done faster?' Jnanakumara asked politely.

'I'm afraid not. You will have to wait for at least a week. You're lucky that I am not postponing your ship,' Mayuri said carelessly.

'A week? Boss, I have got business to do in the city as soon as possible! Should I swat mosquitoes as you unload the ship as slow as a snail?' Jnanakumara demanded.

'Now, don't get angry,' Mayuri said sharply. 'We also have sixteen ships from other nations. Plus, I have meetings with important traders all around the world. You can either wait for a week or do something on your own.'

'We couldn't possibly wait for a week,' Pratipa whispered anxiously.

'Of course not. You haven't seen the tricks of the trade yet,' Jnanakumara said, smirking.

'Ratnachandra!' he called out in a loud voice, such that Mayuri wouldn't miss it. 'Don't bother bringing the bag of silver.'

Turning to Pratipa, he said, 'You know, I was planning to give 100 *tola* of silver to the monthly car festival.'

Mayuri quickly turned around, looking at Jnanakumara, suddenly interested. Noticing this, Jnanakumara sighed, 'But, sadly, since my business will be halted, I don't think the contribution will be possible.' Now looking directly at Mayuri, he continued, 'It's rather unfortunate, isn't it? For 100 tola of silver is a large contribution.'

Mayuri didn't break eye contact with Jnanakumara. Instead, he raised his hand and snapped his finger, summoning his assistants. Smiling forcefully, he said, 'Please unload Jnanakumara's ship as soon as possible so that he can, ahem, *donate* to our festival.'

A servant came up and offered to drop them off at their living quarters.

As they walked towards the city, Pratipa looked around, astonished by its size and splendour. Everyone from commoners to important officials and foreign traders rushed by, occasionally stopping to exchange a few words in a foreign language. Even after sunset, every street in Kedah bustled with activity. Oil lamps were lit every few steps, illuminating the whole area. Tall houses lined both sides of the street. Pratipa marvelled at the architecture and the elegance with which the houses had been designed. Shops, twice as large as in his village, were stocked with goods. Sacks of grain were arranged in one corner. Hawkers walked by with their carts, wrapping up their business for the day.

A group of weirdly dressed people passed by them. They had beards and wore long flowy robes, and their hair was wound up with cloth into elaborate headwear.

'Who are they?' Pratipa asked.

'The Chins call them *Dashi*. Like them, they never bathe.' Jnanakumara chortled. 'Barbarians,' he added after a pause.

'Where do they come from?' Pratipa asked.

'Arabia, a place hundreds of yojanas west of Aryadesa.'

'Is it the westernmost country on earth?' he inquired, unable to imagine such a distance.

Jnanakumara laughed. 'Of course not! There are many other countries in the far west. Thousands of yojanas from Aryadesa.' After thinking for a moment, he said, 'The westernmost country is perhaps Fulin.'

'Who's that?'

'It's not who. It's the name of a country. The people there are *mlecchas* too. They are extremely fair and pale though.' Jnanakumara explained.

'Wow!' Pratipa pondered upon how one could travel so far.

They reached a building with Srivijayan soldiers guarding the entrance. Jnanakumara exchanged a few words with the guards in a foreign language and then went in. Pratipa followed.

Entering a large and comfortable room, Jnanakumara said, 'Our home for now!'

'Where are we going next?' Pratipa asked.

Jnanakumara looked at him, surprised. 'Merchants don't go to new countries every day. We will now stay here in Srivijaya for a few weeks. Hence, we always have a reserved place to stay. We people of Kamboja have a separate colony for ourselves.'

'Do other countries have their own colonies?'

'Definitely. Many of them have bigger colonies, and some even have several big ones,' Jnanakumara said. 'By the way, Ratnachandra will be there. He is the most experienced and the biggest trader from Kamboja. You should talk to him, first thing tomorrow, about your plan to go to Aryadesa. Perhaps he can help.'

Pratipa visited Ratnachandra early in the morning as advised. He entered a huge mansion, decorated with gems and designs carved on the walls. Doorframes were adorned with fresh flowers. Long lamps hung from the ceiling. They were lit even during the day. Elegant and beautiful statues of *apsara*s stood gracefully in the corner. A luxurious and multicoloured carpet lined the floor. Pratipa was stunned by the opulence of the place.

He breathed in the various scents of sandalwood, camphor, and pepper. Unable to suppress his curiosity, he peeped into one of the rooms. It was stocked up to the roof with various wooden boxes containing pepper, nutmeg, cloves, cardamom, and a hundred other spices he had never seen in his life. He noticed a guard eyeing him suspiciously, so he backed away from the room.

He asked the guard, 'I would like to meet Ratnachandra. Could you tell me where he is?'

The guard nodded and escorted him to one of the rooms at the far end of the passageway. He spotted a distinguished man dressed in expensive clothes talking to what looked like his assistant.

'*Bhauman*, I want the silk consignment to be loaded onto the fifth ship today. Also, figure out what happened to the ship arriving from Chinadesa. We were supposed to receive twelve cartons of porcelain, one casket of ivory, and eight bottles of perfume yesterday from that ship.' He continued, 'And I want to visit the frankincense market while we are here in Srivijaya. Their quality is unbeatable. After you have done tha—' He broke off, noticing Pratipa.

Pratipa smiled and said, 'Namaste. I am Pratipa from Kamboja. I was wondering if you could do me a favour.'

Ratnachandra waved off his assistant before saying, 'Hmm … so you are Jnanakumara's scholar friend. He told me that you dream of going to Aryadesa and other countries.'

'Yes, sir.'

'Well then, you will need to stop dreaming,' Ratnachandra said bluntly, striding across the room and opening a large casket.

'What?'

'Yes. Forget going to Draviḍa, Aryadesa, Kalinga, or *anywhere* to the west of Srivijaya.'

'Why?!' Pratipa asked, flabbergasted.

Ratnachandra raised his eyebrows. 'You are really naive about trade, aren't you?'

Pratipa said, 'Look, if it is about the cost, I can—'

'It's not about the cost,' Ratnachandra picked up and began examining a porcelain bowl. Then, with a sigh, he laid it down. 'Just as air and water are extremely important for normal people, for businesspeople, there are two things that are even more important; first, favourable winds, and second, and more importantly, favourable governments, not only in our country but also in all other foreign countries.'

'I do not understand.'

'It is a ruler's duty to make sure that seas are safe and secure. The straits of Srivijaya are known for their notorious pirates. It is a nightmare for any trader.'

'Why doesn't the Srivijayan government do anything?'

Ratnachandra laughed. 'Why should they? They wish to establish their monopoly over the region.' In a more hushed voice, he added, 'While they do not say it aloud, we are pretty sure that the pirates operate with the approval of the government. No action is ever taken when any merchant guilds approach the local courts with complaints of piracy. King Suryavarman has been busy with internal wars over the last decade. He cannot provide a contingent for us, and neither are we rich enough to raise our own army.'

'Since when—' Pratipa began, but Ratnachandra waved his hand to quieten him, for a servant had peeked his head round the side of the door.

'Yes?' Ratnachandra asked sharply.

A messenger was ushered in.

'Greetings from the merchants of Ainurruvar, having thirty-two *velapuram*s, eighteen *pattanam*s, sixty-four *kadigai tavalam*s, and *ashrama*s at the four points of the compass and known in every direction in all eighteen lands. With the blessings of the almighty God, we are pleased to inform you that we are going to inaugurate a new *mandapam* in our temple. As a part of the celebrations, we cordially invite all the scholars in the city to a colloquium on *tarkasastra*[3] that will be held on the first Friday of the month of *Tai*, that is, *Pausha*.' Saying this, he handed over a platter containing betel leaves, areca nuts, and a coconut.

'Huh? I have no idea about all that. I can't debate to save my life,' laughed Ratnachandra. 'Wait! Hey, Pratipa, aren't you well versed in tarkasastra? Why don't you attend this event on behalf of Kamboja? You may meet people who can help you with your work,' he added.

'Um ... very well, I suppose that is a great idea,' Pratipa said, smiling.

A seagull flew towards the sea, away from the fort that stood magnificently, its dark stones contrasting with the light blue sky. Srivijayan guards stood armed at every gate, protecting the flourishing market inside. Excited chattering could be heard, and exotic smells wafted in the air. The guards could see a man climbing up the Kedah Hill in the heat of the afternoon sun.

Pratipa could not help but marvel at the polished and well-laid steps that led to the enormous fortress on top of the hill. As he climbed up, the sound of waves crashing on the rocks down below grew fainter and the cacophony of the settlement grew clearer. No sooner had he reached the entrance of what seemed like a massive fortress wall than a guard stopped him.

'Identification, please,' he asked, holding his hand out.

'What?' Pratipa said, confused.

'Don't waste my time. This is the colony of the celebrated trade guild Ainurruvar and is not your father's estate,' the guard replied, quite irritated.

Pratipa was not accustomed to the practices of a large and international city. He raked through his bag and pulled out one of the seals that Jnanakumara had given him.

'Will this do?' He handed over the seal bearing the Kamboja emblem.

'From the Kamboja merchant guild, eh? I haven't seen any scholar from there before, only sandalwood traders now and then,' the guard murmured while examining the seal and Pratipa. 'You may go.'

A feeling of excitement and nervousness crept into him as he passed through gigantic wooden doors. As he stepped into the busy townlet, he was overwhelmed by the crowd and the bustle. He needed only to keep upright—the thrust of the crowd took care of the rest. Unseeing hands dragged him this way and that. Pratipa wished he had extra pairs of eyes to see the multitude of people, activities, and goods.

Near the middle of the fortified settlement was the marketplace. Separate lanes were dedicated to a variety of goods: rice, beans, mustard, nuts, tamarind, and a million other things. Some streets were grander and sold items of luxury such as Chinese porcelain, sandalwood, perfumes, and wines.

Pratipa nearly forgot the objective of his visit. He looked around to see if he could spot any school or temple.

'Excuse me, can you please tell me where I can find the central temple?' Pratipa shouted over the counter of a shop.

'Enna?' the shopkeeper replied.

Thinking that he wasn't audible, Pratipa repeated the same thing more loudly.

A few passers-by suddenly stopped, and he understood that he was very much audible but they did not understand the language.

'Deva … Pray,' he gestured, joining his palms and pointing towards the sky.

'*Kovil*?' the shopkeeper said and pointed in the north-west direction.

Pratipa proceeded in that direction, hoping that the shopkeeper had understood what he was referring to. He had, for he could now hear the temple bells and muffled sound of chants.

The colloquium seemed to have started, and Pratipa quietly slipped into the back of the temple verandah.

An anchor, standing in the middle of the mandapa, was thankfully speaking in Sanskrit. 'Before we begin, I would like to express gratitude to the patrons for today's proceedings with special mention of Sri Kulasekaran, the honourable head merchant of the Kadaram branch of the Ainurruvar.'

He paused. Pratipa noticed a scribe near him, working with different types of chisels and hot wax to engrave on a copper plate.

'On behalf of all the patrons, I welcome all the *mahajanas* and learned men assembled here today. We, the Five Hundred of the Thousand Directions, known in every direction in all the eighteen lands, in this prosperous town of Kadaram, on the auspicious day of the Friday of Tai Māsam, hereby inaugurate this mandapam dedicated to Matankari. I invite Heramba, who will be the debate moderator for today, to start the colloquium.'

The anchor bowed and retired to the back while Heramba came forward to take his place.

'Before laying down the preliminary propositions, I request that all the participants make sure they are sitting on the correct side. Those who would like to represent the Yogacara school may occupy the section on my left, and those representing the Advaita school may be on my right.'

Pratipa realised he was sitting on the left side and stood up to cross over. A dozen others too crossed over from left to right and the other way round. Pratipa found himself a seat near another young scholar who appeared to be of his age.

'First time here?' the guy asked, smiling.

'Yes,' Pratipa replied. 'I'm Pratipa from Kamboja.'

'Nice to meet you. I'm Aiyaaran Pennorbagan, but you can call me Sadashivan.'

'You seem to be familiar with this place.'

'Yes, my father was previously a senior priest for the Ainurruvar. I live here for six months of the year but I am from—'

Pratipa did not find out where Sadashiva came from, for Heramba rang the bell to keep silent.

'I now lay down before all of you the preliminary propositions. The first proposition goes thus: We undergo different awareness events with different representational contents at different times. The second proposition adds to the first: We can undergo different awareness events with different representational contents at different times only if there are mind-independent objects, which are distinct from the awareness events and which cause these awareness events. These propositions lead to the conclusion that there exists an external world.'

A bald middle-aged man broke the short silence that followed. 'I object,' he said.

Sadashiva whispered to Pratipa, 'Mallaputta, principal of the Prithvi Vihara in Pannai.'

Mallaputta continued, 'The law of karma gives rise to different impressions that mature at different times and give rise to new awareness events with different forms at different times. So there is no need to accept the existence of an external world. Hence, the conclusion stands incorrect.'

Another man named Sanaya from Sri Lanka added to Mallaputta's argument. 'Whatever exists is momentary, by virtue of its existence—as, for example, the jug. All things about the momentariness of which we are discussing are existent and are, therefore, momentary.'

Applause rang through the left side of the mandapa.

Vardhisnu from Kalinga disputed their logic. 'Explain, then, how impressions can be distinguished from each other, and, as a result, how can impressions give rise to awareness events with different forms?'

Arur Agattiyar from Choḷa Mandala elaborated on Vardhisnu's point (Sadashiva, in the meantime, whispered, 'He is my relative on the maternal side.')

'An impression, which just arises from an awareness event, only gives rise to a recollective awareness. Different impressions are just memory traces left by past awareness events that have different forms. But, if our minds (*citta*) are momentary, then we can't explain how different impressions are created by different awareness events.'

Silabhadra from Gaudadesa reasoned, 'At every moment, all objects of the world are suffering dissolution and destruction. Just as the flame of a candle is changing every moment and yet it seems to us as if we have been perceiving the same flame all the while, so all our bodies, our ideas, emotions, and all external objects.'

Pratipa wondered if he should put across his arguments too. Even though the environment felt daunting, he took a deep breath and stood up.

'Since minds are momentary and their destruction is total, there is no co-existence between that which is impressed and that which impresses. So, there is no impression. The later time slice is not impressed unless it is produced by the previous time slice. Since the previous time-slice is destroyed by the later one, it does not leave an impression. Even if they could co-exist, there is no relation. So, there is no impression. Moreover, since they are momentary, they do not operate on each other. How can an object that is about to be destroyed be impressed upon by that which is being destroyed? Something that persists is impressed upon by a positive or negative entity that also persists.'

Applause rang through the mandapa again, but this time, it emerged from the right side.

'That was very succinctly put,' Sadashiva said as they made their way out during the midway break. Sadashiva was very chatty and easy-going, and Pratipa found him a good company.

'Oh, thank you,' Pratipa replied.

'You seem to be well versed in the school of Advaita and acquainted with the practices of Yogachara as well. I've never known anyone from Kamboja either. Sankara's Advaita Vedanta seems to have percolated to all corners of the world.'

'Yes, my uncle studied medicinal sciences in a Yogachara school. And as far as the doctrine of non-dualism is concerned, yes, we did have an ancestor, Sivasoma, who was a pupil of Sankara Bhagavatpada.'

'Kamboja isn't very well known among the international mercantile community,' added Sadashiva apologetically.

'Yes, it is not surprising. I've learnt that the merchants of Kamboja do not trade as extensively as other countries.' He added after a pause, 'But it is said that this has not always been the case. In the last few decades, our country has been at war with itself. When your house is on fire, how can one go to another's house, or why would others come to your house?'

Both of them then fell into an agreeable silence, broken eventually by Sadashiva.

'So, what brings you here to Kadaram?'

Pratipa grinned. 'Our king, His Highness Suryavarman, broke the long spell of anarchy. He united the three parts of the countries, and all nobles took an oath of allegiance to the nation. So, it is safe to say that we now look forward to a brighter future. On a personal note, everyone needs a little bit of adventure in their lives. Ours is a very closed society. To travel the seas and make friends with faraway nations, I say, is something I've always wanted to do.' He paused, remembering something. 'By the way, where did you say you come from?'

'Thiruvaiyyaru,' said Sadashiva. 'Chola Mandalam from the Dravidadesa,' he added after seeing a bemused Pratipa.

'What a stroke of luck that I should befriend you!' Pratipa said very excitedly. He scrambled around in his bag and brought out a neatly wrapped bunch of manuscripts. 'Can you read this?' he asked, passing them over to Sadashiva.

Sadashiva peered into them very intently and then looked up, astonished. 'Wow, the script suggests that this is probably more than a hundred years old. How on earth did this land in your hands?'

'These were found in my temple's library. But can you tell me what is written? Which language is this?' Pratipa asked anxiously.

'Hold on,' Sadashiva said and started reading aloud, '*Thillaivaz andhanartham adiarkkum adiyen.* This is the work of Sundarar!' exclaimed Sadashiva, excited.

'Who's that?'

'You know what? Words won't do justice. Let me show you something.' Sadashiva got up hurriedly and beckoned to Pratipa to follow.

Confused but excited, Pratipa went with Sadashiva, who navigated through the packed streets and the busy shops. Finally, they approached a silent lane where a large three-storeyed building stood. After a brief exchange with the guard, Sadashiva rushed inside.

They entered an airy, large, and beautiful room through bronzed double doors.

Pratipa gasped. Lined along all four walls were large shelves filled with more books than he had ever seen in his life.

'Must be somewhere here,' Sadashiva murmured, running his hands along one of the shelves.

'Ah! Look at this!' he said, opening the book and showing it to Pratipa. 'This is the entire text of *Thirumurai*. It is a compendium of all Shaivite literature. We are so lucky to have this here. Do you know why? Let me tell you. For a long time, the works of all the great saints were lost. Over time, corrupted versions became mainstream, and the authentic ones went into obscurity. Our emperor, Rajaraja Cholar, embarked on a quest to retrieve them after listening to excerpts. They found some manuscripts stored in the cellar of the Thillai Nataraja Temple, half of them infested with white ants. I do not know what happened exactly, but it is said that they could only find it due to divine interference. What we have today is what had been saved from the manuscripts saved from there. That is why our emperor is also known as Thirumurai Kanda Cholan.'

'Oh, this is wonderful!' said Pratipa, carefully rifling through the pages. 'You know what? Can you help me translate it? I want to take it back to Kamboja to show it to my people.'

Sadashiva thought over it for a minute before replying. 'Look, I might not be the best person for this. I know a person back home who could probably help you with this. Why don't you come to my country with me and have it translated there? I could show you all the magnificent temples we have too.'

Pratipa exclaimed ruefully, 'Ah, I wish I could do that. But you see, the Srivijayan government doesn't allow any ships from Kamboja to travel to the west beyond their own country. It's something to do with them establishing a monopoly over trade.'

'Hey, that's similar to our situation too!' Sadashiva said. 'Ships from Chola desa rarely cross Srivijaya to the east.'

Both of them stood in silence, thinking. Finally, Sadashiva spoke, slowly. 'You could do one thing. Board my ship along with me to Chola kingdom as my personal guest. That way, you will be allowed to cross the country legally.'

'That's a great idea! Thank you so much!' Pratipa said gratefully.

Back in the Kamboja colony, Ratnachandra was astounded by Pratipa's narrative and discovered that he had received an invitation to journey west. 'Despite all the efforts and strategies we've been employing for years, an inexperienced newcomer to the land and trade receives the opportunity,' he expressed with envy. Pratipa commented that in situations where money and power fall short, scholarship becomes instrumental in establishing connections.

Pratipa boarded the next ship to Naagapattinam on the kind invitation of Sadashiva and then went to the imperial capital, Thanjavur. From nearly falling backwards trying to count the number of steps in the *shikhara* of the Rajarajesvara temple to trying to peek into the chamber of white ants from where the *Thirumurai* was obtained in Thillai Nataraja temple in Chidambaram, Pratipa spent several months in the Chola country. In time, he returned to Kamboja to tell his king about the success of his mission.

The *Margali* wind blew over the waters of the Ponni. An extraordinary monsoon that year had ensured an excellent crop. Bullock carts overflowing with grains pulled over the *Raja Raja peruvali*[4]—traders eager to get to the market. A little farther on, in the suburbs of Thanjavur, dancers brought to life Andal's verses. Still further, against the backdrop of the majestic Rajarajesvara Temple on one side and a multi-storeyed royal palace on another, Pratipa was engrossed in a conversation with Visarada. Surrounding him stood a troupe of soldiers, scribes, accountants, and others from Kamboja. On a *thinnai* nearby sat Ratnachandra and Kulashekara, also engrossed in work.

Sitting on the riverfront, a bard immortalised the scene around him in words:

வாழிஅம் போதத் தருகுபாய் விடயம்
வரிசையின் விளங்கலின் அடுத்த
சூழலம் பளிங்கின் பாசல ராதிச்
சுடர்விடு மண்டலம் பொலியக்
காழகில் கமழு மாளிகை மகளிர்
கங்குல்வாய் அங்குலி கெழும
யாழொலி சிலம்பும் இஞ்சிசூழ் தஞ்சை
இராசரா சேச்சரத் திவர்க்கே.

Round the Tanjai runs a crystal-green by-pass
Lined with herbs and flowers, in plein air as if,
In circular scatter by *Vadavaar* tides
Imprinted with floral foliage, embossed.
There black *akil* incense rises from mansions;
There maidens play their *yaazh*
Straining tunes of nocturnes-sweet

> To please my Lord`s ring`d Ear! (Translation by S.A. Sankaranarayanan)

The palace doors opened, and a Chola official came outside. Addressing Pratipa, he said, 'His Highness is most pleased to welcome the embassy from Kamboja. You may please present yourself in the Kilakku Vasal.'

As they formed an orderly group and went inside, trumpets were blown, and drums were beaten. Chola soldiers were stationed all along the pathway from the entrance to the verandah where the king was already seated on the throne. Several ministers and officials stood by the side.

Pratipa and his team wasted no time getting down to the matter. All the technical aspects of the treaty were long over, all discussions had already taken place, and today was only the official ceremony in the imperial fashion to bring into effect the accord between the two empires.

Pratipa spoke in a clear and loud voice. 'May prosperity prevail always. Representing His Highness Sri Suryavarman, lord of Kamboja and ruler of the earth, whose feet shine with light emerging from the crowns of kings surrounding, who is ever victorious in battle and whose side the goddess Laksmi never leaves, I, Ambassador Pratipa of Isvarapura, seek to establish friendship with your empire. In hardships and victory, in trade and religion, on land and at sea, we extend our hand of friendship.'

A scribe had quickly written Pratipa's words on paper, and some others were inscribing the same on copper and stone. Visarada took the paper and handed it over to a Chola secretary.

A Chola minister came forward and stood in front of Pratipa. In a similar vein to Pratipa's statements, he announced, 'In the tenth year of the reign of Ko-Parakesarivarman, alias Sri Rajendra Chola Devar, who, while the goddess of fortune having become constant, increased and, while the goddess of the great Earth, the goddess of victory in battle, and the matchless goddess of fame having become his great queens, rejoiced in his extended happy lifetime, conquered with his great army Idaiturainau; Vanavasi, shut in by a fence of continuous forests; Kollippakkai, whose walls were surrounded by *sulli* trees; Mannaikkadakkam, whose fortification was unapproachable; the crown of the king of Ilam, which was surrounded by the impetuous sea; the exceedingly beautiful crown of his queen; the beautiful crown and the necklace of Indra, which the king of the South had previously surrendered to thc kings of llam; the whole of the Ila-mandalam surrounded by the clear sea; warlike Kerala and 12,000 ancient islands. The king accepts with great pleasure the hand of friendship extended by the king of Kamboja. I, the minister for foreign affairs and war and peace, on behalf of Sri Rajendra Choladevar, promise to maintain the friendship in times of hardships and prosperity alike. May the fire and the Brahmanas bear witness to this treaty.'

He came forward and handed over the document containing the text and secured it with the Chola emblem of a roaring tiger seated beside two fish with a bow and a boar above.

Pratipa signalled something to Visarada, and immediately, servants brought forth a variety of gifts—gold, silver, and expensive gems. But what stood out was a chariot.

A low whisper emerged among the bystanders as it appeared.

Pratipa addressed Rajendra Chola, 'Our king has sent a very special gift, his personal golden chariot with which he was victorious in every single battle.'

Then Pratipa waited anxiously to see how this gift would be received, and to his relief, Rajendra Chola smiled.

'Today, the sea bears witness to the pinnacle of human advancement. Seamless trade and cultural exchanges will make way for development and prosperity for all. However, some countries today want to show their power by monopolising the sea. In such a situation, the coming together of two powerful kingdoms shall begin a new chapter in history.'

After 985 CE, as Rajaraja Chola ascended the throne, the Chola empire rose swiftly, soon encompassing the entirety of southern India and penetrating the oceans with the conquest of Sri Lanka and the Maldives. In around 1020, Rajendra Chola, victoriously marched through Kalinga, all the way up to the Ganga. In the same decade, he conducted his famous naval expeditions to Southeast Asia against Srivijaya, attacking fourteen port cities. Alas, today we are unaware of the exact reasons and the intricacies of the political situation in the continent, but trade reasons cannot be ruled out. Chola influence increased in the archipelago, and so did the activities of the merchant guilds of Ayyavole (Ainurruvar) and Manigramam. The Karandai copper-plate inscription of Rajendra I, dated 1020 CE (eight regnal year of Rajendra Chola) records this embassy from Suryavarman I, referring to the gift of a chariot. The inscription states that the Kamboja king Suryavarman I presented him his war chariot 'for the protection of his own royalty i.e, *atma-laksmi*'[5], indicating possibilities of a military alliance during these intense face-offs. There is more: the relations between the Cholas and the Khmers continued for many decades. Nearly a hundred years after the embassy of Suryavarman I, Suryavarman II, the famous builder of Angkor Wat, sent another embassy to the Chola court, presenting a precious stone to Kulottunga Chola.

4

The Magic of the Dragons

Dr Swetha Prakash

Boo Wants to Be Human

Once upon a time, there was a great flood in Cambodia. Many people were shocked, and they consulted occult powers to understand the situation. An occult power suggested that there was an Indian witch who knew the way of floods and storms, and she alone could stop this one from recurring. So, a team of prominent people travelled from Cambodia to India in search of this witch. She was very powerful because she worshipped a goddess who was snake-faced and had the same name as herself—Latha Parameshwari.

I knew this story because my mother and my grandmother told me about it. They also told me that we were the descendants of this very Latha Parameshwari, the witch, and they specifically told me this story many times because they had named me Latha Parameshwari. Even while I was a child, they encouraged me to dabble in the dark arts—witchcraft and the like. None of my requests for cauldrons or magic wands went unattended in my home. Soon, I grew up to be exceptionally intelligent and exceptionally talented in the art of witchcraft. I had hair that reached my knees, eyes dark as watermelon seeds, and creamy skin like art paper. I knew many spells and was always immersed in magic. I used to spend time practising Tantra, black magic, *jadu tona*, and *shava sadhana* (the corpse practice) at cremation grounds. I had a close friend, and I was trying to solve her problem with my magic.

My friend, too, had been a witch. *Had* is the operative word as she is now a ghost called Bhootre—Boo for short—who haunts the Chennai Memorial Cremation Grounds. I, too, live in Chennai, and my house is conveniently situated right next to this cremation ground. Boo wants to be a witch again or, at any rate, human. She badly, badly wants a human body. I am trying to help her the best I can. I have used many spells and tried many corpse practices, yet so far I have failed. Boo remains ghostly, and I remain unhappy. She is, too. Boo is long in the face, and her skin is stretched over it like translucent rubber. She wears the de rigueur costume for Indian ghosts: a white chiffon dress that gleams and glitters in the dark.

Boo came to me with a fresh plan two days ago. 'Let's go to Cambodia,' she said. She is the resident ghost haunting my Chennai home and is around me quite a lot, something I don't mind since we can both chat for hours.

'Cambodia? But why?' I asked.

'We may be able to resolve all our problems there, and I may be able to turn human again,' said Boo.

'What! No way!' That was me, in my excitement.

Boo was as excited as I was.

'But what is in Cambodia?' I was curious.

'Dragons, and with the magic of dragons, I can become human again,' said Boo.

'Dragons? Are you sure there are dragons on Earth?'

'Are you sure there are ghosts and witches on Earth?' Boo retorted.

'You got me there,' I said. 'But how can a dragon help you turn human again?'

'Well, the dragons in Cambodia are winged. If you can get one feather from their wings and make a special potion, I can turn human again. Yeeeeeeeeeeee!' screamed Boo in excitement.

'So, we need a dragon feather?' I asked cautiously.

'Yes, dragons have magic, and the magic contained in their feathers is such that it can make anyone's wish come true,' said Boo, as she was rushing out through the window in great speed.

'But—' However, Boo was gone.

I don't know where Boo learnt about the magic of the dragons and the power of dragon feathers to make any wish come true. I thought I would call my mother to find out more about dragons. She is a practising witch too.

'Amma, do you know anything about dragons and their magic?' I asked my mother, who was boiling dal for sambar in the kitchen.

'What are you saying, Latha? Let me finish cooking. Then I will talk to you,' Amma said.

I didn't mind. I wanted to taste my mother's sambar mixed with freshly cooked white rice too. Boy, was my mother's sambar worth the wait! It was the most scrumptious sambar in the world. The consistency was just right, and so were the myriad spices mixed into it. My mother ground her own sambar powder and did not rely on ready-made mixes. She made her own rasam powder and pulliodariaye powder too. Our house was always alive with the smell of varied spices like coriander and cardamom and traditional Indian ingredients like tamarind. I loved herbs too. I know that my mother got her love of herbs because she was a practising witch. All witches love herbs and the magic of herbs. I use herbs for healing.

Amma and I discussed dragons over hot sambar and even hotter rice. Amma ate with her hands, slowly relishing each morsel and regretting that she had not made red chilli–flavoured aloo sabzi to go with the meal.

'It may be difficult to get a dragon feather,' said Amma. 'I know there are winged dragons living underground near the Seam Reap river in Cambodia, but I also know that if you try to steal from a dragon and stealthily get their magical feathers, they will curse you,' she added. 'Yes,' Amma went on between bites, 'what Boo said is true. Any wish, any magical and outlandish wish, can be made true with a genuine dragon feather due to the magic of the dragons.'

'That is great news for Boo,' I said.

Amma said, 'Tell me about the time when Boo was last human.'

I told her.

Ramali Travels from Cambodia to India

When Boo was last human, her name was Ramali. She had left her home in Cambodia and had recently arrived in the land of the Tamils in Bharatavarsha. She had fled Cambodia because she was being pursued by a strange man, who was elegant and wild. She did not know his name, but she knew he ate human flesh and sang with the animals and the birds. He had wanted to devour her from the minute he had set eyes on her. She, being young and foolish, did not understand his true intention. She thought he was soft on her, the way guys in her tribe were soft on certain girls who wore their animal skin cloths well and cooed whenever these same guys made everyone laugh. No man in her tribe was soft on her. They all thought her strange. It was not that she had desired anyone or anyone's affection. She was much too wild to desire human affection herself.

Or so she thought. However, when this man, who was tribeless and free, started watching her from a distance, she felt a strange nibbling pain in her stomach.

He would follow her tribe around when they assembled outside the caves, stealthily sometimes, hiding behind bushes and tall trees. He would keep his eyes trained on her. The men in her tribe would laugh at her, and the women would giggle. But the old storyteller told her the truth: the man following her around was a cannibal who was trying to hunt her for her flesh. She fled Cambodia within three weeks, took a magic boat, and arrived in India. Finally, there, she was able to sigh, remove her animal furs, and replace them with tree bark.

She had come to India for a specific reason. She had heard that, in India, there were certain tribes that never wore animal skin or ate animal meat. Ramali was born a witch and, because of this, was always very close to wildlife. Wild animals and birds would talk to her. Trees would teach her the language of the animals. This had been so ever since she was very young. However, no one else in her tribe was like her. They hunted animals and wore animal fur. She had not been able to eat animal meat. She would vomit the meat if it was given to her. She did wear animal fur, however, because the chief of their tribe insisted on this. He said that fur clothing was the insignia of their tribe and she had to wear it. She did so but with some reluctance.

Because of this, she never felt comfortable in her own skin. She was always teary-eyed. She would keep shivering, as if something icy had been placed on her. The women in her tribe wore a coat of deer skin and a sort of crown made of decorated deer antlers. They spent hours decorating the deer antlers with deer teeth and tree gum. They also painted the deer skin coat with designs made with natural dyes and paints. The coats were dyed in the same colour (blue) and had designs drawn on them with ochre tree gum.

Everyone in the tribe worked on the cloths, everyone made the same patterns on the cloths, and everyone wore the same cloths. She, because of her aversion to animal skin, did not have to work on the cloths. She had heard of India from the old travelling storyteller with a long, grey beard that touched his toes. He met their tribe when they were all living in the caves by the riverbanks. The caves were moss-covered, cold, and slippery. Still, to the tribe, they offered protection from the wilderness and wild creatures. But she, Ramali, knew that she needed no protection from the wilderness or wild creatures. She was truly Earth's child. She spoke with the wind and the sea waves. She spoke to the animals and the birds. The trees were her teachers and her instructors. She was always one with nature. It was the humans whom she could not fathom.

When Ramali arrived in Bharatavarsha, she fed on roots and shoots and made her way to the first forest she could find. She wanted to get away, away from the Indians and their cow dung–laced village homes. She wanted to avoid their noisy temples and their ritual fire sacrifices where they offered rice grains to the fire and to Indra, the god-in-chief. These fires caused so much smoke that she would cough as she passed by. The Indian people were harmless and never paid much attention to the fact that she, a small-eyed stranger, a woman, was wandering by herself in their country. Her skin, pale and clear, would glisten with drops of sweat in the hot Indian sun. The Indians were a busy lot, and they lived differently from the Cambodians. While the Indians lived a settled existence, living in permanent huts in villages, the Cambodians lived in the forests, in the caves, and on the riverbanks, carrying arrows and hunting animals. In India—and Ramali watched this new, strange country closely—they worshipped snakes and tigers and offered fire sacrifices to the snake and tiger gods. Snake worship was so prevalent and widespread that Ramali wanted to cry. She would bite into a mango she had plucked and, as its juice wetted her mouth and dripped down her chin, she would hide behind a Peepal tree and watch them (the Indians) decorate large stone sculptures of snakes with white and red powder.

Ramali had other uses for the mango juice too. Being a witch, she knew that if she applied a spell-charged mango juice coating on her smooth, never-out-of-place, silky hair, it would change, transform, and mutate. She knew this instinctively, using her witch instincts. She coated her hair with mango juice, and still, the Indians who watched her wander around did not care. They themselves decorated their hair with areca nut powder to make it wiry and thick and wild.

Ramali felt safe and happy in India. In this country, they accepted wild women. They never followed her, shooed her, or threatened her. She loved India. Nevertheless, she wanted to leave the village area the boat had taken her to. She was looking for a forest.

In the forest, she hoped to build a little enclosure for herself, stock up on nuts and wild berries, and practise magic. There was a hill nearby, and it was covered with wild trees. Ramali decided to climb up the hill. The journey was arduous and painful, but the isolation and solitude elevated her. The hill was known as the Arunachala Mountain. It took the form of the Indian god Shiva. She knew this because the birds and the trees spoke to her and told her. When she realised she was walking on the body of the god, she shuddered and turned back. She returned to the village.

In the villages, they were celebrating a festival dedicated to a lion-faced goddess. Ramali peered at her. The goddess had been carved on a long black granite stone. The figure had the head of a lioness and the body of a woman. They called her Pratyangira. The crows told her that these villagers were not human like her. They were a class of beings called *betala*s. They were vampires in temperament, but, being religious also, they rarely killed the victims they sunk their fangs into.

The crows flocked around her as she sat down on the soft mud to watch the festival dedicated to the goddess Pratyangira. They told her that the betalas had just brutally defeated the dragon queen and her clan of dragons. These dragons were on the battleground nearby, bleeding and injured.

Just as they didn't have villages in Cambodia, they didn't have battlegrounds either. All this sounded strange to Ramali, and she followed the crows to the nearby battleground. After three nights of travel, she reached the place they had told her about. It was a vast field covered with sand. On the sand lay bloodied and dejected dragons. Ramali cried when she saw the carnage.

The dragon queen and her dragon herd were severely wounded after the battle with the betalas, the vampire tribe who worshipped the goddess Pratyangira, who dwelt in the cremation ground. The dragon queen and her dragon herd were worshippers of Shiva in his form as Sarabeshwara, the lord of dragons. Pratyangira and Sarabeshwara were eternal consorts. So Sarabeshwara did not send power to the dragons since they were fighting his wife's devotees, the betala clan.

The dragons were howling in great pain. They were lying in a circular formation. In the centre of the circle lay their queen, who was dying. They were grieving because they were wounded and their queen was dying. Their queen had the face of a dragon and the body of a woman. Her gown was bloodied. A sword was jutting out from her heart.

Ramali's heart started beating against her chest. She knew that she could save the dragon queen. Ramali walked up to the dragon queen and placed her limp head on her thighs. She cast a magic spell and pulled out the sword. Then, with an enchantment, she healed the dragon queen. The dragon queen looked at her in confusion and then passed out.

Ramali walked up to each dragon and cast a spell on each of them so that their wounds would disappear.

The dragon queen, recovering consciousness smiled a cruel smile and told her three main dragon generals, 'Tie up this girl who cured us. She will be useful for us—and *only* for us.'

Ramali felt terror when she heard the order. Had she heard wrong? But her shuddering body told her that, yes, this was what the dragon queen had said.

The dragon queen marched up to Ramali with long strides. Her gait was purposeful and noiseless. She was followed by her three dragon generals who had serious and fierce expressions. They were wielding lances in their paws.

The dragon queen pushed Ramali to the ground and put a knife to her throat. It was a curved knife with an eye carved on it. Ramali's eyes widened in shock. She died of fear and turned into a ghost called Bhootre or Boo for short.

After I had told Amma Ramali's or Boo's story, I demanded a story in return. I wanted to know about the origin of the magic of the dragons.

'The magic of the dragons has its origins in the Cambodian Reamker,' said Amma slowly.

'Reamker,' I said, pronouncing the strange name slowly.

'Yes, the Reamker, the Cambodian Ramayana,' said Amma, and she went on to tell me the story of how the magic of the dragons had its origins in the Reamker.

The Origin of the Magic of the Dragons in the Reamker

The story that Amma told me began with a sage who had small crumpled eyes, like folded white cloth. His hair was long, white, and matted. He had a curved nose like a bird's beak. His lips were dark and cracked. His forehead was creased and marked with sacred ash. He looked very ancient. He was bent over a curved rosewood stick. He carried a rosewood begging bowl. He was wearing a single piece loincloth. His hands were shaking, and his voice was loud and angry. 'I will kill myself if you don't step out of the line and give me alms with the respect I deserve.'

Neang Seda trembled, and the basket of fruits she was holding almost fell. Luckily for her, she held on to the basket of freshly plucked pineapples, apples, mangoes, and watermelons. It was a heavy cane basket that her husband Preah Ream had himself shaped and sculpted. He would create these baskets, ten at a time, each week to give alms to passing sages.

The sage once again tried to enter the hut. But the minute he took a step forward, a line of fire flared up from the ground, preventing him from proceeding. 'What is this magic?' he yelled at the girl.

She took a step back, biting her lower lip and tightening her hold on the fruit basket. She was wearing a single-piece saffron sari with jasmine flower garlands. Gold adorned her neck, earlobes, hair, and wrists. Though she was dressed in the manner of a forest dweller, it was apparent that she was a princess.

'It is a special circle that has been drawn around this hut to protect me from wild animals and demons,' she whispered.

'Do I look like a wild animal or perhaps a demon?' thundered the sage. 'There is no option for me but to starve myself to death after this affront.'

Neang Seda considered her options. She could stay inside the magic line and hope that Preah Ream, her husband, and Preah Leak, her brother-in-law, would return soon and restore the sage's faith and stop him from harming himself.

Almost as if he read her mind, the old sage chanted a magic spell, and there, to Neang Seda's horror, manifested—

in his reddened, roughened hands—a sword. He held the sword beside his head as if to behead himself.

'No, no, stop!' cried Neang Seda in alarm. 'I will step out of the line.'

Then, without thinking, she stepped out of the line.

The minute she stepped out of the line, she knew she had made a mistake.

The old sage changed into a rakshasa. His skin became rough and hardened. His red eyes shone with cruelty. His long hair, which reached down to his waist, was decorated with a string of mammoth teeth. He had pointed fangs, which gleamed as if polished. Neang Seda was not sure if he was a betala (a vampire) or a rakshasa (a shapeshifting demon who fed on human flesh). She tried to run back into the hut, but the line would not allow her. It flamed up as if she, too, were an intruder. Neang Seda looked again at the demon. She knew that her husband, Preah Ream, who was an expert demon slayer, could kill this demon in seconds. But where was he? Oh, what a big mistake she had made by crossing her brother-in-law's line!

'Compassion, my favourite sin,' smirked the demon.

He had large, curved nails, again polished. At that moment, Neang Seda recognised who was in front of her. It was Krong Reap, the king of the rakshasas. She recognised him from his nails. His sister, Surpanakhar, had her nails shaped the same way. Surpanakhar was the *rakshasi* who had attacked Neang Seda with her sharp painted claws when Preah Ream had refused to marry her. Surpanakhar had tried to kill Neang Seda, and in the agitation, to protect Neang Seda, Preah Leak, her brother-in-law, had cut off Supernakhar's nose and ears. Even then, Neang Seda had known that a great mistake had occurred—the disfiguration of the demoness who fed on the flesh of sages and humans. Neang Seda and Preah Ream knew that Surpanakhar would return for revenge, and she did. She brought her two rakshasa cousins and their army of 60,000 murderous demons. However, Preah Leak and Preah Ream had effortlessly scattered the lot. There was a rumour among the sages of the forest that Surpanakhar's real brother was Krong Reap, the king of the rakshasas. The demon standing in front of Neang Seda with gleaming fangs was meanwhile enveloped in smoke and flames.

'What magic is this?' Neang Seda screamed and called out for Preah Ream. The monster laughed out loud, and from the flames and smoke emerged his ten heads.

'Neang Seda, you are mine,' said the rakshasa, and he gripped her left hand tightly.

Neang Seda moved back in revulsion and fear. She jerked her hand to force the rakshasa to leave her so that she could run into the forest. But the grip of his well-muscled hand was like an iron clasp.

Neang Seda screamed and called out to the birds and the animals of the forest to inform her husband, so that he may swiftly come to her rescue. The rakshasa started dragging the unwilling Neang Seda, and she howled in rage and shock. The rakshasa's flying chariot was hidden behind some trees ,and the moment Neang Seda saw it, her heart sank. He was going to place her in that awful, winged chariot and take her to his city. Neang Seda, in that moment of deep pain and crisis, had a flash of self-knowledge. She, Neang Seda, was the supreme goddess, the energy force behind all the universes that existed. Her husband, Preah Ream, was the source and origin of all the universe. He was the supreme consciousness personified. They had both taken human birth to put an end to the plight of sages and humans who were being terrorised by the scornful, flesh-eating rakshasas, who were given to plunder and murder. If Krong Reap, the king of the rakshasas, abducted her in his aerial chariot and took her to his kingdom where the flesh-eating rakshasas lived, there would be a war between her husband and the rakshasas. Her husband, Preah Ream, would use the kidnapping as an excuse to put an end to the rakshasas living on earth. Knowing all this, Neang Seda resigned herself to the iron grip on her wrist.

In the same manner as the rakshasa was abducting her, he had stolen away tens of thousands of women in the past and taken them with him to his island home, Lanka. Such women—some human, some the daughters of sages, some sages themselves, some Vidyadhara, some Siddhars, some Yoginis—had all been manhandled by him and then abducted and taken to his city where he had forcibly married them. Some of these women had been previously married and cried in pain and suffering every night in Ravana's demonic palace. Neang Seda, the goddess supreme, when she heard of the plight of these women, had vowed to relieve their suffering, and her husband, Preah Ream, had vowed to kill Krong Reap and his rakshasas himself.

The purpose for which she, the great goddess, had descended would become apparent soon enough—in fact, the minute Krong Reap dragged her into the chariot, not knowing that he had dragged the goddess of death herself.

However, the revulsion and hate Neang Seda felt for Krong Reap was real enough. He glared at her with triumphant, lustful eyes, even though her brother-in-law had disfigured Krong Reap's sister (purportedly for attacking Neang Seda but actually for being the demoness queen who led the rakshasas in attacking and devouring the sages of the forest). He was so enchanted by Neang Seda that did not even care for his sister. Neang Seda was disgusted. She turned her face from Krong Reap and started scattering her jewels in the forest. Her bracelets, her necklaces, her earrings—she threw them all down so that Preah Ream might follow the trail and swiftly come to Lanka to destroy the demonic hordes.

Krong Reap had shiny bronze skin, and his ten heads were decorated with mammoth teeth strung on gold thread and set in carved golden ornaments. His laughter would have dampened anyone's spirit. In her distress, Neang Seda thought of Preah Ream and continuously repeated the mantra with his name. The separation from her beloved was going to be real, but they had descended to earth for a particular purpose and that purpose would soon be fulfilled.

Krong Reap, jackal that he was, was abducting her the same way he had abducted tens of thousands of women. This time, however, the results were going to be very different. Neang Seda was cursing Krong Reap under her breath and screaming Preah Ream's name loudly so that he may find her soon and kill the monster.

Just then, Jatayu, an aging brown eagle, saw Neang Seda being carried away in the aerial chariot. Jatayu was tired. He had flown to a distant mountain and was on his way back to the forest. He spotted the aerial chariot from a distance and identified it as belonging to Krong Reap. Jatayu fought mightily with Krong Reap once he realised that Neang Seda was being kidnapped. However, Krong Reap first cut off Jatayu's wings and later struck a lethal blow. The eagle's wings hit the ground and turned into magical dragons with wings. Because these dragons had been created from Jatayu's wings, Neang Seda, once rescued, blessed all winged dragons with great magic. That was the origin of the magic of these dragons.

'Wow,' I said.

Amma continued, 'I must tell you a rare version of the Tamil Ramayana that has dragons in it too.'

So, Amma told me another story.

Dragons and the Tamil Ramayana

In the city of Lanka, where virtue goes disregarded and unrewarded, it is better not to be too chaste, to speak with exactness or to wear white, a colour its king, Ravana, abhors. Today, however, a hundred and eight priests are sitting in a square—with fires blazing in front of them—all dressed in white silk *veshti*s and *angostram*s. Their topknots indicate an awakened *brahmarandhra*[1]. A *yantra*[2] is drawn on the ground with turmeric, rice powder, and kumkum. The air smells of *homam* smoke, bitter herbs like neem, and sandalwood incense. While they pour ghee and other oblations into the fire altars in front of them, the priests recite mantras that evoke the most destructive powers in the cosmos. There is an earnestness in their expressions that is touching. Sincerity, it must be admitted, adds a great deal of charm to wickedness.

The chants are from the *Atharva Veda*, the Veda of sorcery, secret syllables whose correct pronunciation can ensure *vashikaran* and *sammoham,* which can bring any being under the control of the host—words and signs situated in a web of terrifying intent. Here, the gruesomeness of primordial desires has been turned into a cinematic episode.

The priests invoke subtle currents of energy that can alter the fundamental energy field and psychology of a person, making the individual vulnerable to subjugation by Ravana, the king of the flesh-eating rakshasas and patron of this bizarre *yajna* (fire sacrifice). The sacrifice is being made to the mother goddess, Nikumbala Pratyangira, the *kula devata* (family deity) of the rakshasas. Nikumbala Pratyangira, a terrible form of Kali, the goddess of the cremation ground, is the patron deity of the *Atharva Veda*. She is depicted as a ferocious and intimidating goddess with a fierce lion face, seated on a lion. If the ceremony is not successful, the priests will be sacrificed to her. Ravana is, after all, a just ruler. He treats his allies and enemies alike, killing them when they don't serve his end.

The priests are not intimidated by the death clause. They have performed, with success, many such sacrifices to Nikumbala Pratyangira before. This is how Ravana *Dasamukha*—winning over *Kala* (time) and the *dik pala*s (guardians of space)—brought the entire matrix of spacetime under his sole control. Thus, Indrajit, Ravana's son and heir, the hero of the Vedas and the king of the heavens, conquered Indra. Today, the target is easy: a mere mortal and a woman at that, feeble and unaided, an *abla stree*. The chief priest, Shukra, had felt that Sita Videhi, the daughter of Janaka, was entirely unworthy of such a grand ceremony. However, Ravana Dasamukha, ruler absolute, had insisted.

Ravana thinks that knowing Sita's unshakable obstinacy and her fixation with that unworthy mortal, Rama Dasarathi, there is a possibility that this great Vedic and Tantric ceremony on which he is exhausting half of Lanka's coffers may also fail to meet its end.

As with any obsession, the essence is itself abstract. Within himself, Ravana feels the primordial battle, the tension between passion and reason. He wishes that he didn't have to force Sita into submission by using supernatural means. This is what he has yearned for all these months—that she would desire him as much as he desires her.

Ravana views the whole universe as a sphere of consumption. Lanka, the golden city built on barbarism, affectation, and decadence, belongs to him. Having some acquaintance with the Dharmashastras (the ethical books), he prefers to ignore them. Looting, rather than trade, is responsible for Lanka's expansion. Ravana is used to everything in the cosmos giving in to his will, and this woman who refuses to do so for a bark-clad, begging bowl–carrying monk, inflames him with yearning and wrath. At the heart of Ravana's fixation with Sita is her devotion to Rama. He can't believe that she is refusing a *Trilok Vijayta* (conqueror of the three worlds) for that drifter Rama who roams around forests conversing with other drifters who call themselves woodland seers. Sita was a princess after all, used to the comforts of a palace. Yet his City of Gold doesn't seem to enthral her at all. Any other woman would have joyously married Ravana by now. This singular attitude intrigues him, deepening his obsession—the most intense mode of egotism that the world has known.

Churning

Sita's only possessions in Lanka are toy building blocks. With these, she builds models of her experiences in Mithila, Ayodhya, Chitrakoot, and Lanka. The building blocks are shaped into metaphors and ideas. But she isn't sculpting now.

Her human eyes, often compared to fully bloomed lotuses by Sanskrit poets writing in the *shringara rasa* (erotic mood) are closed. But she is not sleeping. She sits with her back against the Ashoka tree, legs crossed in the *padmasana* (lotus position), and her palms rest on her knees in the *chinmudra*, with the thumbs pressed on the index fingers to form a circle on both hands.

Circles. Her father, Janaka Videha, found her under a prehistoric rock marked with circles and spirals when he was ploughing. At her *swayamvar*, Rama Dasarathi had bent Shiva Mahadeva's bow into a circle. Their eyes met briefly through the frame before he broke it. Her brother-in-law, Lakshmana Dasarathi, had drawn a circle around her in Panchavati, a circle of vowels and consonants charged with the potency of ancient mantras, forbidding her to step across the line. But she had, and now she is sitting in another circle, made with dried Kusha grass sanctified with Rama's name.

Sita concentrates on the point between her shut eyes, her *ajna* chakra (third eye). She focuses till the dark, lifeless space becomes luminous and awake. To Trijata and the other rakshasi women standing around her in a threatening circle, Sita looks like a madwoman. Her hair, knotty and rough like coir, hasn't been combed in months. Her ochre sari, coarse and torn, is streaked with old mud.

Sita's face, her beautiful face, is, however, calm and placid. Her calmness puzzles them. They don't understand how this destitute woman with a death sentence pronounced on her could be so serene and so stubborn. '*Bhrastmati*' (fool), they shout at her—Bhrastmati for refusing to be the queen, Bhrastmati for not living in the palace of gold, Bhrastmati for rejecting Ravana. Bhrastmati. Bhrastmati. Bhrastmati.

Sita, however, cannot hear them. Her consciousness is in another spacetime reality. That is why she is also called Vaidehi—she who can transcend her body mind consciousness. Her gross body is in Lanka, held captive by *khadgamdharini*s (fierce-looking rakshasi women with stained cleavers), but her subtle body is free from the restrictions posed by time, space, and causation. She experiences the apparent material cosmos as a vast matrix of psychospiritual energy. In her body mind, the universe revealss itself as an infinite pattern of energy and light, where everything is superconscious. She is Adi Shakti after all, the creatrix of the three worlds and the power behind all creation and manifestation. As scholarly pundits often put it, without her, even her husband, the spirit supreme, is incapable of doing anything and is nothing but a corpse. So only a fool, a bhrastmati like Ravana, could believe that he has any power over her and that he has held her vulnerable and helpless under his control. She doesn't blame Ravana. It is her *maya shakti* (power of illusion) that blinds him. It is his fate, and she is the goddess of destiny, Niyati.

There have been many Ravanas before this, and there will be many more who will come at points after. Spacetime is full of Ramayanas, Sitayanas, Rama Lilas, and Sita Lilas. There are as many Ramayanas as there are universes (*brahmandas*). The narration, plot, crisis point, or climax vary in some, whilst the Adi Ramayana, written by Valmiki in the 'authentic' sloka metre, is ritually re-enacted without allowing for any deviation. In this original form of the Valmiki Ramayana, the relationship between the 'cult of feeling' and the representations of ethical codes are particularly vibrant. In some Ramayanas, the dramaturgy tends to abstractness. In one Ramayana, the emotions of all the characters manifest into gross objects. Another Ramayana excludes the idea of dramatic characters, functioning on countless ideas alone—ideas postulating various social and individual truths.

Right now, in her *sukshma sharira* (subtle body), Sita examines the several Ramayanas, those that have been and those that will be. She watches them, one after the other, like a spectator in a grandiose film festival. As she evaluates the Ramayanas, she considers such factors as the banality of ideas and the absence and confusion of meaning. As a witness, she turns away from empathy and identification, taking a more detached, experimental stance. She likes Ramayanas built on metaphors, where everything rests on nuance.

Like an actress watching old reels of herself, she flinches at the parts where she thinks she is too melodramatic, too predictable. The essential characteristic of the Ramayana universe is its refusal to make things easy for its protagonists. This is the story of gods who suffer and suffer deeply. Sita watches the Ramayanas with affection and detachment. Sometimes she forgets that she is seeing her own life reflected in a million existential planes. Immersed in the plot, Sita forgets that she is its eternal *nayika* (heroine). Now and then, Sita is perplexed, as if she doesn't know how the story will end, as if she is witnessing a Ramayana for the first time. If spacetime is a circle, then she is the circumference and Rama is the centre. Their story is enacted inside. This is her play, her *Lila*. And what is the purpose of this theatre? To delight and instruct, of course. And to deliver.

The universes she has created are built on dualities, positive and negative energies acting on each other. Without the friction between these energies, life would not be possible. But when negative energies overpower all other forces of manifestation in the universe, intervention is needed. Another Ramayana needs to be played out. That is the divine law. The many Ramayanas are, in truth, the bridge upon which one can cross the timeless problematics of human existence, greed and lust. That lust and greed are built into the source code of life (*guna*s of *Prakriti* or attributes of the material world) is itself a comment on the difficult and problematic character of existence, a dilemma tackled, both literally and metaphorically, in the Ramayanas.

The philosophical Ramayanas are better than the action ones, Sita thinks. The desire among the sages for an end to sentimental and romantic Ramayanas resulted in the creation of the extraordinary philosophical Maha Ramayana, the Yoga Vashista, which is a conversation between Rama and his preceptor Vashista on the nature of the world's appearance. Sita loves listening to dialogues between Rama (with palms folded respectfully in the *anjali mudra*) and his gurus. Rama asks, 'On what are these worlds woven like warp and woof?

What eternity sustains everything here?'

Vashista responds, 'These worlds are woven like warp and woof on pure consciousness and its inherent vibratory energy endowed with the omnipotent power to create. Everything else that is experienced here is mere illusion or Maya. Just as reflections in a mirror are insubstantial and never exist outside of the mirror, so too is the world's appearance a reflection on the mirror of supreme consciousness, which is endowed with the capacity of perceiving and reflecting on itself. That consciousness can be experienced as pure bliss, transcending all forms of pleasure and pain. It is present in all objects and is the subject and the very act of experiencing. Being the knower, the known, and the object of knowledge, it is both immanent and transcendent, both the known and the unknown.

'Know this, Raghava, it is beyond the senses. Yet the senses derive their power of perception from it and none other. This consciousness is very subtle and is the form of infinite ethereal space. Here, there is no notion of time, space, or causation—the fabric of material existence. It is *turiya*, beyond the three mundane states of experiencing: wakefulness, dreaming, and deep sleep. When the supreme consciousness is realised, the phenomenal world appears to be insubstantial. When you disengage from both that which is pleasant and that which is unpleasant in the material realms, you become established in this supreme state of self-realisation. When the mind is reined in and freed from its endless cravings and desires, this absolute state of consciousness, which is very tranquil, can be experienced. The endless cravings and desires take the shape of rakshasas and, once they are slain, pure being can be realised.

'*Tat tvam asi,* Rama. You, Rama, are no different from that supreme consciousness, and Sita is your inherent vibratory energy, or *spanda*, continuously creating as the mother goddess. She is the great illusion that causes the world to appear to come into existence and then dissolve back into nothingness.'

Each time a Sita is kidnapped, countless universes are flooded with *pralaya jal* (the waters of dissolution and chaos). It is a strange, subtly perceptive image, that of Sita being kidnapped, projected through a representation that is self-consciousness and tonally hopeless. Each time a Ravana is beheaded with the *Brahmastra*, countless universes are born. Destruction brings vitality and creativity to the next phase of creation, like a rainstorm infusing the earth with renewed fecundity and vigour.

An urge comes over Sita, haphazard and compulsive. 'This time Ravana must be killed sooner,' Sita thinks, 'and then I can create some postmodern universes, built on contradictions and logical impossibilities—planes of existences that are discontinuous and random.' She wants to extend the rubric of technology and create worlds built on deliberate indiscriminateness.

Impatient and excited by the possibilities, Sita wants to start creation instantly. So Ravana must be killed now, before Hanuman crosses the ocean and burns Lanka, before Rama builds the bridge and comes to Lanka. She wants Ravana out of the way so that she can engage in her sport, her lila: creation.

She opens her eyes and tells Trijata, 'Take me to the palace. I want to see Ravan.'

There is complete silence. Nothing moves. *Moola stambham*. Everything freezes at Ashoka Vatika. Finally,

Trijata manages a nod, 'Sure, I will do that.' Finally, Sita has come to her senses. The grand yajna Ravana had organised has achieved its end.

Devi

Lanka is a city of huge, sweeping curves and heavy shadows, in keeping with the spirit of Ravana's daring. Simultaneously addressing and alienating its citizens, Sita walks through its gem-encrusted streets with a look of absolute purity and unconcern. There is freedom in this powerful image of the proud hermit woman in tattered clothes walking through the streets of the affluent city. Her figure has a haunting presence that draws the onlookers to examine their own souls. It holds the enigmatic essence of the ascetic princess separated from everything she knows.

Ravana, swathed in gold and silks, waits with unflinching intensity. His elongated head shakes, denoting his restlessness. The expression in his eyes betrays a painful vulnerability—to desire someone so much, to expose one's weakness to the entire city. He pulls himself together. There is one last thing he needs to do before he receives Sita Videhi. He must thank his family deity, Nikumbala Pratyangira, for accepting his prayer and granting his craving.

Ravana, in a gesture unique and startling for him, bows before the goddess Nikumbala Pratyangira. When he raises his head, the statue of the *ugra* lion-faced goddess riding a lion morphs into a smiling statue of Sita Videhi. Now, with his thoughts reduced to a net of gaudy, heavily impastoed lines, Ravana feels fear for the first time. His brother Vibhishan had warned him that Sita was not a woman but a goddess.

'Lankesh, I am the source of your power. Nikumbala Pratyangira, your patron deity, is one of my infinite forms.' Sita has arrived, accentuating Ravana's primal sense of shock.

'But why?' Ravana asks, unable to speak further.

'Because creation and destruction go hand in hand. Without negative energy, the universe will become static, and it will cease to evolve. All beings will stagnate. All potentiality and possibility will freeze. The universe needs beings like you who feed on negative energy, just as much as it needs the sages and devas.'

Unless there is a struggle with the asuras, *danava*s, and rakshasas, beings can't realise their innermost selves or distinguish between what is proper and what is improper. They can't realise the wisdom of the ancient seers and the import of the great sayings of the Upanishads: *Aham bhramasmi* and *Tat tvam asi*. Negative energy propels beings into positive action and self-realisation.

'As the great goddess, it is I who distribute both positive and negative energy in the worlds to those who pray for them. As Nikumbala Pratyangira, I empower you for a reason, and once your powers go out of control, I and Rama Dasarathi descend to eliminate you. Fools like you think that the world's energies are for personal exploitation, but these energies exist for a particular evolutionary and moral purpose.'

Her passionate speech makes her furious, and Sita transforms into Nikumbala Pratyangira in flesh and blood—Mother Nature at her most raw, as absolute untamed wildness. She has a lion's head with a flaming fire for a crown and is seated on a lion. Hissing cobras, poised to strike, form the ornaments of the blue-black goddess. With *gohra*-like laughter, she noisily crunches bones. Blood drips from her chin and her protruding fangs. Scarlet snake-like shapes form a luminous aura around her head. The scene becomes animalistic and primitive. Ravana takes his ten-headed form, hoping to intimidate the goddess. The goddess, too, multiplies her heads. A thousand lion faces, emerging out of pure psychic automatism, roar. Their exhalation is a dark vortex of smoke. Ravana, in this painful and razor-sharp moment, is impassive and almost detached, as Nikumbala Pratyangira rips his navel open with her curved claws and pulls out the pot of amrita (nectar of immortality). Smashing the pot, which has a highly patterned decorative surface, the goddess tears Ravana's body into two.

Having drunk the demon's blood and been anaesthetised by her own violence, the goddess is in a reckless mood. Her concern is with destruction for its own sake, having overturned the stereotype of female passivity and male belligerence. In this transformation from Sita Videhi to Nikumbala Pratyangira, she questions the equation between vulnerability and violence. Thousands of fearsome dragons emerge from her body and destroy Lanka, killing the rakshasas—Kumbhakaran, Indrajit, Atikaya, Prahast, Naranta, Trisaras, and Devantak—and wiping out Ravana's entire clan except his brother, Vibhishan. They twist and turn their bodies into a joyous circle, losing all self-awareness in the tempo of the blood dance. The faces of the dragons have mask-like angularity, suggesting disengagement with the turmoil all around. Lanka is reduced to a disturbing and chaotic scene of violence and terror, like a sculpture constructed spontaneously from the darkest recesses of the subconscious.

Despite the profusion of ruin and fragmentation, Nikumbala Pratyangira's bloodlust does not subside. The god Brahma, watching from the heavens, sends an akashvanai (heavenly message) to the great goddess.

'Remember your purpose is creation. Think of the new worlds you can create now that this time space matrix is free of Ravana. Use your surplus energy to create newer and stranger worlds. Channel your energy.'

So, Nikumbala Pratyangira stops her dance of death and absorbs the dragons within herself.

Once both Amma and I had spoken of the dragon stories embedded in the Ramayana stories, we went off to sleep. Boo had been listening to these stories too. She was excited about going to Cambodia. So was I.

5

Unsent Letters

Vaishali S.

Sandhya looked at the watch. It was quarter past eight. She wouldn't be boarding the flight to Cambodia till eleven, so she had more than a couple of hours left. She rolled her trolley towards the waiting area, found an empty seat, sat down, and took out her mirror. She kept staring at her reflection for what seemed like an eternity. She examined her features. Her complexion was fair. She was neither too thin nor too fat. Her large, fish—shaped eyes were blue. There were dark circles around them. She had thin lips, high cheekbones, a sharp and pointed nose, and black and curly hair. Her hair was oiled, neatly combed, and tied up in a ponytail. She had a scar on her chin and a brown mole at her temple. She then looked at the sixth finger on her right hand. She called it her 'lucky finger'. She had had it for as long as she could remember.

'Will she look like me?' wondered Sandhya.

She was going to Cambodia to meet her long-lost twin sister who had gone missing when she was hardly a year old. Sandhya had only recently discovered that she had a twin, and she had wanted to meet her ever since. Sandhya wanted to write to her sister before she left India but had neither her sister's residential nor email address.

All the same, she began writing:

Dear unknown sister,

I am Sandhya, your twin. Hope you are keeping well. Currently, I am at the airport in Chennai. I will be boarding a flight to Cambodia at 11 p.m. I am on my way to meet you. Around four days ago, I discovered that I was not born alone. Ever since the moment I discovered that I had a twin, I really want to meet you.

I can't wait to see you. I can't wait to see how you react when you meet me. Are we identical? I hope we are. When I meet you, will I be staring at my replica? I hope so.

Are you, like me, fair-complexioned? Do you also have a scar on your chin? Do you also have a mole on your right temple? Do you also have blue eyes? I hope your eyes are blue too. I love my eyes. I hope I'll love yours too. Are your locks curly like mine? Do you also have a sixth finger on your right hand? I hope you do. Doesn't that make you lucky? I want to know more about you. I want to know your name. I want to know who named you. I want to know who adopted you. I want to know who brought you up. Did they tell you that you were adopted? How will you react when you discover that you have a twin?

I want to know what your favourite colour is. I want to know what your favourite food is. I want to know what your favourite clothes are and I want to know who your favourite actor is. What are your hobbies?

Let me first tell you more about myself.

I love to paint. Do you also love painting?

Unfortunately, it has been six years since I painted my last piece. It was that of a man with a blue hat. I have not touched my painting brush since then.

Blue is my favourite colour. That is the reason why I love my eyes.

Although I am not a foodie, I love cakes, and I love wearing T-shirts and jeans.

I was told that our parents had died in an accident in 1980. I was hardly four then, so I don't remember how they look. I was staying at Mr Vijay's house when the accident took place. Mr Vijay was a dear friend of our father. After the death of our parents, Mr Vijay handed me over to our maternal uncle, Sanjay. Sanjay had never met me until then. He had not met our mother (his elder sister), Radha, since her wedding in 1974. He knew that our mother had fled to Cambodia along with our father immediately after the wedding.

Sanjay was informed that his sister had given birth to a baby girl (me) in 1976. He was also informed that, because of the Khmer Rouge, his sister and his brother-in-law had flown back to India along with his baby niece immediately after the birth of the child. Mr Vijay then broke the tragic news of the accident to Sanjay. Sanjay was sad beyond measure when he heard that his sister and her husband had died in an accident, leaving behind their precious baby girl. He took me under his care. Ever since then, I have been living with Sanjay.

Sanjay cares for me as though I am his daughter. He brought me up with love, and he educated me.

Four days ago, police authorities came searching for me. They informed me that there was a piece of land in Chengalpattu that was registered in the name of our late father, Ramesh. The government wanted to acquire the land and construct a railway track and was ready to pay for the land. I was amused when I discovered that our father had left a piece of land. I travelled to Chengalpattu.

I saw a tiny brick house on the land, which looked as though it had been unused for many years. I entered the house, and an inexplicable joy filled my heart. Never had I felt that way. I thought that this was perhaps where I had lived when our parents were alive. Everything in the brick house was damaged except for a bed. There was an ugly bag on the bed, and I saw an old diary inside the bag.

I saw the pictures of our parents in that diary. I also saw a picture of myself that had been taken when I was hardly a couple of years old. Tears rolled down my cheeks as I saw these pictures. In that diary, our mother had mentioned you also. That was the moment I discovered that I had a twin sister. I was initially shell-shocked, and then I was extremely happy to discover that I had not been born alone. Our mother had mentioned in the diary that you were born exactly three minutes after my birth. She also mentioned that you had gone missing at the time of the Khmer Rouge. You were not even a year old when a thief had stolen you away from us. Both our parents had tried their level best to discover you, but they were not able to do so. With sad hearts, they had flown back to India with me.

As I mentioned, I have been living with Sanjay ever since our parents died. Until I discovered the diary a few days ago, I knew nothing about you, and neither did Sanjay. Even Mr Vijay was not aware of you. The universe conspired for me to enter the brick house and discover I had a twin sister.

Six years ago, the doctors discovered a tiny problem in my heart. Although I am under medication, the medicines will not cure me completely. They have suggested open heart surgery. I have to undergo the surgery the week after next. I am not sure whether I will survive. I have one last wish. I want to meet you before the surgery so that I can die peacefully.

With love,
Sandhya

'Angkor Wat is the largest religious monument in the world,' the guide proudly proclaimed.

'Wow!' Sandhya exclaimed in genuine awe.

The guide, sensing Sandhya's interest, continued, 'Do you know who constructed Angkor Wat?'

Sandhya shook her head, eager to learn more.

'King Suryavarman II began building this magnificent monument, and it was later completed by King Jayavarman VII,' the guide explained.

'Please, tell me more,' Sandhya urged.

The guide went on enthusiastically, 'Angkor Wat is designed as a three-tiered pyramid. Can you see it clearly?'

Sandhya nodded, her eyes fixed on the awe-inspiring structure. 'Yes, it appears to be crowned by five towers.'

'You're absolutely right,' the guide confirmed with a smile. 'What's truly fascinating is that these towers are shaped like lotus blossoms. The temple is surrounded by a moat, and its walls are adorned with intricate bas-relief carvings.'

'How massive is this monument?' Sandhya was curious.

'The temple complex covers an astounding 420 acres,' the guide replied. 'The central tower stands tall at 65 m, and the encircling moat is a staggering 200 m wide. If you appreciate art, you'll be delighted to know that there are 2000 *apsara* carvings gracing the walls.'

Sandhya interrupted, her interest piqued. 'Wait a moment, aren't apsaras celestial nymphs?'

The guide nodded in agreement. 'Indeed, apsaras are celestial nymphs. The walls also depict extraordinary bas-reliefs portraying scenes from Indian Puranas and Itihasas.'

'I truly feel like I'm back in India,' Sandhya remarked with a sense of nostalgia.

The guide smiled warmly and replied, 'Our people share roots, madam.'

As Sandhya explored the magnificent monument, she couldn"t help but capture the beauty with her camera. Suddenly, her artistic eye was drawn to an elegant painting. Having been a painter herself in the past, Sandhya was spellbound by the exquisite masterpiece. It depicted Lord Dasharatha's *Putrakameshti Yagna*. Right beside it, another painting portrayed the grand wedding of Lord Rama and Goddess Sita, all rendered in the unique Cambodian style. Sandhya listened intently as the guide explained that in Cambodia, the Ramayana was known as Reamker.

The figures looked like elegant nymphs, each sporting a royal diadem that reminded Sandhya of little bells. Clad in a variety of colours—scarlet, blue, and violet—and equipped with an assortment of weapons, from bow and arrows to swords, they filled the scene with a vibrant palette of hues and intriguing details. The vivid colours and dazzling artistry held Sandhya in a delightful trance. Time seemed to slip away as she marvelled at the breathtaking tableaux in front of her, as if she had been transported to an altogether different world of wonder. It wasn't until her phone rang that she returned back to mundane reality, though she chose to ignore the call.

It had been six long years since Sandhya had last picked up her paintbrush. Learning of her heart condition had cast a shadow over her creative pursuits, leading to a prolonged period of depression. However, as she stood before the inspiring artwork, her hands quivered with a renewed passion for painting. She felt an irresistible urge to meet the artist to express her gratitude for rekindling her artistic spirit.

At the bottom, at the right-hand side corner of the painting, the name Chanthavy was written in bold letters.

'Someone named Chanthavy must have painted this,' muttered Sandhya to herself.

A tiny picture of Chanthavy was stuck beside her name. Sandhya was stunned for a moment! She could not believe her eyes!

Chanthavy looked exactly like Sandhya. Chanthavy's skin tone was much fairer than that of Sandhya's. She was neither too thin nor too fat. Her eyes were blue. There were no dark circles around her eyes. Her locks were curly. Unlike Sandhya, whose locks were always tied in a ponytail, Chanthavy had left her hair loose.

Tears of joy rolled down her cheeks. These were indeed her twin sister's works! Her beloved sister, Chanthavy, was a painter too!

Sandhya pined for Chanthavy more than ever. She longed for her presence. She longed to tell her that she loved her paintings.

Sandhya jumped with joy. She did not bother about the crowd that was staring at her. She was so happy that nothing else mattered to her. Sandhya was all aflutter! Never before had Sandhya danced this way. Chanthavy's paintings filled her with joy.

Becoming a little dizzy, Sandhya sat down and began writing yet another letter.

Dear Chanthavy,

I just discovered your name. Doesn't Chanthavy mean 'beautiful moon'? I reached Cambodia this morning. I checked in at a hotel in Siem Reap. I rented a car and drove to Angkor Wat. With the help of Google Maps, I was able to locate the place very easily. I am currently writing to you from the grand Angkor Wat.

Angkor Wat is such a wonderful monument. I was amazed when I discovered that Angkor Wat is dedicated to Lord Vishnu. I am awed to know that India and Cambodia share such a wonderful cultural heritage. The guide here explained to me that Angkor Wat is one of the most important archaeological sites of Southeast Asia.

I saw a stone sculpture of Lord Rama, Goddess Sita, and Lord Lakshmana on one of the walls and I was awed by the incredible sculpture. The guide informed me that Lord Rama is known in Cambodia as Phreah Ream. Goddess Sita is known as Neang Seda, and Lord Lakshmana is known as Phreah Leak.

I cannot get the bas-relief carvings out of my mind. The guide mentioned that the bas-relief carving on the walls depicting the sea churning is the longest single bas-relief sculpture in the world.

Yet, among all these wonders, do you know what awed me the most? Your paintings, sister! I have now seen two of your works. One was that of Lord Dasharatha's Putrakameshti Yagna, and the other was that of the grand wedding of Lord Rama and Goddess Sita. You are an amazing artist. Your works have inspired me to go back to the canvas once again. I haven't previously been that fond of Indian culture and heritage. You changed that. Your art changed that. Let me tell you why I chose to visit Angkor Wat first. In the diary that I had mentioned to you earlier, our mother had written that, while they were searching for you, they came across your waist-band in Angkor Wat. She mentioned that it was lying behind a pillar. They had kept it in memory of you.

Instinctively, I chose to visit Angkor Wat first. My intuition did not fail me.

As soon as I saw your paintings, I was as happy as I will be when I meet you in person. As time goes by, I am getting more and more excited to meet you.

I saw your tiny photographs next to your amazing masterpieces. I am extremely happy to realise that you look exactly like me. You and I are identical. Your eyes are blue too, and your locks are curly too. After having seen your pictures, my longing for meeting you in person has increased beyond measure.

Can't wait, sister. See you soon!

With love,
Sandhya

Sandhya read the letter over and over again. How she wished she had Chanthavy's mailing address! She desperately wanted Chanthavy to read her letters. Sandhya folded the letter, tucked it inside her bag, and began to walk.

She roamed through the entire monument once again, and before dusk, she came across yet another Chanthavy masterpiece—a painting of Kaikeyi demanding two boons from Dasharath. At the right-hand corner of the painting, it was mentioned that the story continues in Bakong.

'I must visit Bakong next,' Sandhya muttered.

On the next day, late in the afternoon, Sandhya found herself staring at a work of Chanthavy's in Bakong. It was a painting of Lord Rama, Lady Sita, and Lord Lakshmana dressed in bark garments, ready to leave Ayodhya and stay in the forest for a period of fourteen years.

Sandhya was spellbound by the marvellous painting. The magic of the colours, the strokes of various brushes, and the devotion with which Chanthavy had brought to life the very essence of Rama, Sita, and Lakshmana brought a tremendous amount of peace to Sandhya. She could sense the love with which Chanthavy had created the amazing masterpiece. Sandhya wanted to know more about the life of Lord Rama.

She explored the magnificent monument thoroughly. It was incredible. Her love for Cambodia increased beyond measure.

She came across yet another Chanthavy masterpiece, a painting of Lord Bharat receiving Lord Rama's sacred sandals. Sandhya could feel the nobility of Bharat as he knelt in front of his elder brother. Bharat was holding the sacred sandals of Lord Rama on his head. Sandhya felt she was present at the scene, as if a silent witness to one of the world's greatest displays of brotherly love and duty.

At the right-hand corner, it was mentioned that the next picture had been temporarily moved to Banteay Srei. Sandhya knew where she must go next. She took out an empty sheet of paper and a pen.

Dear Chanthavy,

I am writing to you from Bakong. Google Maps guided me to Bakong perfectly well. As I mentioned in the previous letter, I visited Angkor Wat yesterday. In one of your masterpieces, I found out that the story of Ramayana continues in Bakong, which was why I visited it today.

I am elated to discover Bakong's devout dedication to the Lord, from whose divine locks the sacred Ganga flows. It stands as a resolute tribute to the great Lord Mahadeva. A knowledgeable guide revealed that Bakong, an architectural marvel, was meticulously crafted from sandstone—a pioneering endeavour in Khmer temple construction. In the 9th century CE, it held the esteemed position of Emperor Indravarman I's official state temple.

The temple, with its artful design, is in the shape of a stepped pyramid, and the two seven-headed nagas gracing the causeways seem to venerate Lord Shiva within. The towering structures themselves are crafted from brick, evoking memories of my childhood home—a humble brick abode, once a haven when our parents were still alive.

Here, eight brick towers stand in symmetrical harmony, enveloping the central temple mountain, symbolising the facets of Lord Shiva. This shared connection between India and Cambodia unfolds as a profound and beautiful bond, a testament to our shared reverence for the divine.

I am yet again awed by your works. I came across two of your masterpieces. One was that of Lord Rama, Lady Sita, and Lord Lakshmana in bark garments, ready to leave Ayodhya and stay in the forest for a period of fourteen years, and the other one was that of Lord Bharat receiving the sacred sandals of Lord Rama.

Every day I thank the divine for letting me know that I have a twin. Your incredible paintings and your love for the Ramayana has changed me *so* fundamentally. Not a moment goes by when I am not thinking about the Ramayana these days!

It feels that I have finally found an anchor. Thank you so much!

The day that I meet you will be the most memorable day of my life. I am desperately looking forward to it.

Lots of love and hugs,
Sandhya

Sandhya woke up with excitement coursing through her veins. She was planning to visit Banteay Srei that day. She had rented a car but, unfortunately, had taken a wrong turn somewhere along the route. After getting thoroughly lost and going around in circles for an hour, she parked by the side of a small tea stall. Resting her head on the steering wheel, she sighed helplessly, her mind in a turmoil.

Then she heard a knock. She looked up to find a man in an ivory blazer asking for a lift. Sandhya raised her eyebrows. Even before she could speak, she saw the man come forward and peep through the window. Sandhya could make out that the man was much older, yet, just like her uncle back in India, he had youthful, gentle eyes. She did not sense any danger from the man.

The man requested, 'Madam! Can you please drop me at the hill of Phnom Dei? I have an urgent appointment there. If you could do me this favour, God will bless you with what you are looking for.'

Sandhya knotted her eyebrows when she heard the man speak.

'Does this man know that I am looking for my sister? Is that why he is saying that God will bless me with what I am looking for?' wondered Sandhya.

She shrugged.

She could not refuse his request. Reluctantly, she nodded and opened the door next to the driver's seat. The man quickly got into the car and sat down.

Throughout the journey, the man kept talking about his large family, his rice mill, and his love for pets.

Sandhya asked him the route to Banteay Srei.

The man answered that it was near the hill of Phnom Dei.

Sandhya breathed a sigh of relief. Although she had been thoroughly confused initially, she could tell she was going to reach Banteay Srei without any trouble.

'Maybe it is Lord Rama who has come in disguise'.

She told him all about her search for Chanthavy and about the way in which she had come to know that she had a twin.

Before getting down at the hill of Phnom Dei, the man blessed her, stating that she would indeed find Chanthavy very soon.

Banteay Srei was only a few minutes away from the hill of Phnom Dei. Sandhya drove quickly and, as she neared the temple, realised that Banteay Srei was dedicated to Lord Shiva. '*Om Namah Shivay*,' muttered Sandhya as she entered the amazing temple. There was an information board near the entrance that told her that Banteay Srei, widely praised as a 'precious gem' or the 'jewel of Khmer art', was built of red sandstone and had been consecrated on 22 April 967 CE. It was the only major temple at Angkor not built by a king but by courtiers named Vishnukumara and Yajnavaraha. Sandhya walked in and lost herself in a world where the Ramayana came alive in stone. She lost all sense of time, until she finally came upon what she had been desperately seeking.

In front of her was a huge canvas that depicted Lord Rama receiving a unique weapon from Sage Agastya. The painting had a magnetic quality to it, and she noticed other tourists too suddenly stopping to gaze at it in wonder. As evening approached, it seemed as if the golden light of the setting sun mingled with the colours of the painting, infusing the composition with an ethereal otherworldliness. The word *Chanthavy* was written in bold letters next to her tiny photograph at the right-hand side corner of the painting. Sandhya knew that the painting depicted an episode from the *Aranya Kanda* in which Sage Agastya blesses Rama with a divine weapon with which Rama finally killed Ravana.

She also found a statement mentioning that the next major part of the story can be discovered in Wat Bo Pagoda.

Early next morning, it began drizzling as Sandhya started off towards Wat Bo Pagoda. In no time, it was raining cats and dogs. Sandhya took shelter under the shade of a huge building, where she found a little girl crying piteously, seemingly all alone. None of the people around seemed to know who the girl was. Sandhya understood that the girl was lost.

'How nice would it have been if Chanthavy had not gone missing?' wondered Sandhya. 'My life would have been entirely different if Chanthavy had been with me. I would not have been here now, in Cambodia, had it not been for the thief who stole my precious sister,' muttered Sandhya to herself.

Sandhya smiled at the girl, 'Don't worry. I will help you.'

Even though the girl couldn't understand a word of what she was saying, there was perhaps something in her smile that made her grasp Sandhya's fingers.

When it stopped raining, Sandhya walked the girl (her name was Sophea) to a nearby police station where she found a man and a woman. They were in great distress. The woman resembled Sophea.

'They must be Sophea's parents,' thought Sandhya.

Sophea sprang towards the couple and hugged them tightly. The couple was extremely happy at being reunited with their beloved daughter.

'My parents would have been happy too had they found Chanthavy,' thought Sandhya. Sophea's parents thanked Sandhya wholeheartedly and asked if there was anything they could do for her in return. Initially, they wanted to gift her a lump sum of money, but Sandhya stubbornly refused.

'Kindly drop me at Wat Bo Pagoda. That would be of great help,' she told them.

Sophea's parents readily agreed and took her in their car.

While travelling to the Wat Bo Pagoda, Sophea's father told Sandhya that the most respected and important monastery in the area was Wat Bo, with over 100 monks living there. These monks were responsible for taking care of the paintings and valuable items in the monastery.

When Sandhya got out of the car, she thanked Sophea's parents for dropping her off at Wat Bo Pagoda. Inside the main temple, she showed her respect by bowing to the monks there. She was amazed to see many paintings, some dating back to the 19th century. Even though Wat Bo was a Buddhist temple, there were paintings that told stories from the Ramayana.

'Wow!' Sandhya couldn't help but exclaim as she looked at the paintings. She remembered what Sophea's father had told her during their drive to Wat Bo Pagoda. He had said that Wat Bo Pagoda was built in the 18th century, making it the oldest pagoda in town.

In the far corner, Sandhya could see several of Chanthavy's works.

The first one was a painting of Shurpanakha's nose being chopped off by Lakshmana. She had read somewhere that Shurpanakha was known in Cambodia as Surpanakhar.

Next to it, she found yet another of Chanthavy's works. It was a painting of Ravana abducting Sita to Lanka. These events form a part of the *Aranya Kanda*. The guide she had met on the previous day had informed her that Ravana was known in Cambodia as Krong Reap.

On the wall adjacent to it, Sandhya discovered four more works by Chanthavy. There was a painting of Rama and Lakshmana meeting Hanuman. Next to it, there was another painting of Rama killing Vali.

'These two incidents form a part of the *Kishkinda Kanda*,' muttered Sandhya under her breath.

The third painting was that of Lord Hanuman leaping across the ocean, which forms a part of the *Sundara Kanda*. The fourth was of Rama killing Ravana, a scene from the *Yuddha Kanda*. There was an empty space in the place where the fifth painting was supposed to be with a note beside it mentioning that the final painting was in a building adjacent to the Phnom Penh National Museum.

Sandhya wanted to write to Chanthavy before she left Wat Bo pagoda.

Dear Chanthavy,

I had a smooth trip to Banteay Srei yesterday, and I owe it to Lord Rama's blessings. It was there that I stumbled upon your incredible masterpiece depicting Lord Rama receiving a unique weapon from Sage Agastya. Your talent is simply magical.

While exploring Banteay Srei, I met a guide who was well-versed in the Ramayana. They shared some great recommendations for me to learn more about this epic and the Cambodian version, Reamker. Today, I'm at the Wat Bo Pagoda, and I'm writing this letter from here. Once again, Lord Rama made my journey here effortless. Just like before, I'm completely blown away by your incredible creations.

Wat Bo Pagoda is like an artist's dream come true. It is filled with amazing paintings that would make any artist or painter jump with joy. One painting that stood out to me depicted the intense battle between Indrajit and Lakshmana. What's even more incredible is that the entire Ramayana story is beautifully painted on the main building of Wat Bo Pagoda. I was absolutely fascinated by these paintings. There are nearly two hundred murals and paintings on the walls, inspired by stories from the Ramayana, Thai Ramkien, Cambodian Reamker, and a few from the Jataka and the Puranas.

Oh, by the way, last night, I caught a play about the Reamker at a local theatre, and it was fantastic. After the show, I got to meet one of the actors, who told me about dances like 'Robam Tep Apsara', 'Lakhon Pre ricTep', 'Lakhon Luang', and 'Lakhon Kabah Bohran Khmer' that pay tribute to Phreah Ream, known as Sri Rama in India.

Tomorrow, I'm off to the Phnom Penh National Museum and the nearby building where your last painting is said to be.

I just can't wait to meet you in person.

Lots of love,
Your sister,
Sandhya

Sandhya's heart sank when she saw the ancient, dilapidated building beside the impressive-looking museum. It was almost deserted.

'Why did Chanthavy choose to keep her painting here? Does she live nearby?' wondered Sandhya.

She took a deep breath and, brushing aside her sense of foreboding, entered the complex through a broken stone arch covered in creepers.

'Is this an ancient school? Or is this a ruined temple?' wondered Sandhya out loud. There were broken stone walls and pillars everywhere, most of it covered in some form of vegetation. Yet there seemed to be a faint track through the ruins, which indicated that a few folks still visited the place.

The track took her to a huge, rippling banyan tree, under which Sandhya found one final canvas. It was from the *Uttar Kanda* of the Ramayana, the very last part of the divine tale. The painting showed Lav and Kush singing the story of the Ramayana in front of Lord Rama. There were small offerings around the painting—some flowers, a few lamps, and splashes of vermillion. The power of bhakti that radiated from the painting was such that Sandhya sank to her knees, without understanding why tears filled her eyes.

'Sister! I was not searching for you. I now understand that this was a pilgrimage!'

In the right corner of the painting, the word *Chanthavy* was written in bold next to her tiny photograph. Below the photograph, something had been scribbled on the wall in extremely small letters. If Sandhya had not looked keenly, she would have missed it. Blinking away her tears, she brought her face so close to the wall that the tip of her nose was almost touching it. She narrowed her eyes and read the messy words.

'One can find Chanthavy if one climbs down the stairs.'

Sandhya let out a gasp as she read what was written. Her eyes widened in excitement. She was extremely thrilled. She could not believe her eyes. She read the sentence over and over again to make sure that she had not misunderstood any word.

She quickly turned around and saw a staircase. With extreme excitement coursing through her veins, Sandhya joyfully ran down the staircase two steps at a time.

As soon as she reached the bottom, her heart almost stopped at what she saw. She stood there gaping, horrified! Her lips trembled, and her knees buckled. Her head began to spin. She felt like her entire life was splitting apart. She was about to fall, but she balanced herself with hand on the wall.

Not even in her worst nightmares had she ever imagined seeing what was in front of her.

It was a tomb. There was a board beside the tomb on which the name 'Chanthavy' was written in bold. Below her name, she could see the date of her birth as well as the date of her death.

Chanthavy
Date of Birth—14 August 1977
Date of Death—30 March 2018

There was a huge photograph of Chanthavy next to the board. She looked extremely pretty in this photograph. She was fair-skinned and lovely. Her blue eyes radiated peace. Her curly locks were adorable. Dimples glorified her already gorgeous smile. From the photograph, Sandhya could guess that Chanthavy was as tall as she was. She was wearing a blue kurti and white pants. Blue and white suited her well. Sandhya could see a sixth finger on her sister's right hand. Hot tears rolled down her cheeks, a stream of lava from the unbearable eruption of sorrow inside her. She closed her mouth with both her hands and screamed—a scream audible only to Chanthavy's soul, a scream that expressed the sorrow that overwhelmed her to the core, a scream that expressed her misery from the depth of her being, and a scream that conveyed her extreme pain.

Sandhya knelt in front of the tomb.

'Did I come all the way from India only to discover Chanthavy's tomb? Did I come all the way to Cambodia only to find my sister dead? Why is destiny so cruel? Why did fate take her away from me when she was a baby? After several years, why did fate make me discover that I had a twin? Why did fate make me take this journey to Cambodia? Why did I discover her amazing masterpieces? Why was I inspired by her works? Why was I so excited and thrilled to meet my sister in person? Did everything happen only for me to discover her tomb? To whom shall I give all the letters that I have written? What will I tell Sanjay when I go back to India? Is this a terrible nightmare? Who will wake me up from it?'

'Chanthavy!' screamed Sandhya and fell on the ground.

She cried with uncontrollable sobs. Her body shook vigorously.

'Let me just keep travelling in search of my beloved Chanthavy.' Saying this, Sandhya cried out loud again.

A few minutes back, Sandhya had been thrilled with joy, but she was now mad with grief. Her desperation to meet her twin had now increased beyond measure. Her misery was more than she could bear. She beat her breast, banged her head on a wall, and cried miserably. She felt like a calf that had gone astray only to come back home to realise that her beloved mother was dead.

Sandhya bit her lip and passed out.

A hand gently nudged her. Sandhya opened her eyes and saw a woman dressed in blue and white. As the woman came nearer, Sandhya could see her face clearly. It was Chanthavy. Chanthavy looked as brilliant as the sun. She was smiling joyfully. Dimples adorned her gorgeous face. Her face was round, and her thin lips were beautiful. Her curly locks gently fluttered in the air, and her blue eyes radiated peace and serenity. She looked like a goddess.

Sandhya sat up.

Chanthavy sweetly spoke Sandhya's name.

Sandhya, mesmerised by her beloved sister's sweet voice, could not respond.

Chanthavy repeated, 'Sandhya!'

She gently touched Sandhya's cheeks. Sandhya closed her eyes and cherished the fragrance of Chanthavy's touch.

When Sandhya opened her eyes again, she saw Chanthavy sit down beside her. Chanthavy said, 'Dear sister! Do not cry for me. As it is said in the Bhagavad Gita, one's soul cannot be destroyed. It is the body that gets destroyed. I no longer live in my body, but that does not mean that I have ceased to exist. I live in my masterpieces, I live in your heart, I live amidst the birds and butterflies, I live as the sun shines brilliantly, I live in the gorgeous rainbow, I live among the trees and plants, I live among those that give peace and serenity to everyone, and I live in all the beauty that exists in the world. I rejoice when you smile, and I weep when you cry.'

Sandhya gave a slight smile as tears rolled down her cheeks. Chanthavy wiped them off and made Sandhya rest her head on her lap.

'I don't remember resting my head on our mother's lap, but I can feel our mother's fragrance as I now rest my head on your lap' said Sandhya and closed her eyes.

Caressing Sandhya's head, Chanthavy said, 'I live happily with our parents in the heavenly abode of Lord Sri Rama. We are always looking at you from the heavens above. Make us proud.'

'I will,' answered Sandhya with her eyes closed.

Sandhya promised herself that she would make her parents and Chanthavy proud.

She remained lying in her sister's lap for what seemed like an eternity.

Chanthavy gently nudged her to wake up.

Sandhya sat up, rubbed her eyes, and looked around.

She realised that she was at the cemetery, leaning on Chanthavy's tomb.

Sandhya got a grip on herself. She knew what she must do. She was on a mission—a mission that would make her parents and Chanthavy proud of her. Sandhya had to continue Chanthavy's legacy.

Epilogue

Sandhya looked at all her paintings. Just like Chanthavy, she had let her curly locks fall free. The dark circles around her eyes had disappeared. She had purchased a lot of blue kurtis and white pants. She was wearing them now. Immediately after the successful completion of the surgery, Sandhya had begun to paint, retracing the Ramayana journey that her sister had undertaken before her. Unlike Chanthavy, who had painted various incidents from the Cambodian Reamker, Sandhya used the Valmiki Ramayana as her inspiration.

The paintings of the two sisters were displayed beside each other at the Phnom Penh National Museum. The gallery was called 'Sisters across the Sea'.

6

A Cambodian Enchantment

Sunil Kumar

'The Curse of Phnom Bakheng.' The ominous words seethed and crawled through her insides, crushing them to an amorphous pulp.

Jayalakshmi Vijayan Mehra awoke with a start, her palms and forehead drenched with sweat. Night after night, she was plagued by the same nightmare, each time more vivid and horrifying than the last. The surreal dreamscape, interlaced with a blood-soaked story, felt like a past life regression.

Long corridors fill her with dread and anxious anticipation. The Cambodian king's soldiers stamp their feet in unison, and hound dogs follow a scent, as she rushes, trembling, through an interminable maze. Rain splashes in puddles through the cracked roof. She can see bark scorpions and giant rats. Sculpted gods on intricately carved pillars mock her with their cold, unfeeling stares penetrating right through her soul.

A flickering light peeps through a passage. Freedom at last, she thinks, rushing towards the source—like a moth to the flame, burned by the fire. Just as with everything in her life, this is not a happy ending. The tall, imposing figure of the king's prime minister appears out of nowhere, blocking the entrance.

The dream always ended this way, abrupt and unresolved.

'You okay there, honey?' her husband, Dhruv Mehra, asked, half-asleep in their four-poster canopy bed. His voice was drowsy and tired.

'Go back to sleep, Dhruv. Busy day for both of us tomorrow. Don't you have jet lag?' she winked, her intonation soft and silky.

Leaning forward and planting a gentle peck on his cheek was not something she did very often, but she managed it in that instant.

'Right, Lakshmi. Red-eye flights always suck, even though the company booked first class,' Dhruv said, dozing off again.

Dhruv Mehra was the dynamic India business head of one of the world's most prestigious advertising agencies. Back from New York Advertising Week, he was catching up on some much-needed rest.

To Lakshmi and Dhruv, their daughter, Ananya, was like a beacon of light, a glimmer of hope that shone amidst the tedium of their stressful existence.

Professionally, Jayalakshmi's resume read like a dream. She had an MTech from the prestigious Indian Institute of Technology and a PhD in Biochemistry from the acclaimed Indian Institute of Science (IISc).

As she was an ambitious go-getter, her work spoke for itself. Awards on her shelf displayed innovative prowess.

Rajiv Kapadia, a titan of Indian industry and the billionaire owner of Biopharm, had hired her straight from the IISc campus, recognising the potential of a shy, introspective but brilliant student.

Lakshmi's mother, Padma Vijayan, lived by herself in a beautiful bungalow in a serene and verdant suburb of

India's IT city, Bengaluru. It was worlds away from the cacophony of sounds and smells surrounding Lakshmi's condo skyscraper apartment in Lower Parel, Mumbai.

Subramanian Vijayan, her late father, was the first person to enlighten her about the curse of Phnom Bakheng.

Descended from an ancient lineage of Tamizh Brahmins who were involved in the coronation of the first Khmer king at Siem Reap a thousand years back, Subramanian had noticed years back when dark dreams fractured Lakshmi's mental peace.

A retired scientist, Vijayan doubled up as a reclusive Sanskrit scholar.

Studying scriptures and mystical Vedic mantras, as well as charting star positions and planetary conjunctions, took up most of his free time.

Vijayan's bottle-thick glasses adorned a wrinkled, broad forehead with white *vibhuti* (ash) in three horizontal lines and a red *tilak* (mark). This mark indicated the Saivite third eye—the cyclic dance of creation and destruction in Hindu cosmology.

'Get me that old palm-leaf manuscript from the bookshelf, Lakshmi. You need to know a very important thing.' His voice still resonated in her mind, years later.

'Where exactly, Appa?'

'Behind that big fat Harry Potter book you like so much, Lakshmi,' Subramanian replied.

In that moment, imagining herself to be a cross between Hermione Granger and Lara Croft, the queen of Jhansi and Indira Gandhi, Lakshmi leapt up in excitement, causing her books to topple over and crash to the floor with a resounding thud.

'Found it, Lakshmi?' her father's loud baritone asked.

A green jade amulet and an old manuscript covered with a thick layer of dust lay abandoned on the bookshelf slat. Intricate snake-like motifs crisscrossed the outer surface of the amulet, the slithery look creating an ominous and haunting impression.

'Yes, Appa. Bringing them to you,' she said.

'Hurry up. We don't have all day,' Subramanian replied.

She leapt over the books strewn across the floor and raced back to her father, thrusting the pulsating amulet and well-worn manuscript into his outstretched hands.

The sound of his voice crawled under her skin, causing her to fidget and avert her gaze.

'Lakshmi, come closer and listen to me. The curse of Phnom Bakheng is a story that spans generations. It's a saga of light and darkness, timeless like your Potter–Voldemort stories or the dichotomy explored in our ancient epics. The fight between good and evil is eternal. It's a never-ending chess game with its pawns, combinations, sacrifices, and stratagems, which anybody can possibly win anytime. There are truths hidden from our limited senses, beyond the mundane, as real as this world we see. Life is not merely black and white, my child. Whoever tells you that is too lazy, privileged, or plain stupid. This earthly palette is filled with infinite shades of grey. This is something that will unravel as you grow older, shaking every bone in your body. There will always be a choice, my dear. Deep inside, I know that you will make the right decision.'

Biopharm Office, Central Business District, Mumbai—Present Day

'All stories have a beginning, a middle, and an end, Lakshmi. You need single-pointed focus. Get on with the action. No clunky, irrelevant exposition.' Rajiv Kapadia barked. With beady eyes and bushy eyebrows, his stern, pock-marked face suggested a Kafkaesque cockroach to Jayalakshmi.

For a fleeting moment, Lakshmi fidgeted with her hands and braced herself to respond but then hesitated, wondering if her tough-as-nails workaholic boss had tossed his mind in the garbage.

Was this man a cryptic soundbite–spouting writing coach or a corporate boss? What exactly had transpired in a day to make Kapadia go off on an unrelated tangent? Had his voluptuous wife left him for some boy toy?

Shalini, Kapadia's better half, graced the front pages of tabloids as a local fashionista and minor celebrity. She was the wealthy proprietor of the Mumbai franchise in the Indian Cricket League, the most affluent cricket club globally.

Kapadia and Shalini, a power couple, regularly featured on the covers of umpteen business magazines as well as in the photo on her boss's desk smack in front of her face. Would such a woman give up all that opulence and attention?

Highly unlikely, Lakshmi thought, bringing herself back to the present.

'I know what's on your mind, Lakshmi. You're probably wondering if Kapadia's lost his marbles. But let me set the record straight. What I'm about to tell you has nothing to do with research. It's all about marketing savvy. It's time to sharpen your skills and close every deal with finesse,' Kapadia said authoritatively.

She couldn't breathe for a second. Despite believing that Kapadia could have a good heart and cared genuinely at times, she knew he was first and foremost a businessperson and her boss. Lakshmi always felt that her true strength lay in research. Kapadia had plucked her straight off the IISc campus after graduation, even before the final results had come in. By now, ten years later, Lakshmi had dual responsibilities—marketing as well as R&D.

The big boss was animated today, insisting that she rush to Siem Reap and Phnom Penh. A Cambodian business delegation had met with him earlier that day, and he was in back-to-back meetings for hours.

'The situation in Southeast Asia requires a woman's touch, Lakshmi. It's not a job for beer bellies and gauche, self-important jokes. I'm sure you can handle this, and I can do what I damn well want. I trust no one else but you, Lakshmi Vijayan Mehra. The Cambodians specifically requested your expertise after reading about your ground-breaking API molecular research in the latest trade journals. You can ace this, and I need you to.' Rajiv's voice was insistent and demanding.

Lakshmi's gaze swept across the meticulously arranged books on Kapadia's shelves, the art pieces adorning the walls, and the polished mahogany desk dominating the centre of the room.

Family photos, numerous awards, and other accolades dotted the plush interior. She always felt that Mumbai corporate life was like unabashed Americana, a cookie-cutter replica of the West. Slam, bam, keep it movin', M'am. She missed her carefree youth now, caught up in the stress of a monotonous job and family responsibilities.

'Agreed on this, Lakshmi? Sending you to Siem Reap, pronto. Either way, you don't have a choice. Clear?' Kapadia's smirk was unmistakeable.

'Sure, sir. Anything you say,' Lakshmi replied, her heart sinking as she resigned herself to the inevitable.

The weight of expectation on a woman to juggle multiple responsibilities and excel in every role was immense. While a few men showed genuine empathy, Lakshmi knew that they were the exceptions rather than the rule. Most men strutted around like shallow, entitled brats—a sweeping generalisation but tinged with truth

Tired of her present predicament, Lakshmi's mind painted a vivid scene, like a high-definition movie, of herself sprinting along a pristine beach, the salty sea breeze whipping through her hair. She then lounged on a beach hammock, reading the latest bestseller. Imagining her muscles unwinding after a relaxing spa session and the gentle stretch of her body after morning yoga practice added colour to the idyllic picture.

'The name of the company again, sir?' Lakshmi inquired, knowing that his pompous highness, Rajiv Kapadia, would not remember it at first.

'Ah, the Cambodians. A rising star in the local pharma industry. Led by Cambodian-American Noel Nat. Mother's a senator in the US Congress, and the father is a Phnom-Penh big shot rumoured to dabble in the occult, according to Rajan. Phnom Boobeng, was it? Nah, Phnom Rapheng. Not good with these names. Hmm, yes, Phnom Bakheng.'

Lakshmi's heart skipped a beat. She slunk lower in her chair.

'Listen to your boss, Lakshmi. Go to Cambodia, Siem Reap, whatever, wherever. Can't figure out this hesitation.'

Dhruv's handsome, square-jawed face clearly showed his agitation.

'Dhruv, I've said this before. Something feels off. I've got a gloomy feeling about it all. Awful things will definitely happen,' Lakshmi replied.

'What do you base this on? Clairvoyance? A sixth sense perhaps? Ah, no, I forgot about your world-famous father's astrological prowess.' Dhruv's voice dripped with sarcasm.

Lakshmi was so shocked that she stood there frozen, mouth gaping, a half-formed response struggling to escape her lips.

Never before had Lakshmi seen Dhruv display such insensitivity. His callous words cut her like a knife, leaving her reeling with pain. She couldn't help but wonder if her parents had been right when they warned her against marrying outside their community.

'It's all these little things that keep adding up, Dhruv—recurring nightmares, conversations with my father, strange car with snake motifs on the doors following me today while dropping Ananya off at school. If that's not serious enough, someone messed with my Kia's brakes,' Lakshmi said.

'Well, if you put it that way, Lakshmi … why didn't you tell me any of this? Sorry for everything I said. Tell you what, the best thing you can and must do is talk to your mother about all of this. If anyone knows how to tackle the situation, it's Padma,' Dhruv replied.

'What is your entitled lordship going to do about it? No concern for your wife or child at all?' Lakshmi was ballistic with rage.

'I've got a job to do, Lakshmi. My calendar is blocked for the next six months. I need to put food on the table.

Your mother is retired. On top of that, she's an erudite, experienced professor. No disrespect. She's much more intelligent than yours truly.' Dhruv's impish charm softened Lakshmi up a little.

'Male chauvinism. I can earn enough for the both of us,' Laxmi responded, a tad acerbically.

'So, listen to your boss on the career trajectory, Lakshmi. You know I've never been jealous of your job. I'm genuinely proud of my better half and brag about you every chance I get.'

She feigned surprise as Dhruv planted a goodbye kiss and ran out the front door.

'Late for an official engagement,' he waved, stepping into the elevator.

Reluctantly, Lakshmi conceded to herself that Dhruv had offered unwavering support all these years. Also, Padma, her mother, was always the go-to person to answer any questions that popped up in her mind.

The real challenge remained getting past the banal small talk they always indulged in and delving into something more profound or pertinent.

Lakshmi often sensed a reticence on her mother's part to talk about family history. She always seemed more willing to speak about generalities rather than specifics. Maybe, this time it would be different.

Her mother's cell number was on the speed dial. Padma picked up the call at once. A devotional ringtone was followed by a long pause, then a coughing acknowledgment as the familiar voice of the intellectual, reserved matriarch at the other end answered.

An anxious Lakshmi blurted out every doubt and niggling concern at break-neck speed.

'I knew this day would come. Our long story needs some detailed clarification. Kings and adventurers, artisans and craftspersons, priests and traders—the contact between India and Cambodia lasted multiple generations,' Padma said.

'Yes. I know that, Ma. Easy on the history lesson! I don't have time. How is our family connected, and what is this Phnom Bakheng Appa used to talk about?' Lakshmi asked, the agitation messing up her mood.

'Patience, child. Living in Mumbai has spoilt your manners. Always in a hurry. No time to listen,' Padma replied.

'Well, forgive me for being rude, Amma. I've a major life decision to make. I could get fired tomorrow, divorce my husband, and lose my daughter, and you're the only person who can maybe help me out. No two ways about this.'

'You want me to condense a thousand years of history into two minutes. So, here's a news flash for you: almost every problem we face stems from an ancestor's misdemeanours.'

Lakshmi tapped her feet as she listened. Her fingers twitched. Maybe she was getting somewhere; maybe she wasn't.

'Hmm, something to do with our blasted family, yes. All those manuscripts, mantras, and planetary astrology that Father dabbled in.'

'Yes, indeed. When you were born, Lakshmi, a priest and an itinerant monk both uttered the same prophecy about you and our family lineage. As you very well know, your father had unconventional acquaintances.'

'What is the connection, Amma? The mystery. What are the links with me or the family, I mean?' Lakshmi inquired with curiosity.

Padma paused for a moment. 'All paths lead back to the first Khmer kingdoms and the magnificent temple seated like a colossus at the centre of it all, Angkor Wat.'

'I do know that the Tamizh kingdoms had extensive trade with every nation in Southeast Asia, Amma. The language scripts resemble India, they revere our epics and gods despite changing faiths, and all that,' Lakshmi said. Her knowledge of history had always been scanty compared to Padma's expertise.

'Much more than all that, Lakshmi. A lot, lot more. One of your father's ancestors ensured the coronation of the Cambodian potentate Suryavarman. He worked his way to the very top like a Cardinal Wolsey, Thomas Cromwell, or Richelieu, for instance.'

'So, what's the big mystery, Ma?'

'Never jump the gun, dear. Life and fate always dish out surprises.'

'I'm going to Siem Reap and Phnom Penh, Rajiv sir. Wherever and whenever you want,' Lakshmi told her boss the next day.

Kapadia seemed pleased by her decision. 'That's what I like to hear, Lakshmi. I need my top executives to be proactive. Business has stagnated in the past few years in Southeast Asia. Get your tickets through Babu, and get moving,' he said with a hint of urgency in his voice.

'Definitely, Rajiv. On it right away,' Lakshmi replied. She walked past the office cubicles with all the secretaries and office staff into her plush, inviting cabin.

The conversation with her mother had been a turning point.

She now knew that her father's ancestor was Divakar Pandita, the chief priest at the coronation of Suryavarman, one of the Khmer Empire's most illustrious monarchs. Suryavarman, the builder of the world's biggest temple, Angkor Wat, was so pleased with the Brahmin Divakar that he bestowed upon him a great deal of land, wealth, jewels, and a golden Shiva Nataraja idol.

Unfortunately, despite the piety of the priest Divakar, his descendants were anything but virtuous. Nagaraja, his profligate gambler son, and Shashi, his vile and debauched grandson, were the black sheep of the family.

It was Shashi who became the driving force behind the infamous 'Curse of Phnom Bakheng'. After Divakar's demise, the family fell out of favour with the king. Shirking his priestly vocation, Shashi, who had a strong and robust build, joined the Khmer military.

A flake who frequented all the taverns in town, Shashi even had the audacity to pick a fight with the prime minister's son and carry on an illicit affair with one of the numerous princesses the new leper king, Yashovarman, had fathered.

The abrasive but brilliant prime minister, Devaraja, dabbled in the occult. Power-hungry to the core, Devaraja manipulated the king with various totems and convinced him to wear a cursed crown infused with malevolent energy to control him.

Devaraja despised Divakar Pandita, Lakshmi's ancestor, who kept him out of the capital, Angkor, as long as he was in power. As a result, Devaraja got Shashi's head chopped off and displayed publicly for months on an elevated spike in Angkor Wat's main square. He banished Lakshmi's ancestors from Cambodia.

Local legend maintained that Devaraja put a curse on the family, which could be overcome only by a Cambodian princess reborn in Divakar's lineage. Apart from that, an ancient golden treasure guarded by the demigod Macchanu would remain buried until the reborn princess set foot on Khmer soil. Until then, Devaraja's descendants would continue to prosper.

The only thing Lakshmi's family had had in their possession for more than a thousand years was the manuscript and the amulet of their illustrious predecessor, Divakar Pandita.

Buzzing with excitement, she entered Suresh Babu's small cubicle.

'Boss wants you to go to Cambodia, right? I have put together a tentative booking and itinerary. I need you to confirm this, so I can process it fast,' Babu rattled off, even before Lakshmi had settled in her seat.

She had known Babu for years, and they had yapped about everything from their families to the dark net.

Babu's whole existence centred around Biopharm. Lakshmi wondered why Kapadia kept him around for HR and ticketing, rather than IT or finance. His shrewd, underused business brain was wasted here.

The only negative was that Babu's cubicle reeked of nauseating odours, another reason she rarely visited him in person.

'How much do you know?' Lakshmi asked.

'About what, Lakshmi? Seriously, easy on the riddles. The way you said that, somebody would think that there's a big mystery and Kapadia is sending you to some profound peril.'

'Did you know the Cambodians asked for me by name?'

'Yes, who do you think gives Kapadia updates about everything? Without me, where would that fatso be? The great philanthropist, bon vivant, and media darling. Nobody ever gives me credit for anything. I'm underpaid and overworked, sitting in this shithole.'

Lakshmi ignored his diatribe.

'Phnom Bakheng is the name of the company, right?'

'Yes, so what?' Babu countered.

'What more can you tell me about them?'

'Ah, so you're concerned about Phnom Bakheng. I heard through the internal grapevine that you needed time to consider. Nothing stays hidden in this place. News spreads faster than wildfire in a drought. I was shocked, you know. Nobody tells Kapadia that they need time to think. It just isn't done. Well, about this Phnom Bakheng group, there's nothing at all out of the ordinary. They have grown rapidly over the last few years and are very interested in cutting-edge research. The company is named after an ancient Shiva temple close to Angkor Wat, the big temple city in Cambodia. What else do you want to know?'

'Who owns it? Anything unusual?' Lakshmi asked.

Babu leant in, his voice lowered to a conspiratorial whisper. 'I only have information that's in the public domain, Dr Lakshmi. For instance, the CEO, as I already told Mr Kapadia, is forty years old, pretty young. The mother's a Republican senator in the US Congress, while the father is a local bigshot in Phnom Penh. There's a floating rumour that the father's a practitioner of the dark arts. With a country having a shady and bloody history like that, that's nothing at all out of the ordinary. Business-wise, they have strong fundamentals, increasing revenues, and potential prospects of synergy. They could even go public on Wall Street. Kapadia always says it's all about the money. So don't let your scruples get in the way.'

Lakshmi's eyes sparkled with a fierce determination. 'I'm not one to settle for surface-level information, Babu, especially when it comes to something as important as this. Along with my job and this trip, I need to keep on digging and peel back the layers until I get to the truth. It's personal, a matter of life or a trip to the great beyond.' She gave Babu a nod of thanks. 'If you come across anything that could help me, you know how to reach me.'

'Bam, bam, bam. Killing all the bad guys!' Ananya squealed with delight as she threw a toy gun across the room, narrowly missing Lakshmi's packed bags.

'Little girls don't play with guns, Ananya. That's what all the stupid boys like. What about the dolls Grandma gave you for Navaratri and Diwali last year?' Lakshmi admonished her young daughter.

'What will you get me from Cambodia, Amma? Sweets, dolls, what?' The child pretended to cry.

'Quiet, baby. Amma keeps you safe in her heart, you know. Papa will take care of you. Listen to him, and do what he says. Amma is going to the airport as soon as Dad gets home.' Lakshmi's tone scared her daughter.

Dhruv was late.

He had a near-mystical ability to create unnecessary tension, she thought. Mumbai airport was pretty close, but traffic was always unpredictable. Dhruv's laissez-faire attitude increased her anxiety, a strict no-no in her mental books.

Lakshmi had never been short on love and acceptance, although even people who liked her a lot remarked unfavourably on her fastidiousness and conformity, which they perceived as cowardice.

'I'm home, Lakshmi.' Dhruv's loud voice catapulted her back to the present.

'You had me worried, Dhruv. Can't you be on time for once in your life?'

'Don't be such a drama queen. We still have a lot of time. I've been on so many flights in my life. Sometimes I've boarded just before the damn aeroplane was going to take off. Take it easy! Nothing's gonna happen,' Dhruv replied.

'Easy for you to say, Dhruv. Are you dropping me at the airport, or should I book an Uber?'

'Husband forever at Her Majesty's service, my precious. License to thrill. So, flight to Siem Reap via Bangkok or Singapore?'

'Rajan booked it via Thailand, Dhruv. I forwarded it to you a few days back. You would know that if you read the mails your wife sends. I guess that's not important enough,' Lakshmi said.

'Cut it out, Lakshmi. I do my level best to be supportive. Now, cheer up, and let's go.' Dhruv's lips curved, but the half-formed smile did not reach his eyes.

Traffic was minimal, and the drive to Mumbai's Chhatrapati Shivaji Maharaj Airport was a breeze.

Riding shotgun, Lakshmi listened to the radio. The channel 105.1 Capital FM was playing a 1990s Depeche Mode song, 'Walking in My Shoes'. She found the lyrics—'Try walking in my shoes. You'll stumble in my footsteps'—strangely soothing.

She cursed herself for her rudeness with Dhruv. Lakshmi's stomach cramped a little when she noticed a few tattooed Asian-looking people in an SUV travelling alongside their sedan, but she brushed it aside as paranoia.

'I love your slender, fine nose and those full lips. Kiss and make up,' Dhruv said in the most childish tone possible, taking out her baggage and placing it on an airport trolley.

'Dhruv, Dhruv, Dhruv. I forgive you. Just try to be a bit more involved in our lives. Take care of Ananya when I'm gone. Get breakfast made, and drop her at school on time. Anything else, you can find in the bedroom diary,' Lakshmi said.

'Yes, madam. Don't worry! Just focus on the job. I'll hold the fort and not let you down. Forget all the supernatural nonsense. There are no such things as ghosts, spirits, or curses. It's all just make-believe to sell movies and books,' Dhruv replied.

'Famous last words. Usually, when ghosts overhear such overt scepticism, they attack.' Lakshmi was trying a bit too hard to be funny.

'Hear me, spirits. If you mess with my wife, I'll bash your non-existent skulls and send you straight down to hell,' Dhruv said in a faux serious tone.

'Bye for now, Dhruv. I'll ping you when I reach Siem Reap.'

Lakshmi smiled and moved rapidly towards the entrance gate and check-in counters.

The Bangkok flight was not as uneventful as Lakshmi had hoped. The security queue was painfully long. By the time she boarded the Thai Airways Airbus A320, she was so tired that the seat felt like manna from heaven.

All she wanted to do was doze off, but a smartly attired male flight steward rushed up from the first-class galley.

'Madam ...'

'Yes?' Lakshmi replied, impatient and irritated.

'This gentleman is in Seat 12F,' he said, pointing at a middle-aged, spectacled Asian man with an expression on his face that appeared to be a curious mixture of seriousness and restrained mirth.

Lakshmi realised that she had settled in the wrong seat and quickly checked her boarding pass.

'Oh, I'm sorry, sir. Mine is 12E,' she shrugged.

The man's laughter was infectious, as if he was amused by a secret joke. He kept his briefcase in the overhead bin and settled down in the window seat.

'Namaste. I am, Dr Nhik Ban Sihanouk from Phnom Penh, Cambodia. Pleased to meet you.' He greeted Lakshmi in a voice that reminded her of Yoda, the Jedi guru from the Star Wars movies.

'*Choum reap sour*. Oh, Sihanouk like your ex-king Norodom Sihanouk,' Lakshmi responded.

'Hahaha! Good, good. Not many people know about my country and our great king.'

Lakshmi directed a piercing look at him to fathom whether he was truly sincere or joking.

'Dr Sihanouk, if you don't mind me asking, are you a physician or do you have a doctorate in something?'

'I'm a cardiologist. Royal Phnom Penh Hospital. Best in Cambodia. Attend conference in Mumbai. Like India, very kind, nice people. Going back to my home city, Phnom Penh, via Bangkok and Siem Reap.'

A medical doctor, Laxmi thought. She blamed herself again for suspecting everybody and tried to relax her deep, anxious breathing. It was alright. This man was above board. There were no curses or villains lurking around.

The plane's drab decor and dimmed lights again lulled her to sleep. Lakshmi wanted to read up on some company presentations for upcoming business meets in Cambodia, so she got up to wash her face in the aircraft's lavatory.

She looked back and saw Sihanouk's round face. His lively back eyes were closed, and he was seemingly asleep. On his slightly exposed forearm was a curious tattoo that looked like an occult symbol—snakes coiled around a pyramid of skulls.

Lakshmi brushed her apprehensions aside, smiled at a flight attendant, and closed the lavatory door. She snuck inside the small and cramped toilet and started washing her face.

A shocking three-dimensional vista unfolded in front of Lakshmi's eyes. Instead of the mirror, there was a primordial forest with dense shadows everywhere, ancient trees blocking out all light.

Remember your true purpose, Lakshmi. Something whispered in her head. *Never mind the rest. Time and space are an illusion, a self-created barrier. Believe and the path shall be revealed.*

'Help me! Help me! Somebody help me!' A woman's voice shattered Lakshmi's immersion in this otherworldly spectre.

Opening the lavatory door, she saw a young woman hysterically crying over a fainted child.

'Don't worry, madam. Do we have a doctor among the passengers?' an attractive, stiletto-wearing flight attendant called out.

To Lakshmi's surprise, Nhik Ban Sihanouk volunteered. A cardiologist was not a general physician, but he was a doctor, nevertheless. This man must be good after all, she thought.

Turbulence made the plane lurch sideways.

The watch showed 10.15 a.m. Lakshmi checked her calendar for the next few days.

Courtyard Marriott, a plush Siem Reap hotel, was convenient and centrally located. The greenery in the resort and around her room enhanced her mood.

Babu always chose well. Lakshmi felt that his knack for researching and finding the best places anywhere on the planet was uncanny.

Dr Sihanouk, the nice man she had met on the Mumbai–Bangkok flight, was also staying at the Marriott. Business trip and personal engagements, he told her. Sihanouk's heroic intervention had been interpreted as saving the young girl's life, winning applause from the staff as well as the passengers.

However, for the life of her, Lakshmi had not been able to figure out what had been wrong with the young girl.

With a sense of urgency, she bolted out of the elevator and charged towards the hotel lobby like a sprinter at the starting line, heart racing with anticipation.

'Can I ask you something?' Lakshmi leant forwards, talking to the suave man at Reception.

'Sure, madam. Anything I can assist you with today? Glad to help,' he replied.

'Is travelling here in Siem Reap safe for a lady?' she asked, lowering her voice.

'Of course, madam. Unless you plan to go out late at night. There have been rare instances of handbag or chain snatching. Apart from that, Cambodia is the safest place in the world.'

Lakshmi felt this was hyperbole but let it pass. This was the land of the Khmer Rouge and Pol Pot after all, one of the worst genocidal maniacs in the world. All of that was yesterday's news. She wasn't going to let feelings of impending disaster plague every breath and squeeze every last ounce of joy. Nothing was going to happen. It was just a question of positive visualisation—mind over matter and all that self-help jazz. Was she a damsel in distress? That is a cliched trope, overused in movies, literature, and even in real-life news.

Never! Lakshmi was a strong, confident woman willing to take on the world. After a few power meetings, she would take in the local culture, food, sights, and sounds, all the touristy stuff that is overhyped but enjoyable. The pool and the spa in the hotel were perfect, but leisure needed to wait.

Glancing at her watch, she decided it was time to get a move on. Lakshmi felt a tinge of sadness looking back at the impressive facade of the resort, sad that she couldn't spend more time there.

'Where you wanna go?' a tuk-tuk driver near the entrance asked Lakshmi.

She looked at the small, smiling, wiry man. The tuk-tuk itself was bigger than auto-rickshaws back home in bustling Mumbai, but it was a dingy contraption with a motorcycle in front.

'Empress Convention Centre,' she said.

'Thirty-thousand riel. I also take dollar, madam,' the tuk-tuk driver replied.

'Too much. *T'lai na*,' Lakshmi tried negotiating in the pidgin Khmer picked up from the hotel guidebook.

'Seven kilometre, madam. Too faaar. Fair price,' the driver insisted.

As she was getting late, Lakshmi decided not to bargain further.

Once she was seated in the smelly tuk-tuk, it was some time before she felt comfortable.

'Fast, fast,' she said in basic English, intelligible anywhere. Getting late, she muttered to herself.

The city exuded a laid-back colonial charm, but the chaotic traffic and continuous road construction again reminded her of India. She saw tourist buses overflowing with Western and Chinese tourists and a disproportionately high number of station wagons.

She had only moments to take in the scenery, when the Cambodian driver made an unexpected detour, pulling into a secluded side road.

'Where are you taking me? What's this?' she shuddered in horror. Maybe this man wanted to mug her for money, assault her, or do something far worse. The possibilities raced through her mind, intensifying her fear.

'Special delivery, Lakshmi!' He flashed a crooked, knowing smile.

In the blink of an eye, a large Ford Lincoln SUV screeched to a halt besides the tuk-tuk. Four balaclava-clad men brandishing guns jumped out. The tallest among them raced towards Lakshmi, knocking her out with a single powerful punch.

'Welcome to heaven on earth, Angkor Wat. It's the largest religious structure in the world. It was originally built as a Hindu temple by the Khmer king Suryavarman to serve as his capital city. Dwarfs all the puny riffraff everywhere, don't you think?'

Lakshmi opened her eyes to see an odd-shaped man with a scar straight down his left cheek. His fingers were callused and filthy, and his eyes were cold and merciless. The world snapped into focus around her, colours sharpening and sounds intensifying as if someone had cranked up the volume around her senses.

'Who are you? What's the meaning of this?' she asked, even though her head hurt as if it had been hit by a ton of bricks. The realisation that she was in a bad place washed over her like a cold wave, leaving her breathless and disoriented.

'Wow, Lakshmi Vijayan finally awakes! Glad you decided to join us in the land of the living. Come to think of it, trapping you was way too easy. I wonder what all the fuss was about.'

She sat dazed for a minute before recovering her composure. 'You are a coward, that's all. Assaulting and abducting a woman with four masked men is not bravery, you condescending and patronising piece of shit!'

The man clapped. 'Full marks for courage, Lakshmi. But I'm still disappointed. Anyways, let me introduce myself. You deserve that much. My name is Noel Nat, and I'm the man who invited you to Cambodia.'

Hate blazed in Lakshmi's sparkling eyes. She looked around, her face still sore from where Nat's hired goon had hit her. Was this the fabled temple complex, Suryavarman's ode to Lord Vishnu?

'How do you know so much about me? Why the special interest?'

'Patience, Lakshmi. I have invested, sorry, wasted a lot of time and effort to get you here,' Noel glared at her.

One of his brawny henchmen spat at her.

'Witch,' he said. Probably the only English word that could pass through his thick, dirty skull, Lakshmi thought.

'The man's right, Lakshmi. You're a psychic witch, inextricably linked with our land, my beautiful country. I'm not usually a misogynist, but our families have a long history together. Way too much if you ask me.'

If looks could kill, Lakshmi would have murdered this wimp ten times over.

'Hmm,' he smirked, pure malice gleaming from the whites of his eyes. 'You're wondering what I want. Mama dearest, oh yes, what was her name? Padma. She only recently revealed some of the secrets of the childhood jigsaw troubling her little pet. Damn insensitive if you ask me.'

Lakshmi suppressed any show of surprise. How did this man know intimate details of telephone conversations. Had he been eavesdropping on her all along?

'You're so intellectually inferior. You couldn't even see through Sihanouk, the genial doctor on the flight. Yes, yes, don't be surprised. I planted him to keep track of you. Frankly, I expected you to be a worthwhile opponent. Moriarty to my dazzling Holmes,' Noel Nat continued his pompous rant.

'Shouldn't it be the other way round? You're the bad guy, remember,' Lakshmi seethed.

'People are directionless fools, oblivious to the truth, Lakshmi. They only see what they want to see. I want to change their entire perspective on reality.'

'How do I fit into all this?'

'It was prophesied a long time back that a psychic witch would be born in Divakar Pandita's land. Yes, your august ancestor. Personally, I didn't believe all this bullshit until the manuscript I got hold of correctly predicted every goddamn major world event to date including this blasted crapshoot of a pandemic,' Noel Nat said.

'A regular Nostradamus,' Lakshmi remarked snidely.

'Blah, blah, blah,' Noel tugged at the roots of his hair. The man was a certified nutjob, Lakshmi thought. The wind pressed and pulled around her.

'Glad to see that bondage has not dented your sense of humour. Listen to me carefully. Your psychic powers have been increasing ever since you got here. There's a surefire way to ramp them up using my favourite resident *kru thmup*. That's a sorcerer for the uninitiated.'

'Why would I collaborate with you, a murderous lowlife?' Lakshmi's eyes felt as if they were about to pop out of their sockets.

'Simple enough! The rates in your country to kill people are very cheap. Let me start with your precious daughter, Ananya. Isn't she pretty? I generally don't like murdering children, but then everything is fair in war and war. Oh, sorry, was it love and war? Then your stupid husband, Dhruv. I'll take a special joy in torturing the bastard. I'll start with his eyes. No, I prefer nails. People scream like frightened chickens and piss their pants. I love that. Then it gets really interesting—bloody, slimy, and yummy. So, for your own good, don't try to resist me, ever. You'll make things so much worse than you could ever imagine. If you try to save the world, witch, you'll only ruin it.'

At that moment, every last cell in her body was writhing in a real nightmare. The only difference was that Lakshmi was not asleep, about to wake up in her comfortable bed. Everything bad and ominous was staring right at her face in exotic and beautiful daylight.

Afraid of losing her mind. A vortex of conflicting emotions. Freefall into nothingness.

Noel Nat, the nefarious mastermind and influential business tycoon who had abducted her, now whisked Lakshmi away to Phnom Bakheng in his opulent private helicopter.

The majestic temple complex, currently in ruins, stood as a reverent tribute to Lord Shiva, one of the most enigmatic and creative gods of the Hindu pantheon. The intricate architecture was a symbolic representation of Mount Meru, the central axis of the universe in religious cosmological narrative.

Bound securely with new ropes, Lakshmi recalled what her father had told her about Shiva or Mahadeva. With two of his eyes, Shiva pervaded all space and, with the third, all time. If anybody could get her out of this predicament, it was Shiva, the lord of the space–time continuum.

'You know, I'm amazed at social media these days,' Noel Nat said.

'There he goes again,' Lakshmi thought.

'Hashtags are an ocean of publicity. A single tweet can ignite a revolution and incite political and societal turmoil among judgemental readers with fleeting attention spans. The moronic idiocy of instant gratification.'

'Is there a point to this? I'm really tired of your windbag speeches, Schmuckstein. Just kill me, and get it over with,' Lakshmi said.

'So transparent and conformist, Lakshmi. I expected a great fight, but this is a walkover. Not the greatness I expected to be pitted against.'

'Whatever,' Lakshmi's response was curt.

'Getting bored, are we? Haven't we entertained you enough? Free helicopter tours, breathtaking aerial views, the whole shebang. Let me regale you with a story.'

'Quite frankly, I don't give a damn,' Lakshmi said. She wanted to snap the man's neck into two.

Noel Nat grabbed a bag from one of his scrawny henchmen and pulled a wand out. It was long and ornate with engravings in what looked like a mix of Sanskrit, Tamil, and Khmer to Lakshmi's eyes. The air around him crackled with an ominous energy.

'Feast your eyes on this,' he said with a sinister tone. 'Beautiful and mystical, isn't it? It's been in my family for countless generations since Devaraja. Does that name ring a bell?'

Lakshmi's mind immediately flashed back to the detailed conversation with her mother, Padma.

'Yes, Devaraja, enemy of my ancestor Divakar Pandita and murderer of his grandson, Shashi.'

Nat let out a howl of delight. 'Excellent! So you do know about the curse of Phnom Bakheng and, more importantly, the buried treasure.'

'Aren't you forgetting something? If I'm the person who leads you to the treasure, the curse on my clan will finally end,' Lakshmi replied.

Noel Nat's smile grew wider, relishing the power play. 'How stupid do you think I am? Of course, I know. The treasure is precisely the reason I kept tabs on your family. I was expecting some great fighting heroine with supernatural powers, a full-service package, the reincarnation of an ancient princess. Instead, what I get is you, nothing more than a glorified housewife. I would rate my chances highly.'

Lakshmi ignored the degrading taunts aimed at her. 'So, tell me, what exactly does your wand do, Lord Voldemort?'

'Childish, Lakshmi. This wand was used by Mihirakula the demon worshipper, who invaded your country, India, many times. In Rajaraja Chola's time, it passed through the hands of the Tamizh kingdoms and finally found its way east to Cambodia, where my master magi ancestor, Devaraja, used it. A symbol of power throughout history, this wand was around when Angkor was founded, right down to the time of the savage French colonists, murderous Nazis, and the genocidal Khmer Rouge. This wand is the original reason for your clan's misery—the curse of Phnom Bakheng.'

'What do you intend to do with it now?'

Nat's response was simple but ominous. 'Just wait and see.'

Mumbai

Rajiv Kapadia's face reddened, his throat constricted. Lakshmi had not contacted him the entire day, nor had she shown up for business meets with furious Cambodian pharma majors, who were flooding his inbox with irate mails.

'Get me Vijayan's home number, quick,' he bellowed at his secretary, who nearly spilt the tea she had brought for the boss.

'Yes and no, sir. I mean I can get it ... definitely ... I mean ...' The secretary's voice trailed off into a whisper.

'Move it, then,' Kapadia said. 'What do I pay you for?'

As it was 10 p.m. in India, the time was close to midnight in Siem Reap, Cambodia. The time difference was the same as in Thailand, the other Southeast Asian country he visited for business.

Kapadia had noticed the hesitation in Lakshmi's eyes whenever Cambodia was mentioned. He had ignored it, thinking she'd rather live it up in the snazzy streets of Singapore, Kuala Lumpur, or Bangkok. Lakshmi not turning up meant that something was seriously off kilter.

His personal life had been spiralling downwards. When he had chastised his wife for abusing an unrestricted expense account, a no-holds barred shouting match had erupted. Threats of divorce were straining his already fraught marital relationship to potential breaking point.

Still, Lakshmi's disappearing act was way more serious than the usual office affairs or noisy media fracas Kapadia handled with panache.

In the ten years since he had hired her, Lakshmi had gone from strength to strength, handling every work engagement like a consummate professional. Kapadia never saw a smile on her lips though. A sinister spectre seemed to hang over her every action.

He decided to call the number given by his secretary.

'Hello,' a groggy voice answered.

'Lakshmi Vijayan Mehra's residence?'

'Yes.'

'Is that Dhruv?'

'Of course. Who's this? Why call me at this time of the night?'

'Sorry to disturb you this late, Dhruv. But it's urgent. Rajiv Kapadia here, Lakshmi's boss. Has she spoken to you today?'

'No, but I wasn't worried. She does that sometimes—not call for several days on a hectic business trip.'

'Hmm, yes. Lakshmi hasn't shown up for multiple business meetings. She left her hotel in the morning around 10.30 a.m. That was the last time anybody saw her. No email follow-up. We can't get through to her cell. This is very unlike the Lakshmi I know.'

Kapadia heard laboured breathing on the other side of the phone in a marked contrast to the nonchalance of a few moments back.

'Well, Mr Kapadia, bad news for sure. There still might be a legit reason. Let me try and contact Lakshmi on a private number she carries in her valise.'

'Okay, Dhruv. Since she's an old employee, we will give her some leeway. Don't contact the Courtyard Marriott by the way. Last time anybody saw an Indian lady was in the morning. She was heading towards a tuk-tuk.'

Rajiv slammed his phone shut, struggling to control his anger. He couldn't believe Lakshmi's audacity. After all, he had put her in a top-notch hotel, not to mention his generous compensation package.

Why couldn't Lakshmi have just taken a cab? Then again, navigating transportation in an unfamiliar city could be a nightmare. Maybe, she wanted to save a few dollars for future family trips.

Speculation was futile. Only God or Lakshmi knew what she was up to.

Everything around Lakshmi felt alive—the foliage, like an insidious monster, twisting and cavorting through the cavities of her mind.

'Stay away,' she shouted at a snake that slithered past her.

She thought about the deeply mysterious and mystical past of Cambodia. Legend had it that the kingdom of Kamboja or Cambodia was formed when an Indian prince married a *naga* (snake) princess.

A glimpse at her father's old manuscript had told her that the number of heads the naga people had, whether that was odd or even, was believed to be auspicious or inauspicious determinants of fate, good or dark omens.

Maybe she had not transcended to the quasi-mystic plane yet as the snake she had just seen had just one head.

The omens right now were all bad. Noel Nat's sorcerer (thmup) had arrived.

His garland of skulls and long, sharp fingernails added to the already surreal atmosphere, making Lok Baran Saran's dark, bloodshot eyes look even more menacing.

'Welcome, Lok Baran Saran, I am honoured by your presence. Meet the enemy of my family, Divakar Pandita's descendant, this black Indian witch, Lakshmi,' Noel Nat greeted him with a distinctly theatrical flourish.

'Glad to be here, Mr Nat. I will make this insignificant worm vomit the location of the treasure in no time.'

Lakshmi heaved a partial sigh of relief. There was no black magic for the time being, just the oldest temptation in the book—money, the root facilitator of all evil. She had been conjuring up different situations in her mind, each progressively worse.

'What do we have here, a goddamn dirty Indian half-blood? My powers and King Mihirakula's wand will make you squirm,' Lok Baran Saran, the sorcerer, said in a tone that made Lakshmi both cringe and want to laugh.

Saran's incantations began, the psychedelic sounds steadily rising in tone and volume as he vigorously pounded a loud drum. The language sounded like Khmer to Lakshmi, with mellifluous Sanskrit regularly interspersed.

'You think your mind is inaccessible to us, wench? I speak with the power of the dark lord pulsating through every vein, every nerve, all the cells of my body. I can stare deep into your subconscious, your soul, every tiny fibre of your existence,' he taunted.

'I'm not scared, lowlife scum. Come at me with everything your puny little brain can think of,' Lakshmi shot back.

As the mad frenzy of the chanting and the moaning grew louder, Lakshmi felt that the man earnestly believed that his words could open a portal to other worlds, past, present, and future. Her father's manuscript had hinted at the potential for destruction or boundless power that lay buried in the cavernous depths of Sanskrit mantras.

His words were not an idle boast. Was this man opening the gates to hell? Lakshmi's eyeballs nearly popped out of their head as a whirlwind started to form, spinning violently and seemingly sucking in the darkness. The thousand-year-old stones amplified the intensity of the moment, lending an eerie and foreboding backdrop for this tryst with the dark side.

The Hindu/Buddhist temple symbolises Meru, the haloed abode of the gods. However, it felt as if the asuras or demons were running riot.

'Descend, O great god of time. I pray to Lord Vamachara, the fierce one, the mighty and cruel embodiment of the infinite universe, the overseer of all events across space and time. Vajrabhairava, Dandapani, Swasva, Yamantaka, hear my call. I beseech your benevolence as a humble servant,' Lok Baran Saran's voice echoed in the wilderness. The wind howled, and the trees creaked in protest.

As Saran shook his body, jumping up and down, swaying and gesticulating like a madman, Lakshmi implicitly understood that this was a ruse to appease the deity and extract buried secrets from her subconscious.

'Give me light, Master. Great god,' Lok Baran screeched. The swaying wand, intermittent flashes of light and darkness, and eerie sounds contributed to create a thrilling, heart-stopping spectre.

The majesty of the surrounding temple was awe-inspiring. It felt alive, like a living, breathing organism and not the lifeless artefact that scores of tourists treated flippantly every day.

Amid this eerie atmosphere, two men etched a black magic symbol—a yantra known as a pentagram in Western satanism. As the sorcerer's chants grew louder,

Lakshmi felt an otherworldly force attacking her from within, attempting to squash her soul and squeeze out her vital life force.

It was nearly an hour past midnight. Gusts of wind shook every tree around her, right down to their gnarled roots. She felt like she was losing her grip on reality as the unsettling laughter of ancient spirits echoed in the darkness, permeating her last lines of defence. Everything grotesque had come alive, suffocating Lakshmi with their ominous presence.

'Behold, Kala Bhairava, Lord Mara, descends,' Lok Baran's eyes burnt like overflowing lava from a volcano.

She shuddered with revulsion when she saw the wind contorting into an ogre-like figure with slimy, dripping fangs. A vial overflowing with a green, frothy concoction passed from the ogre's hands to the sorcerer, Lok Baran Saran.

The dead had invaded the world of the living, and Lakshmi was now utterly terrified.

'Get the Siem Reap police to investigate. Find my employee ASAP. I have contacts at the highest level in both the Indian and the Cambodian governments. Crank up the pressure,' Rajiv Kapadia's voice over the phone was so loud and threatening that everyone around him shuddered.

Shirin, Kapadia's secretary, hurried in. 'Sir, Dhruv is on the line. He says Ms Vijayan's mother, Ms Padma, has some strange ideas on her disappearance and a possible explanation about what happened to her. She lives in Bengaluru and can connect via a conference call.'

'Okay, let me see. I recall Lakshmi once telling me that her mother was an award-winning professor. Everything that comes out of her mouth can't be trash,' Kapadia replied.

'Hold on, Dhruv. Sir says he's willing to talk ... Y ... yes to your mother-in-law.' The secretary looked disconcerted to Kapadia.

Even though Lakshmi was not verbose, sociable, and pretentious like some of her more flamboyant, extroverted colleagues, most people never had a bad word to say about her.

'Patching you through, sir. Please pick up the line,' Shirin requested Kapadia.

'Hello, Padma madam. Hi, Dhruv,' Kapadia said.

'Call me Padma, please. Dhruv tells me that you haven't been able to trace Lakshmi since yesterday evening. Things are pretty much going to get worse, even apocalyptic. I'm afraid this is just the beginning of a colossal shit-show,' Padma Vijayan said.

'No time for mysticism, mumbo-jumbo, and doomsday scenarios, Padma. Tell me something real that makes sense. Lakshmi is a valuable asset, and so I've put in all this time and effort. Also, she went cattle-class to Cambodia on my insistence. So I feel personally responsible,' Rajiv replied.

'Very considerate. However, I'm afraid her father and I committed an unpardonable sin, Rajiv. We concealed our family history from her, apart from the millennium-old curse on our clan.'

Lakshmi's mother succinctly summed up what she had told her daughter a few days back. Rajiv suppressed his incredulity and scepticism, as he knew there were many strange and unexplained things in the world. Lakshmi had not jumped ship due to some corporate poaching or malicious masterplan, but he couldn't fully bring himself to buy into the mother's story. Curses that lasted for a thousand years existed only in fiction or the movies, not the real world of power, strife, and money.

'It's also about Jaimini and the missing Mahabharata, Rajiv.' Padma's Pandora's box of tales unfurled like a Russian doll, layers within layers.

'I'm a man of science, to be specific, pharmaceuticals. I don't have the bandwidth for legends, Padma.'

'A tragedy, Rajiv. All our scriptures are always interlinked with science. It's a pity that we have been so brainwashed by the West that you see no value in our literature. These aren't fairy tales.'

'Go on, Padma.'

'Coming back to the lost Mahabharata of the sage Jaimini. Vyasa, the original composer, encouraged his five disciples—Vaisampayana, Jaimini, Sumantu, Paila and his son Shuka—to come up with their own versions. The one extant today is Vaishampayana's narration at the king Janamajeya's snake sacrifice. Similarly, Jaimini had his own take on the Ramayana and the Mahabharata. On the walls of the Silver Pagoda in Phnom Penh, Mairavana's abduction of Rama and his brother Lakshmana and their rescue by Hanuman is depicted.'

'What has this to do with Lakshmi?'

'Patience. I'm getting there. Even Buddhist lore, such as the Anguttara Nikaya, says that the 'end of days' would happen when the earth burns under the heat of seven suns blazing.'

'What's that, a nuclear holocaust?'

'No, that's when the earth degenerates into chaos in case the dark side gets hold of the *amrita* obtained by the gods post the ocean churn or *sagara manthana,* if you remember ancient stories.'

'What's the connection here?'

'Devaraja, the prime minister who deported our clan after getting Divakar Pandita's grandson beheaded, also opened a portal to the netherworld along with his curse on us.'

'So?'

'Devaraja believed that the netherworld door, a vast ancient treasure, and Buddhist apocalyptic predictions were unrelated. As a great wizard, he knew how to open the netherworld door but couldn't seal it shut. The gods told him that the door would only open and close after a thousand years when Divakar Pandita's female descendant named after the goddess Sri or Lakshmi came along. By that time, Devaraja had either killed or deported most of Divakar's lineage.'

'Please don't mind me saying so, but all of this sounds too outlandish to believe, Padma. I will try to get Lakshmi found via the local police,' Kapadia said.

'Okay, Rajiv. I still don't think you will find her through normal means. The only hope is an Anjaneya (Hanuman) mantra her father taught her in childhood. I've told you many times that you're dealing with a blazing, uncontrollable volcano. My daughter's life is on the line.'

'Witch, be ready to meet your maker, the great god Phnom Bakheng,' Lok Baran Saran, the moronic sorcerer said, making his way towards Lakshmi with the green, frothy vial.

The foliage and darkness around her symbolised Mount Meru, the abode of the gods. She remembered the novelist James Hilton's Shangri-La, an ode to the secret, mysterious lands of Hindu and Buddhist lore.

'Do whatever you can, infernal ugly scum!' Lakshmi maintained a brave veneer. Coming face to face with death had strengthened her resolve. A burden lifted, and all the mysteries of the past swept away, dissolving into nothingness.

All the self-pity and depression from her unknown past and recurring nightmares evaporated in an instant.

'I will escape and kill every last one of you.'

Noel Nat and his henchman guffawed with malicious glee. 'We'll see about that, witch. I'm impressed that you're fighting till the bitter end. But your last-minute bravery won't save you. Lok, force the putrid liquid in the vial down her throat.'

As Lakshmi writhed and screamed, the burly members of Noel's goon squad pinned her down to a more supine position.

'Silence, you wretched woman. By the power of the great Lord Kala Bhairava and Noel's noble ancestor Devaraja Vajrapani, this witch will be a slave to our every whim. You will reveal to us the location of that treasure and the entrance to the netherworld, whether you like it or not.'

'How courageous of you to torture a helpless woman! My mind is shut forever, even if you kill me,' Lakshmi said.

'That can be arranged soon enough,' Noel said with a cold sneer. He snatched the vial from Lok Baran's hands, yanked open Lakshmi's mouth, and forced the vile green concoction down her throat.

Lakshmi recoiled in agony at the sheer malice in Noel Nat's eyes, which were glowing bluish green in the darkness like a predator stalking its prey. In that moment, she felt her father's ghost materialising above the goons along with a wizened old Indo-Cambodian man wielding an ornate Hanuman staff.

'Divakar Pandita, my great ancestor,' she thought.

'There will be times in your life when you will face extreme danger.' A latent memory of her father, buried deep somewhere in Lakshmi's subconscious, emerged as the nauseating green concoction wound its way through her insides.

'Whenever and wherever that happens, recite the Anjaneya mantra I am teaching you now with complete faith.' Her father's words echoed in the vast depths of her mind.

'What are you thinking, smelly witch?' Lok Baran Saran kept up his condescending rant, sprinkling dirty water on her face. His wide, bloodshot eyes spewed fire. 'Scared yet? Don't keep us waiting. Be prepared for the deepest pits of hell because you're soon going to pay them a visit.'

Even in her drowsy state, she sensed a paranormal entity gradually gaining control of her cognitive abilities, heart, feet, and every last bone in her body. Death was waiting in the wings.

From her earliest days, Lakshmi's heart had been entwined with the tales of Lord Hanuman, her family deity. His adventures and feats of strength had been a constant source of wonder and inspiration, shaping her childhood in ways that she could never have imagined. His courage and devotion made him a god beloved across India and a vast expanse of the ancient world, particularly East Asia.

Her father often told her that the Chinese Ming dynasty classic *Journey to the West* had been inspired by Lord Hanuman's exploits and the Buddha's wisdom.

Even Barack Obama, the former American president, apparently carried a Hanuman statuette in his pocket for luck and inspiration.

However, the most interesting take she had heard was the Cambodian version. In Cambodia, the Reamker or the local Ramayana had its own saucy and romantic take on the Hanuman story. Lord Hanuman meets Sovanna Maccha, an alluring mermaid who is the daughter of the antagonist, Ravana, as the monkey army builds a bridge to Lanka.

Falling in love with the petite Sovanna Maccha is an unintended consequence of Hanuman's battle with the mermaids.

Nevertheless, Lord Rama's foremost devotee successfully woos her, convincing Sovanna of the justness of his cause. The celibate and intellectual god of Indian tradition has a son with Sovanna, Macchanu.

When Lord Hanuman embarks on a mission to rescue Sri Rama and his brother Lakshmana from the netherworld king, Mairavana, he encounters a fierce opponent who eventually reveals that he is Hanuman's son, Macchanu, and unveils the entrance to the netherworld, which is through a lotus pond he is guarding.

As Noel Nat and Lok Baran Saran argued over the best way to access her memories, Lakshmi's mind flashed back to the Lord Hanuman story and the Anjaneya mantra her father had made her memorise a long time ago.

'I need to cure you of your inordinate fascination with Western literature. India's wealth of knowledge and fables is greater than any other place on the planet. Read and respect every culture but be aware of the treasures within. That is the gist of what our ancestors taught us.

Always remember the syllables of this Anjaneya mantra I am teaching you. All of them flow like a river, carrying with them the power and divinity of Lord Hanuman. The final syllable is like a burst of energy, releasing the full force of Hanuman's power into the universe. Even if you face the darkest night of the soul, when everything seems lost, it will surely help you.'

The potion Noel Nat had forced her to ingest was having its desired effect. She felt as if chakra whorls were opening in her body, from the genital region (*anahata*) to the roof of her head (*sahasrara*).

'How long now? I'm losing patience. The sun will be up soon. We work best under the cover of darkness. Get what I want from this witch, or I'll finish both her and you,' Noel Nat said, his raised eyebrows fuming with impatience.

'Soon enough, Noel. Never dare to threaten me. Both of us know that I have great occult powers,' Lok Baran replied.

'Bah, humbug and stinking bullshit. Granted you made Kala Bhairava appear and you obtained that smelly vial. Nothing my father couldn't do.'

'But you can't, Noel, can you?' Lok smirked.

'Who's holding the purse strings and has all the power here, Lok? It helps to have an American senator for a mother. Never forget your place in the world. You're like a bug I can crush anytime.' Noel's eyes breathed fire.

Lakshmi realised that Lok was going to trawl through her karmic memories like somebody using an internet search engine. The man's occult powers were intent on finding something even she didn't know on a conscious level.

Baran pointed his Mihirakula wand at her, muttering incantations and saying loudly, 'By the grace of the great god Lord Vajrapani, reveal everything that is hidden. O Macchanu, come forth and reveal to us the location of Mairavana's treasure.'

A powerful gurgling force ran through Lakshmi's head like a piston thump. Every bone in her fragile body felt that a supernatural entity was in firm control of her consciousness, speaking through her.

'Who dares to find Master Mairavana's treasure?' The voice was so loud it resonated throughout the forest, shaking it to its core. This was a tone that demanded attention, a voice that carried the weight of ancient power.

'I am the servant of Kala Vajrapani, the ancient sorcerer supreme, Lord Macchanu. I have summoned you invoking the ancient protocols, harnessing the power of Bhairava's potion,' Lok Baran said.

'Indeed, you have. But do you realise the enormity of what you have unleashed, fool? Once the door to the netherworld is open, it's impossible to close. Unimaginably powerful forces will descend on this earth, destroying cities, villages, and continents in a split second. Only a person who knows the secret mantras used by my father, Hanuman, to seal the fissure can close the gates to this perilous dimension.'

Instead of Baran, Noel cut in. 'Never mind, Macchanu. Enough of this scorching hellfire and apocalyptic nonsense. I just want to get my hands on a treasure that's worth billions, possibly trillions. I'm not scared of your death and damnation party trick if I can become the richest and most powerful man on earth.'

'As you wish, foolish human. Behold,' Macchanu replied, his eyes aflame with anger and irritation. The earth around them shook so hard that it felt like every tree, insect, and animal would fall off the blue planet. It then parted to reveal a very old and deep subterranean passage.

As Noel Nat's men dragged her along, Lakshmi was amazed at what opened in the ground beneath her feet. Buried treasure, demons, magicians, and flying dragons were fictional—only in books and movies, she had always felt.

By now, Dhruv and Rajiv would be worried sick. Even in their wildest imaginations, they couldn't fathom the dire situation she was in. Only Padma, her mother, would have a vague inkling of what she was going through.

'We need to kill and dispose of this witch now, as soon as we get all the gold, diamonds, and jewels loaded up. It will take only a few hours by my estimate. What's your opinion, Baran? Should we kill her now or later?' Noel said.

Their words made Lakshmi's blood run cold, but she put on a brave face. There had to be a way out of this, but it had to be extremely quick.

'Let's see if Hanuman descends from the heavens and saves you, Vijayan. That's your surname, right? Victory in the face of inevitable defeat. Isn't that ironic, since you're about to be stamped out like a slimy cockroach?' Baran was at his stinging best.

Facing the eerily glowing Noel, he added, 'We can finish her off as soon as the convoy of empty trucks are loaded with as much as we manage to get our hands on. Wouldn't want to incur the wrath of any supernatural force till then.'

Unwittingly, the moron Lok Baran had opened an escape door that Lakshmi could squeeze through. She then realised the true import of her father's words and the universe-altering power in every pregnant syllable of the Anjaneya mantra.

Lord Hanuman was her clan deity, honour-bound to save her. Hanuman symbolised the power of good, the victory of light over darkness. He was also Shiva's incarnation, custodian, ever-vigilant protector, and principal deity of Phnom Bakheng.

Baran had addressed the supernatural force as Macchanu, the son of Hanuman in the tale her father had often told her as an inquisitive teenager.

Immediately, Lakshmi started a loud, incessant chant of the Anjaneya mantra. This time, the unexpected sound caught Noel Nat and his henchmen unawares.

'What are you doing, you wicked witch?' Noel Nat shouted at the top of his voice.

'Showing you what real pain looks like. Your insatiable greed has led you to tinker with the immutable laws of the universe and mess with transcendental dimensions across space and time. Now, feel anguish, anger, helplessness, and pain like never before. Rot in hell forever,' Lakshmi replied.

The ground shook again.

If the previous time was vigorous, it now felt like the earth would split into two shards floating in space.

A mighty and great figure clutching a mace in his right hand appeared overhead, his face dazzling with the brilliance of a thousand suns.

The ground gradually gave way, treasure and gold dropping and disappearing into an infinite hellish vortex blazing with volcanic intensity.

Lok Baran, Noel, and his henchmen shrieked in agony as they were sucked in. Their feet and legs burnt as if in an atomic blast. Their eyes popped out of their sockets, scalded skin fell off like flaky paint, and heads exploded like shot watermelons. It was all over in less than a split second.

Lakshmi felt the blinding divine presence lifting her up, which she believed was no other than Lord Hanuman. A brilliant radiance enveloped her, and intense light filled every corner of her vision. Every frayed nerve was now as calm as a gently flowing stream.

She slid down a gigantic arm, which gently set her down in a snug enclosure within the main Angkor Wat temple complex. The walls were adorned with intricate carvings, and the air was filled with the sweet scent of incense. Standing before her was an awe-inspiring eight-armed Vishnu statue, its exquisite beauty leaving her breathless.

'Follow your heart, Lakshmi, and stay true to yourself. Never let doubt cloud your mind. Always remember Sri Rama, lord of this eternal multiverse,' the divine figure said and disappeared.

As she walked out of the complex, her body still sore, Lakshmi realised that nobody would ever believe what had just transpired.

If she talked about soul-damning thousand-year-old curses and saving the world from destruction, many people would simply ridicule her or recommend a lunatic asylum.

The Supreme Lord, his foremost devotee Hanuman, and her wise, intellectual father had pulled her back from the brink of a perilous fate, and she would be indebted to them for eternity.

The disappearance had to be explained some other way. For now, she would head back to so-called civilisation, her job, her loving husband, and her daughter.

As the sun set over the glorious remnants of Cambodia's past, Jayalakshmi Vijayan walked gently towards the vast horizon. She had exorcised the ghosts of her past, forming an eternal, new, effervescent connection. The end of this road held the promise of a new adventure.

7

The Search for Iravan

Pranshu B. Saxena

The Good Ship Kutsa

Elaputra *uvacha* (Elaputra tells us)

The serene waves of the Eastern Sea laved onto the coast of Lobpuri with a rhythm reminiscent of a mother breathing as she nestles a child against her bosom—a sound perfected through millions of years to assure and assuage the future of humanity and the trade of the seafarers. Like a child in a mother's arms, the ship was rocking in the calm night. The coruscating lights of fires lit by our landing party on the beach provided a gentle illumination, helped by Mamu Moon, which was halfway through his cycle.

Being a landlubber and a lover of land from head to boot, I was reminded of the sounds of the snoring of my father and my uncles from my childhood. The villagers used to say that our household did not need to spend money on midnight oil for the torches to scare away wild animals from our front yard. The *singhnaad* (lion's roar) of the snores was enough!

I could not sleep then, and I could not sleep now! Then, the solution had been simple—a bit of cottonwool! Tiny solutions for modest times. Now, the rollicking creation of Lord Varuna was pitching the ship this way and that, reminding the landlubber of the existence of the third dimension. No wonder Varuna is called Jhulelal (the rolling god of the ocean), swaying in time with the sea. Lying in my bed in the cabin was like undulating in the swing in my childhood, close to my snoring uncles! Eventually, giving up on sleep, I got up and made my way to the forecastle.

I will never get used to this life of a naval trader.

'Elaputra, once you told me that you were never going to be a warrior,' Yudhamanyu, my dear friend 'Danu', observed, 'but you have been a tolerable one for the past five decades!'

'Decades is the key, Danu. You can always teach a young pup, but you cannot teach an old dog new tricks,' I replied, drawing attention from the night shift mulling around on the deck, looking at this strange old man talking to himself.

'Elaputra, you were never a builder before you helped rebuild the seven ashrams of the Saptarishis at Naukabandhan Parvata in Kashmir during the Vanavasa,' countered Uttamaujas, my dear friend 'Anshu'. 'Never stop learning.'

'Look what you've done. It is midnight, and you got the gurudeva and his lectures started,' whined Yudhamanyu.

'As if ghosts care about whether it is day or night. Stop fighting,' I mock-complained, a tad too loudly, scaring the lad at the watch, the captain's page, standing next to the captain at the forecastle. The lad's eyes bugged out, trying to discern my compatriots. The *naunetra* (captain/navigator) of the ship, Jaimini Turvasya Kutsa, threw his head back and laughed at the expression on the young lad's face.

'Don't let Mamaji spook you, Pradyota, with his spooked phantoms,' the captain chuckled at his own alliteration, mirth and hope visible in his eyes as they, too, searched in anticipation around me, all calm and efficient but missing his mother all the same.

'Mamu, welcome to the night watch. Who did you bring with you this time? Uncles Yudhamanyu and Uttamaujas, I bet! Did you get a chance to talk to my mother recently?' enquired my 'nephew', at ease with the fact that I talk to dead people like some people do in our homeland. He respectfully saluted the ones who were present yet not present.

His salutations as usual drew a chuckle from me and my friend-tasms. 'No, Kutsa, your mother, Poorva, comes just to scold me when I forget to take *shana* seeds and the *Jangida* plant medicine she prescribed to me for my *madhumeha*.'

'Aye, she does that a lot. Scold, I mean! I feel like she sits beside my bed watching over me while I sleep,' shared the captain, suddenly looking wistfully at Pradyota standing at attention.

Kutsa was the master shipbuilder at Dantapuri who had built this great ship for us, the spearpoint of our expedition to the golden land, Suvarnabhumi (Cambodia). One examination, one cursory glance at the size and complexity of Kutsa's creation, was enough for Svyambhavu Kaundinya, our *Sarthavaha* (expedition leader), to understand that he would not be able to control this ship without expert guidance. He selected Kutsa to be the naunetra on the spot. As per the tradition, the ship was named after him, Hastinapur Mahajana Shallika Kutsa (Hastinapur Trader Ship Kutsa)—HMS Kutsa for short.

Kutsa calls me Uncle for, like his mother, the other quiver on this old archer's back contains the medicine bag of a *vaidya* (healer). Poorva had literally bumped into me on a battlefield a long time ago, in the dark of twilight, moving through broken, blood-spattered bodies, trying to give succour and make the last moments comfortable for the warriors of Dharma. We had struggled through that night to save a warrior, beginning a lifelong friendship. For her life, that is!

Four years ago, she had died with Yudhamanyu and Uttamaujas in the fires lit by Asvathhamma at the Pandava war camp at Asandivata. Braving those flames, she had used her body to shield a young child (no relation to her). She burned to death but saved the child, Pradyota! Now, her son's page was taking part in this voyage with his captain to find another lost son for another mother forlorn far too long. Somehow, this ship named Kutsa nestled in the arms of the Eastern Sea (Poorva Payodhi) seemed as stable as the swings of my childhood.

Suddenly, the bright jewels on the twin *Makara*s, the ship's figurehead, caught the light from the forecastle torches lighting up the bowsprit (the 30 ft long extended arm at the head of the ship) and the half-golden mongoose sleeping on its edge. This fantastic creature, the immortal son of Brahma, Krodha Nakula, travelled the world in the form of a half-golden mongoose and was our guide for this expedition. The gilded left side of his body caught the light and brought into focus the young man standing next to him. The leader of our expedition—Vela Asvathhamma Svyambhavu Kumbhayana Kaundinya Kamboja, to give him his full name. He is the person you might blame for my being on this ship so far into the Eastern Ocean.

Dear reader, imagine him on this inaugural voyage to Suvarnabhumi: a young man of around thirty years of age, tall, powerful in gait, features from his Vanara and naga ancestors on his physique, and the unmistakable handsomeness of his ancestress, Urvashi. I always remember him as the newborn bundle I coaxed into swallowing a tonic as I struggled to save his nascent life, a constant situation in Svyambhavu's childhood, as the babe and toddler fought death and illness to earn the right to grow a moustache one day.

The poisonous hatred inside the Kuru family ended up creating walls across society and the nation. Svyambhavu's father, Yogacharya Kaundinya, chose to stay on at Indraprastha as an officer under Kaurava rule rather than come with me into exile after the game of dice. He chose to stay back to save the public of Indraprastha from casual, capricious Kaurava cruelty but still earned opprobrium from his family and, in time, scorn from his son. The decades of exile, the Kurukshetra War, and the Ashvamedha campaign had passed quickly.

By the time I returned from the Ashvamedha campaign, Yogacharya had retired to Naukabandhan Parvata in Kashmir to pursue his lifelong ambition of setting up the original university of Svyambhavu Manu, the forefather he named his son after.

Wrestling with my own demons for my failure to protect Arjuna at Manipur in the Ashvamedha campaign, I ran into Svyambhavu, grown into a fine man but bereft of purpose and in constant agony because of his rift with his father. Having healed his body as a child, I could not bear to see his soul in pain. I decided to leave Arjuna's service and accompany the young man to Kashmir to help repair

Svyambhavu's relationship with his father. The best laid plans of mice and men, as they say. *Jaate thhey Kashmir pahunch gaye Cheen.*[1]

Yuvaraj Bhima instead ordered Svyambhavu to direct our naval expedition to an unknown faraway land called Suvarnabhumi.

'Well, you did choose to accompany Svyambhavu to the ends of the earth on this expedition. You cannot blame him for your being here,' commented Yudhamanyu.

'No! I wanted to retire to Kashmir. It was Yuvaraja Bhima who sent us here on this expedition,' I countered.

'Bhima chose young Svyambhavu as the expedition leader to wipe the taint of cowardice from his reputation and to show that ex-Kauravas are welcome and given responsibilities in the Pandava administration after the horrors of the Great Civil War. It was a wise decision,' spoke Uttamaujas, as usual looking at the third side of the coin.

'The aim of the expedition is to search for Iravan, son of Arjuna. We all thought he died at Kurukshetra. Elaputra here, as a naga and a Maharathi, is the right person to escort Iravan's mother, Ulupi, on such a voyage. Bhima chose Svyambhavu because he is part of a package deal with Elaputra,' countered Yudhamanyu. The irony of a ghost talking about a maybe non-ghost was not lost on me.

'I beg to disagree, my sinistral colleague. Exposing Iravan's true fate was a reward for Ulupi for saving Arjuna's life at Manipur,' Uttamaujas retorted, as my ghostly friends argued with each other as they had done when they were … I suppressed a sob.

'And why did we need Ulupi to save Arjuna's life? Arjuna was slain in battle because of overconfidence—' Suddenly, Yudhamanyu stopped speaking, his eyes lowered, full of apology.

'You protected Arjuna for forty years. I could not protect him for forty weeks! Whatever the curse of the sons of Ganga, whatever the skills of the son of Arjuna, I failed in my duty to keep my Rathi safe.' My failure to keep Arjuna safe has tormented me ever since Arjuna's head went for a walkabout.

'*You just have survivor's guilt, healer!*' empathised Yudhamanyu.

'Is that your medical opinion?' I inquired, mimicking Yudhamanyu's similar taunts in the past to me.

'Well, you tell me. We are most likely a figment of your imagination. Your shattered mind is trying to hold on to this hurtful reality, not willing to accept the pain of our loss at the field of Kurukshetra, buddy. Heal thyself, physician!' my ghostly pal said sincerely.

After the great Mahabharata war and its accompanying tragedies and trauma, Yudhishthara had decided to send Arjuna and the army on a nation-wide campaign to heal the wounds and unite the populace again under one umbrella. Performing the Ashvamedha Yajna to cleanse the evils of kin slaughter was the perfect excuse for the national jaunt. Ahh, the Ashvamedha campaign! Specifically, at the battle of Manipur, under my watch, my Maharathi Arjuna lost his head literally, and we lost his head literally and ours figuratively.

Guided by Arjuna's naga paramour, Ulupi, we travelled to Nagaloka[2] to retrieve Arjuna's head, which had been stolen by Naga Dhrtrashtra and his sons. Fighting a

Dhrtrashtra and his sons is an old pastime for us! However, that is someone else's story to tell. *Pages to Pages, dust to dust if Vaisampayana*[3] *doesn't get to it, Jaimini must.*

Long history lesson short, Arjuna was reattached, revived, and back in the land of living.

'And it was Alambusha who had to pay his *Brahmahutanirmoksha*[4] to Queen Draupadi, who eventually put Iravan on a ship through the Maritime Jade Sea route. Elaputra *suna*! Danu has finally acknowledged that you are a healer,' chortled Uttamaujas as I joined in the mirth.

'So, we all agree. Jatasura is to blame for us being on the Maritime Jade Sea route,' I completed, catching the words in a fit of laughter.

Back in the land of living, alerted by my words in the dark, Svyambhavu Kaundinya remarked, 'Did Tarkshya's singing wake you, O Left Wheel?' The confusion on his face reflected in the lights from the golden mongoose while I conversed with my ethereal acquaintances. My eyes narrowed as I focused on the other end of the bowsprit 30 ft away and the braveheart sitting nonchalantly on the thin beam of wood jutting ahead of the ship. My uncomfortable sea stomach lurched on observing Tarkshya's precarious perch—suspended over the tossing waves, keeping watch on the front of the ship.

'Uncle, now you are talking to Jatasura! In which *rahukala* did my mother decide to send me to join your service? You talk to dead rakshasas! Your boss loses his head and lives on! And we are here, far far away from Hastinapur under KKKK[5] boss, searching for a dead hero! Bhootein ki hai yeh toli, macchhar ka thikana, hai hai re meri maa,'[6] snapped back young Tarkshya, before continuing his singing.

The rolling of the boat lulls me,
The dusk has fallen,
Alone in the sky like a soaring feather,
Below waves stretch opulent,
Lapping their earth mother,
O where can the one I search for be,
will someone hear me?

Little did I know at that point that all the problems we would face on this voyage to Suvarnabhumi could be traced to Tarkshya Arishtanemi and his defunct love life.

I know, dear reader, that you are confused. How come the warrior tasked to guard Arjuna all his life ends up on a ship off the coast of Lobpuri 'far far away' from hard-won Hastinapur?

'What is the Maritime Jade Route?' inquired little Pradyota, appearing by my side, picking on one term from my exclamation.

'I think this is a perfect time for a history lesson for your readers,' intoned Gurudeva Uttamaujas in sync with our groans.

The Maritime Jade Route

The nagas, vanaras, panis, and rakshasas—a long time before the gilded days of Vaishravana Dashagriva's golden Lanka—had been great merchants and explorers across the three oceans. Earlier, there were land-based trade routes. The Maritime Jade Sea Route has been the main trade artery of asuras, rakshasas, and panis from Taiwan, Andhralaya (Australia), and Misra (Egypt) and Sumaliratta on Patala Mahadwipa (Africa). The aborigines of Taiwan, the Gaoshan, share ancestry with those of Bharatavarsha and Andhralaya. They excavate the beautiful *Ashvaka* (अश्वक) *mani* (Jade) from their mountains and use it in the trade with their cousins across the Maharlika (महर्द्धिक) Mayadwipa (Phillipines), Tawalisi, Yavadwipa (Java), Varunadwipa (Borneo), Malayadwipa and thousands of islands that sparkle in the Eastern Ocean. This network reached across all the three oceans as the Maritime Jade Route.

The Ashvaka route enriched the cultures and societies partaking in its commerce and is one of the open secrets behind the fabulous wealth of the asuras and the rakshasas. With great power comes great responsibility, and power born from lucre sometimes corrupts. Using the pretext of acquiring jewellery for his wife, Agastya punished the evil actions of the *danava*s Vatapi and Ilavala, the controllers of the southern routes. Agastya would lead two major expeditions to cleanse the entire oceans of the ones who strayed from the 'route' of the right, the asuras Kalakeyas.

Even noble and illustrious trading allies, the Bhargavas and the Haihayas, turned blood-oath enemies under the influence of the riches of this trade. The likes of Vashishthas and Kalampashada could not escape the cycle of mistrust and tragedy. There was, however, a sunny side to it.

The descendants of Druhyu, the Vaibhojas, who live and travel on ships and rafts on this route, creating a perfect democratic society with no kings.

Bhima had explained, when giving us our marching—er, make that our sailing—orders, 'The idea to relaunch the Maritime Jade Route has been percolating like a cooking *khichdi* stuck far up in a pot on a tree above the fire. The Mahabharata War has been hard on the people of Bharatavarsha. Widows and orphans encumber the economy of this great Bharata. We need to revive the economy, give guidance and fresh purpose to the young men and women who survived that great calamity and the old men brutalised by that conflict, provide soothing balm for their memories, and defeat the demons of regret and terror that continue to devour their daily endeavours.'

'So, it is Agastya or Dhrtrashtra's fault that Elaputra is here!' said Yudhamanyu, sharply.

The ghosts of my friends or their phantasms or, maybe, the effects of my shattered mind act as panacea for losing them at the battlefield called Kurukshetra.

We served the Pandavas for so many decades as an extended family. Asvathhamma's treachery seared my soul on the night called Sauptika. Kutsa lost his mother, Pradyota lost his family, and I lost my sanity that night.

The irony is that now I seek balm for my wounded heart in the far oceans in company of a young man named Vela Asvathhamma, the spear of Asvathhamma. Svyambhavu was Asvathhamma's favourite student. The sense of humour of the chap above is indeed strange!

The Miss-understanding at Lobpuri

Elaputra *uvacha*

At Lobpuri, on the west coast of Malayadwipa, our expedition was given a grand welcome by the princes and the people. The ladies seemed the most interested, with matrons of the society visiting our ship in droves and enquiring for eligible young men to marry their daughters.

The flow of trade—wares of all sorts, including human ware—has linked these countries to Bharatavarsha by delicate strands of affinity more powerful and tensile than shackles of iron bought by gold. A new ship in the port represents an opportunity to renew all sorts of ties.

There was also a dark secret behind the insistence of the matrons. The local king had passed away recently, and his eldest son, mature and wise in years, was to ascend the throne after a regulation period of mourning. We were looking forward to participating in the coronation of the new king, who would thus start a new reign with a renewed flourishing of ties with Bharatavarsha.

The coronation involved a dark ritual: the oldest virgin daughter of the king is sacrificed to the gods. That's why the matrons were desperate to tie their daughters in bonds of matrimony—to rescue them from being the sacrificial victim. Realising her sisters were too young to be sacrificed in her stead, Princess Jyeshthaarya had volunteered to be the sacrifice. That is where dear Tarkshya Arishtanemi took revenge on me for spooking him through his formative years!

The idiot fell in love with the princess, especially because of the nobility she showed in what she was willing to do for her sisters, and he advocated her rescue.

'Mahanubhav, for a father's future success, where is it proper that a daughter should sacrifice her life? Why only the daughter? Why not the son as well? Every father, wherever he is and to whatever culture he belongs, would give his own life for his children, male or female. Isn't the lesson of the Kurukshetra holocaust that we should follow dharma and revere life, having shed so much of our own blood with callous disregard?'

'Sir, *beti bachao*. O Vela Asvathhamma, you wanted to open a grand university in the original land of our religion in Kashmir valley to teach the Vedas to the children of Bharata, both male and female. How can you *beti padhao* when you can't beti bachao!' he exclaimed.

'The laws of this land and their customs are their own. We should not interfere in them,' advised Kutsa, earning a sharp look from Lady Ulupi.

'How would you feel if the foreigners came and started imposing their cultural values and mores on our customs and traditions?' defended Kutsa, eyeing Ulupi warily.

'The main goal of the mission is to escort Lady Ulupi as we search for Iravan,' reminded Kaundinya.

'Maybe it is a misinterpretation of their teachings, preserved orally over generations, that *kanyadaan* has become *balidaan*,' noted Ravi Bhanu, grandson to both Krishna and Yudhishthara.

Kaundinya looked towards me for guidance.

I knew from experience that Yudhishthara would advocate us interfering. He still carried the hurt of Mother Madri—in whose arms he first opened his eyes—leaving him so callously.

'*Yugadharma* is like a puddle of water. It needs to have a continuous stream of new ideas that will provide the vitalising lifeblood flowing like Ganga, purifying the soul and society. Stuck as a puddle holding germs and outdated notions, it poisons the same society,' I commented.

'*Aur humare daddu kaha karte hain*,[7] do your duty and do not worry about the results,' confirmed Ravi Bhanu. The decision was taken to approach the newly minted king of Lobpuri and his ministers to persuade them to forego the ritual.

We had not counted for the *Makhanchor* element in our crew. Before we left Hastinapur, Dwarka contributed her share to the voyages. They could afford to. Having sat out the Great War, the lazy bums, they had manpower to spare. We got the pick of the litter, literally—the grandsons of the Ashthabharya (wives of Krishna).

The youthful, boisterous, naughty, impish, powerful, and mischievous grandsons of Krishna fell in Svyambhavu's share. These rowdy, ragged rascals were the racked ache in my *rathh* (spine).

Bhai, jab asal aisa ho to fasal kaisi hogi![8]

We advocated the idea to the Lobpuri king-to-be and his ministers, but they were shouted down by the priestly class who saw our intervention as an affront and a threat to their power, as ecclesiastical classes are wont to do. It was a fruitless and very tense meeting. Stuck between a rock and a hard place, our deliberations were interrupted when we learnt that young Tarkshya—with an equally asinine group of youngsters, the grandsons of Kanhaiya (Krishna)—made the discussion moot. They kidnapped the princess and her friends, even younger sisters, as well as their mothers and nurses as well. They struck out as a group into the Malayadwipa countryside, while we hurriedly attended to the safety of our ship.

On the ship, the remaining grandsons of Krishna—yes, he has plenty to spare, not just one for each day of the week but also one for each nakshatra (twenty-seven)— brought us up to speed on Tarkshya's plan. The kidnappers fled across the land towards the east coast of the Malayadwipa Peninsula to Kaladan, famous for its temples. We fled on the ship as the bait to be chased by the angry Lobpurians.

Ulupi, in a great rage, upbraided us for the act of stealing the mothers and the nurses. Logically, it made sense for me that the anger of menfolk will be visited on the female members. Some of the girls were babies and would still be eligible for 'virgin sacrifice'. So the young men chose to steal all the ladies. Also, young men cannot nurse the children.

'You cannot steal calves without their cows, can you?' explained Kutsa carelessly, which merely served to increase the lady's wrath.

'Women are not cows!' she shouted.

'When Grandmother Gandhari, on the occasion of the *vidaai* of Laxmana after her marriage to Samba, asked Balarama, "How many more daughters of this family will you take?" Samba then responded, "Forget daughters! We have a tradition of taking mothers too!"'[9] clowned Svyambhavu.

'The act of the young men has broken the deadlock. It is easier to ask forgiveness than permission. We have learnt that from Arjuna when he barged into a chamber to get his weapons. That's how it all started, this expedition and this search for Iravan! That's how he met you!' I mollified Ulupi.

One great invention of our naval architect, Bhujya, now came to our aid.

Indian merchant ships have a reinforced, non-wooden chamber below the decks. In that chamber, we have a huge fire kiln that boils the water and pipes the steam from the water into the mizzenmast, providing artificial wind for the sails to unfurl and move the ship even if the breezes are becalmed. That innovation, protected for centuries by our merchants, came to our rescue as we moved the ship away from land and into the deep sea, tacking along the coast using our precious reserves of wood. It is always a risky move, starting fires on a wooden ship, but the good ship Kutsa was blessed as if by Indra himself. We managed to avoid the hundred-oared fast boats of Lobpuri amidst a series of close calls and tight encounters.

The main problem would be that this story of Tarkshya and kidnapping of women sailed ahead of us, blackening our name, as the incident was referred to as the 'Rape of the Lobpuri Women'. Across history, many innocent endeavours get blackened by such calumny.

Suvarnabhumi: Phenapa

Elaputra *uvacha*

After fighting monsoon winds and the vagaries of ocean currents, the good ship Kutsa eventually reached the shores of our destination. The Suvarnabhumi coastline shone like gold in the bright sunlight. The welcoming beaches and verdant vegetation were inviting us to partake of their bounty. The shining auric-coloured soil of the land was in beautiful contrast to the greenery that lay beyond and the blue sea that we sailed on. The top of the waves was covered with *phena* (the white foam on the blue) and, in places, dark red sea. The rivers that flowed into this sea from its coastline are mighty indeed, pushing red-brown soil out to sea, giving a distinctive wine-coloured tint to the waters.

We contacted the Phenapa *rishi*s who lived on the seacoast here. Their community subsisted on the mercies and clemencies of the waves and whatever the phena brought onto the coast in its wake. They were not desirous of shiny objects and the riches of the commercial world but were happy in their austere and simple lifestyle. They were still a crucial part of the worldwide commercial enterprise. The Gaoshan, who first mined Ashvaka mani and used it as a catalyst for their worldwide trade, relied on such welcoming communities like the Phenapas to support their Maritime Jade Route—places where the hardworking sailors may find victuals, take a rest, and repair their ships. Phenapas, for all their simplicity, were also great craftspersons. The sea brought in its flotsam of driftwood, and the Phenapas mastered the art of converting the garbage of the sea into beautiful treasures. They shared the tools of their trade with us, including the fantastic curved backwards axe that can be used to create barrels and canoes and was designed for that purpose. It cannot be used as a weapon of war, just as a creative tool, which was fascinating. We had been too long immersed in wars to focus on instruments of peace and prosperity.

We had nothing to give them in return. They needed little that the sea could not provide. They gave us their beautiful creations as gifts and helped repair the good ship Kutsa.

Then, Pairogava (the chef) started the dinner fire. He began putting in the spices Kanka Vyaghrapada had brought back from Gandhara and beyond. The aroma from his dishes spread across the beach and mesmerised the locals, especially that of the rice dish mixed with almonds and spices and dry fruits, a speciality of Pairogava.

Vayu Avatar[10] chose his Svyambhavu to assemble Saptashreshthi (traders) and treasures like lapis lazuli, herbs, and dry fruits. Like the expedition of our great forefather Manu, we, too, have *sadhus* (merchants).

Where the original voyage had *pothi*s of Vedas, we have *potha* full of *vaidurya* (lapis lazuli). They were there in *mevati* (service); we are here with *meva* (dry fruits).

So, now we had something to share with the Phenapas: dry fruits, herbs, and spices from lands they had not heard of. Almonds and, specifically, almond milk became a big hit with the locals.

We did not see many cows with the Phenapas, and there was a reason for that. They do not consume milk in the quantities that *Indu-vamsi*s do. Apparently, their bodies cannot stand too much milk in their diet, and so they replace it with coconut milk.

Almond milk, with its taste and texture, was a ready replacement and something novel to them and won their hearts. That broke the ice with the other merchants from Mayadwipa and Yavadwipa who had taken shelter with the Phenapas as well. They had kept away from us on account of Tarkshya's adventures. The cooking spices of our land, rather than the Lapis-Lazuli, like the *til Ka dana* (sesame seeds) and its oil (*Ilu*[11]) interested them. Another item that was of great interest to eastern merchants was from Gangahridya Magadha itself—foxnuts (*Nakula-ka-dana*), which I used in preparing Ayurveda medicines.

The Phenapas were also surprised by our mixed crew. We had an extraordinary number of women in our company to begin with, and we now had the products of Tarkshya's raid. The Phenapas wondered if we were related to inland naga tribes who also give full equality to women in peace and war.

This was a crucial indicator that we were on the right track for Iravan as per Svarna Nakula's directions.

Speaking of Svarna Nakula, he was an instant sensation with the natives. They have their own legends of mongoose guardian deities and called them M'ring Kongveal, the guardian of fishes. The golden mongoose enjoyed being the centre of attention and worship. I asked him whether he himself is the fount of these legends, having visited these parts before in centuries of travel seeking to acquire a completely golden skin. He told me to wait till early twilight and focus along the tree lines.

Lo and behold!

Next morning, getting up much earlier than the sun, I noticed little creatures the size of children, looking like mongoose, petting the animals we had brought. Mischievous laughter filled the air. I saw children from Phenapa villages and 'our' little girls playing with these creatures, the M'ring Kongveal.

'They are only seen by children and those with a pure heart, these guardians of animals, Elaputra,' Suvarna Nakula reassured me. Two of these elvish creatures became fast friends with Suvarna Nakula. He introduced them as Ngoy and Sothi, massacring their original names.

'They know the route upriver from River Gangeya (Bassaka Pitrshakti), which itself flows out from River Ma Ganga (Mekong). Upriver, there are naga tribes, and Iravan could be found near someplace they call Maton Parvata,' advised Hiranya Nakula.

'Mahendra Parvata! The majority of the crew and the builders of the ships are from the Mahendra Parvata region of Kalinga. Their ancestors must have come in the hoary past and settled here also,' observed Kaundinya. I had no idea how and when he had crept up and joined us, a habit his parents really hated when he was a child.

I suddenly realised the reason why he does not have any siblings!

'You don't seem surprised at the appearance of these creatures,' I said, my eyebrows raised.

'I have told you, back in Indraprastha, in my dreams, I had seen myself walking in strange lands, in unknown forests, accompanied by creatures like this and chasing the song notes coming from an ethereal voice unlike anything I have ever heard,' Svyambhavu said to me. Of course, he had. Many times, as a child, sleep had interrupted by the pains and the effects of strong medicines that coursed through his bloodstream as I nursed him.

'Hmm! Man should remain a bachelor only till the age of twenty-five. You crossed that mark many moons ago. If Yudhamanyu was here, he would have said that your dream meant that you would find your soulmate here,' I joked.

Yudhamanyu raised his hand, 'I am here!'

'How did you know your wife was right for you?' asked our dear leader in all seriousness.

'Well, son, as Yudhamanyu once said, "There is someone put right here on earth for you by Brahma. And one day thanks, to Vishnu, you will find her. And on that day may Shiva give you strength to say, 'Sorry Ma'am, I am married'."' I continued in a jocular vein, a little distracted that Sothi and Ngoy had looked directly at Yudhamanyu raising his hand.

Svyambhavu, Kutsa, Suvarna Nakula, friend-tasms, and the elvish creatures burst into laughter as if they all understood the joke.

I smiled wanly. Then tears suddenly filled my eyes. 'Sridatta, the fortune-favoured!'

'My brother Sridatta was born a few years after me. Months after his birth, it was clear he would not talk or be able to move himself. He would be a burden on the family, and we were a naga tribal family of dyers where everyone worked. Those not mixing chemicals would be mining them or preparing tree trunks to act as forges to cook unguents and mixtures. Sridatta was of no use to us.

'My mother did not even think of any other option. She told us that if they exposed him like people exposed such children, she would also join him. She named him Sridatta, fortune's gift. Vrishabhanu, our village chief, backed her, as did Yajnasena, our king.

'We tried all medicines and cures. Sridatta survived childhood. He stayed in bed and did not disturb anyone. He could not do much else. Whenever someone would look in on him amid their daily chores, his beautiful smile lit up the darkness around us all. He never complained and shared his eternal happiness with us all the time with the sweet sounds he sang.

'After the marriage of Princess Draupadi and the events around it with my role in it, our stock rose in local circles. The local naga chief sent her daughter as a potential bride to our home. We were introduced. It was also time for Sridatta's meal. I took the bowl and spoon and went with the potential bride to Sridatta's corner of the hut. I started feeding him, and his smiling eyes lit up at the prospect of an addition to our family.

'The girl looked most uncomfortable with him and soon excused herself and moved away to sit with my mother and the others. Her family wanted to start discussions on marriage after the rains.

'I had, meanwhile, met a gopi, Pramlocha, from Vrndavana. My mother, of course, got to know of this and invited her to our home. When the time came for Sridatta's meal, I took the bowl and spoon and started feeding him. Looking at that, Pramlocha requested me to pass the bowl and spoon to her, and she then helped me feed my brother, who was delighted with her. I looked up and saw the little pearls on my mother's cheeks. My brother's lifeline is no longer tied to hers.

'Who should I marry, the chieftain's daughter or the poor girl from the next village?

Sridatta guided us to the right answer. Though the only pearls I have given to Pramlocha are the same ones my mother wore that day on her cheeks.' I took a breath.

'What happened to Sridatta?' a tremulous query arose. A lot more had joined in the audience.

'One day, on the northern Digvijay, on the banks of the Salodya river, near the Fourth Ocean (Lake Baikal), an arrow meant for me veered away at the last moment and struck the chariot instead. I saw a vision of Sridatta standing with a being of light in the background. On our victorious return, a messenger from Pramlocha caught up with me at Bahalika (Balkh) and told me that Sridatta was no more. Just as Savitri had asked for the life of her husband, Sridatta had persuaded Lord Yama to take him instead.' I finished, choking off a cry.

'Some people have seen ladies with horses who come to take dead warriors away on the battlefield,' murmured Kutsa.

'Some people claim they see devas and rishis in the sky watching our conflicts,' claimed Svyambhavu.

'War has so much confusion and action. Senses are heightened, and adrenaline floods the body. Visions are what they are,' said Yudhamanyu.

'And I see my dead friends,' I said, still distracted that Sothi and Ngoy reacted to Yudhamanyu.

Battle of the River Pitrshakti (Bassaka)

Elaputra *uvacha*

Knowing we were very close to our destination had animated everybody. Our senses were fired up, and we were scarcely able to contain our excitement. The idea now was to sail upriver around 15 yojanas and join the river Ma Ganga. There we should be able to contact the naga tribes for information on Iravan.

Mother Ulupi was outwardly poised and calm, but her heart was in her mouth. Ladies now surrounded her as if to lend strength through company. Even the Krishna-Paksha were silent and repressed their excitement. The flip side of their wild adventure was that they had all caught the attention of certain ladies they had kidnapped and thus got hitched as well.

Whatever you sow, so shall you reap (Jo boyoge wohi tumhe katenge!)

I have seen this many times growing up in the village. The young, powerful bull calf is never quiet. He is always fidgety and wild, displaying his skill and power, difficult to control. Then one day, the yoke is placed on his shoulders. He is silent then, standing in the corner, chewing the cud and ruminating on his old wild days! He becomes totally docile.

The yokels and the yokes, the young men and their brides, were alert and scanning the riverbanks intently.

We would have left Tarkshya Arishtanemi on the bowsprit, but that would have been a dangerous position in case of an attack. So we stuck him up on the crow's nest. There he was free to sing songs of his travails and separation from his beloved to his heart's content.

We could see that we were being observed and followed on the banks on both sides. This was going to be challenging and tricky.

I was reminded of the Suchimukha vyuha, on the fourteenth day of the war, behind the Shakatavyuha and Chakravyuha defences. Suchimukha Vyuha (needle formation) consisted of two long sides of armoured rathas and elephants with a narrow passage in between for the *ratha*s (chariots) to race in, open to shots from all sides by warriors atop elephants and chariots on the sides.

We conquered Suchimukha that day. However, two Krishnas on one chariot, the inimitable Yudhamanyu and the patient Uttamaujas, were no longer here with us. None of my friends who won the Day of Great Oath were here.

Or were they? The ship was helmed by Arjuneya Kutsa and piloted by Nausarathi Karshni Ravi Bhanu. The portside responsibility was taken by Kaundinya, and starboard was under my watch. On top of the flag post, we had our own Tarkshya Arishtanemi, representing Bajrang Bali.

The faces will change, but the foundations remain the same. Come what may! *Sambhavami yuge yuge*. Individuals do matter, but legacy comes from the entire team.

I looked across at Kaundinya on the other side. It didn't seem right somehow, no pun intended. He looked as if he felt the same. We switched places. Yudhamanyu was always on the left, and Uttamaujas was on the right!

Ensconced in our safe places, superstitions aside, we were alert for an attack. The day faded away, and Ushas (evening) also left us at the usual time to go to the side of her lord, Nasatya.

We slowed the progress of the ship by lowering the sails. The lights were set up across the ship, but we took care not to be directly illuminated to prevent presenting targets to someone shooting arrows from the banks.

Savdhani hati to durghatna ghati! I will not let this happen again. That is why we heard the enemy approaching on all sides long before they were visible. Our watchfulness bore fruit.

We were able to make out multiple boats and canoes heading for our ship.

We hailed them first—in our language, in the local language advised by Ngoy and Sothi, and in the language of the Phenapas. We told them again and again that we come in peace and we do not want conflict.

The boats retreated. They did not answer, which is not a good sign. They knew that we were alert and we would not be taken by surprise. They had retreated to try again later.

We convened quickly at the foremast. Kutsa advised us to take down all the sails except the one on the jibboom at the front and the spanker at the back. That will prevent the attacks from both front and rear. He also advised several soldiers to climb onto the shrouds now that it was dark and sleep on the webbing. When the attack came, they could jump on the attackers from above.

Vel Asvathhamma looked uncertain and asked, 'Vaamchakra, am I the right person for this task? I did not even fight at Kurukshetra. My father forbade it. This could be the last night we experience on this earth. I feel very guilty dragging you and everyone away from your families to the ends of the earth.'

'Vatsa, you were raised in Indraprastha ruled by Drona, and so it was inevitable you became a disciple of Asvathhamma. Obviously, you impressed your guru. He awarded you his great spear. I know you feel the guilt of betraying your guru. Nothing can be farther from the truth.'

'You were born with birth defects and illnesses that beset few newborns. You would have been left to the mercy of the elements under any other king, even under Drona. It was your fortune that you were born in the *Dharmarajya* of Yudhishthira. He had ordained that all children, regardless of their birth issues, will get the best treatments the land can afford and be taken care of. Ayushmaan Bhava! Your father had rushed to my house the night you were born and confided his trepidations and doubts.'

'You never told me that!' exclaimed Kaundinya.

I could just about manage a pallid smile to reassure the child, now a man, with tears again filling my eyes. 'Sridatta, the fortune-favoured! He was the reason your father came to me the night you were born, a sick little child. We persevered with you and fought with Ayurveda rather than Dhanurveda, to save you. Queen Draupadi had brought the precepts of her father, Drupada, to the new Dharmarajya. Every child should have the chance to live and live as well as they can. That is why I followed them across the jungles and battlefields for that is dharma enough to sustain me and buy my loyalty for this life.

The Kauravas did not allow that. That is why your father forbade you to fight for the Kauravas for they have no claim on a child who would not have seen a second sunrise in their rule.

'I left my home and hearth the day Sakuni played Dyuta at Jayanta, travelled twelve years an exile, and spent fifteen months undercover. After the pyres and fires of Kurukshetra had died, I took my broken psyche on the Ashvamedha campaign. My family is waiting patiently. Prabhu went for fourteen years, but my exile from my loved ones is still ongoing.

'When one saves someone's life, one is responsible for them. Your father thanked me and said I have done more than anyone can do after your health got better. Little did he know that you will drag me to the ends of the earth. You are Sridatta's gift that keeps on giving. You are my *karmaphala*, child!'

The youth was overcome with joy, and his expression brightened. An instant smile was born on his lips, which percolated like cool salve to his constricted throat, devoid of any words now. The speechlessness pushed the life blood across valleys and streams to his eager awaiting heart, which started beating in tandem to the joy expressed on his face.

Vela Ashvatthama again repeated the gesture he gave to Bhima in Yatukarna Hall on getting the command for this expedition, the gesture Partha gave to Krishna at Jyotisar—the salutation of an enlightened disciple finding a way out of his trepidation.

'The older I grow, the more everything seems to me to lie in *purushartha*.' Yudhamanyu blessed the young man.

'Older!' exclaimed Uttamaujas.

'So, he IS to blame for your being here,' accepted Yudhamanyu.

'So, you do have some healing gifts?' asked Ravi.

'Well, I have this bald spot on my head. Can you fix it?' Srotas immediately inquired.

'I have this pain in my left knee, especially when it rains,' mentioned Praheti.

'I get frozen shoulder,' added Kutsa.

Ignoring my flippant friends, I turned the focus back. 'Vela Asvathhamma, the attack will come some time before dawn.'

'I do concur, Left Wheel. That will be the right time to attack. The alert watch would be tired from the night's exertions and thus slow to respond,' accepted our leader.

'We will take the first watch and wake you when the moon rises in the third *prahar*,' advised Ulupi. The ladies were prepared for battle, wearing armour with arrows knocked on the bows. I gently held the arm of one of the to-be warrioresses and got her to relax her pull on the bow.

'Amma, do not hold the bow and arrow ready in *Vira Asan*[12]. You cannot bear to hold it for too long and will end up releasing the arrow at one of us.'

Ulupi's idea was sound, and soon so were we—sound asleep—with Ulupi and the women protecting us like mother hens looking after their young.

I had just closed my eyes a moment before when I felt a hand on my arm waking me. The third prahar of the night was over, and there was little moonlight now, enough to attack but not enough for us to see from our high vantage point on the ship where the attack would come from.

Quickly, we drank curd-water and slaked our thirst. As we chewed almonds and dry fruits, energy suffused our bodies, warming and alerting us to the coming danger.

Astrologers would be proud of me. The attack came at the time I had prophesied. Again, many boats and canoes on the water could be heard. We were one ship, and we were going into battle against an army from a nation whose size we did not know. We understood that we would not be able to resist a full-scale attack. So the main idea was to break it up.

Our plan was to allow a certain number of boats to approach the ship and even climb aboard. Then, the archers on the deck would release arrows at the middle group of boats, stopping their progress. Then, when the middle group of boats fell back in panic, the archers, hanging on the shrouds and sitting on the sails, would shower arrows at the banks and the back group of boats. That way, we tried to control who could reach us and hoped that we just had to encounter around a third of the attacking force. We may still not survive the battle. A third of the unknown is still unknown.

The first grappling hooks and lines flew and landed on both sides of the ship, port and starboard. The enemy boarding attack was underway. One thing in our favour was that their canoes and boats were unsuitable for direct gunwale boarding. They were too low, so the attackers had to climb a long way up. That gave us time to cut the ropes and continue to control the sides.

As we suspected, the canoes were so many that they became immobile as the canoes closer to the ship were banging against the stern while the middle group could not move, for the boarding group prevented that. This impromptu floating traffic logjam helped us.

The archers let loose on the middle group, driving back the attackers on those boats.

Battle was now joined in earnest. Quite a few of the attackers had climbed up the ropes on both sides to engage our soldiers, and archers were forced to drop their bows and use their swords to defend themselves.

Lack of arrows from the shoreline and the canoes soon confirmed that the attackers may not risk hitting their attacking compatriots. We immediately set up lights on poop deck and strategic locations to blind the observers from the shore as well as the climbing attackers keeping away from the lighted portions ourselves.

The clash of steel reverberated and broke the silence of the night.

One of the decisions we had taken earlier now worried me. I had suggested that we use the Phenapa axe, which curved backwards, as the main weapon. It is useful as a defensive weapon but would not hurt or kill the enemy the same way a sword can.

Like I said, a third of the unknown is still unknown. We still had to persevere up this river into who knows how many battles. If we do not shed blood, we may convince the attackers of our good intentions. We are at the vela point of the expedition. My family was on the next ship behind us. If we do not create a safe path for them, they will be imperilled.

Not all wars are won by violence. We hoped to win that one by non-violence.

I focused on cutting the ropes or throwing the grapples back. Around me, soldiers fought tooth and nail against the attackers who astounded us with their close-quarter fighting skills. I thought, if we survive, we should ask them about their martial arts and learn from them.

If we survive!

I looked across the ship, and Svyambhavu was fighting like a demon incarnate. 'Well fought, Kaundinya Daitya,' I shouted encouragement.

He thrust at one of the attackers, heard his name, looked at me, and saluted me with his Phenapa axe.

One of the attackers rushed me, forcing me to drop the barrel axe. I was struck dumb. The attacker was a woman. Damnation and holy hells! The Kshatriya training kicked in, and I focused on disarming her rather than harming the opponent. Quite a few of them now appeared to be women.

Kaundinya disarmed one such warrior who was wearing the colours of the leader and then turned his back on her to focus on another warrior.

The attacker was nonplussed by his actions. He could have easily killed her but chose not to. Furthermore, he showed his back to her to tackle another opponent.

She reached for a knife, or another sword in the dark—I could not see. I rushed towards the child I had struggled so hard to save so many years back, my heart in my mouth.

Suddenly, light burst forth across the ship. Suvarna Nakula ran across the lights on the poop-deck. His golden frame reflected the lights a hundredfold, blinding attackers and defenders alike.

The attackers ceased their exertions, fascinated by the golden mongoose. Shouts of astonishment and surprise coloured the air. Sothi and Ngoyalso stepped into the light around the Suvarna Nakula, and consternation spread through the attackers.

They pulled back and huddled together towards the forecastle where, behind them, they saw Ulupi and the women emerge as well. Their leader, the lady warrior who was disarmed by Kaundinya, held up her hand, and the attackers started signalling on conches to their fellow soldiers below on the canoes.

Several of the attackers then started climbing down the ropes while others, with a charm that mirrored their warrior skills on display a few moments back, dived from the ship into the water below.

'Ahead you will find a ford in the river. Take the right channel, and disembark at the large Banyan tree. That is the plain of the Vyadha. Follow the path, and we will parlay for truce and terms there in the afternoon,' the lady leading the attackers said to Sothi. 'I am Mera, the princess of the nagas. I am awestruck by your tactics and valour. Your attempts at avoiding bloodshed belie the reports we have been hearing about your ship.'

She saluted Kaundinya and was the last to leave the ship, jumping like a *hamsa* (swan) hunting for Matsaya, from the top of the forecastle to the river below—with a grace that would put the original swan to shame—where a boat waited for her. I ran up to Kaundinya to see if he was alright.

He was standing as if stunned, mouth open, arms down, and hands unable to lift the blunt axe. Still looking at the retreating head of the warrior lady who had led the attack with skill and knowledge of close-quarter fighting and managed to keep control of the attackers in so little light. I was impressed by the way she was able to disengage at a moment's notice, all the hallmarks of a great tactical leader indeed.

Ignoring me and others, Svyambhavu kept looking at the back of her head as her canoe pulled away from the ship. He kept on looking and looking. Finally, after some time, she turned her head and looked back at Kaundinya and kept looking till she was out of sight.

'*Meri*!' murmured Kaundinya.

'Bhai, *meri nahi*, *mera,*' gibed Kutsa.

'Looks like Kaundinya the *brahmachari* has become the casualty of the battle. As for the bravery that impressed her, we are already known for our unsung valour,' I wisecracked.

'*Teri*,' smiled Ulupi as she kissed Kaundinya's forehead.

The battle tensions drained away in a moment, the aches and pains forgotten. We started looking after banal things like caring for the injured and the hurt.

We survived the battle. This was victory unintentional. Before we had gone on the long Ashvamedha campaign, Yudhishthara had advised us to minimise loss of life, even of the enemy. That training and experience, that non-violent violence, spread like balm across the wounded lands of Bharatavarsha, *Mahan* Bharata (great India).

It may just have created the future called *Brahattar* Bharatavarsha, the Greater India. The way forward!

> जीते हो किसी ने देश तो क्या, हमने तो दिलों को जीता है[13]
>
> Others may have won nations by their valour, but we win by winning the hearts instead.

And dry fruits in our biryani!

Kaundinya and Soma

Elaputra *uvacha*

Captain Jaimini T. Kutsa guided the good ship Kutsa and its *Kutsanauts* to the location advised by Princess Mera. A group of naga warriors waited for us at the landing place.

We lowered the corvus (the side of the ship that turns down to act as ramp) and came down and greeted them. It was an open indication from us that we did not mean them any harm and we did not expect any harm. The welcoming party advised us to follow them to their main village nearby where their leadership would parlay with us.

So here we were—Svyambhavu, Kutsa, yours truly, Lady Ulupi et al.—walking in a strange forest with different hues and colours than those back home. I remembered Kaundinya's dream of walking in strange lands, in unknown forests, accompanied by Sothi and Ngoy. What was missing was the beautiful music that Kaundinya had heard in his dreams.

Then we heard beautiful, unearthly musical notes wafting with the breeze and a soulful voice singing welcome songs in a beautiful tongue (which I would eventually learn in the next few years) and played on instruments we never knew existed, such as ploy, angkouch, sneng, and krapeau.

We all looked at each other in amazement at the fulfilment of the prophecy. Svyambhavu perked up on hearing the sound. He hurried along, taking quicker steps and forcing us to change pace to keep up with him. His dream had come true.

In the clearing waited the chief of the nagas and his daughter, Princess Mera.

The rest of the story is sung in court plays and stories that *Kathavachak*s[14] tell the populace on each Diwali, Choul Chnam Thmey (Maha Sakranti), and the water festival dedicated to *priya* Ma Ganga.

The story of the union of Kumbhayana Svyambhavu Kaundinya Kamboja and Princess Mera Soma, the Preah

Thong and Neang Neak of the people of Kambujya, Cambodia.

The story of the establishment of a new Indraprastha, the city Vyadhpura for the nation of Kambojadesha, populated by, among others, the kidnapped women of Lobpuri.

The story of first recorded Indian expedition to nation of Cambodia, the establishment of our 'Shared Roots'.

What I remember is not in the royal plays and official histories. After the greetings and exchanges of gifts and talks for trade and truce and tales of troubadours, we had a great celebration with our new friends and family. As the party dragged on into the evening, I espied the young Kaundinya and Lady Mera slipping away towards the banks of the river Ma Ganga.

Imagine the sounds of a quiet night, away from the rumbustious sounds of the main gathering, with the shadows of trees lengthening on the land and on the river. Lady Mera walked in step with Kaundinya, both quiet, both afraid to say the first words.

Was it ego, was it shyness, or a fear that the other might not reciprocate the stirrings in the heart? Was that the dread both were feeling, so clear on their transparent faces?

Lady Mera led Kaundinya to a beautiful longan tree laden with fruit looking like lychee.

'This is my favourite tree. I come here often to think and meditate,' said she.

'I like a Neem tree for doing meditation, because when I go to do *sandhya* in the morning, I can break a twig and brush my teeth at the same time,' answered the great lover, the descendent of Ruru.[15]

Satyaanash! Telling the lady in such a romantic setting that you move your bowels and brush your teeth at the same time!

Krishna! You can show the path, but they will still empty their bowels on the sides of that path!

I was afraid to disturb them. Otherwise I would have smacked my palm against my head. I thought I heard a similar sound nearby. The lovebirds were not aware of my presence. Mera looked quizzical following Kaundinya's comment, whose face turned beetroot red on realising his faux pas.

Lady Mera found a small boat tethered nearby and climbed in. Our hero followed suit. It looked like the lady had something very close to her heart to share with Kaundinya. She had stolen away for these few moments from her family to share that something. The import of that was very clear to me. I hoped that *Sandaas*-with-teeth-cleaning got the message also.

The river was calm. Ma Ganga was caressing that boat going nowhere in perfect harmony with the cadence of the waves breaking on the left bank near the spot where the river joins Pitrshakti. The silence of the static *Naukavihar* reigned. The evening was beautiful, the climate was cool and, on the banks, the moonlight fell like silver, reflecting the greenery of the surroundings.

They were alone in the world and only had eyes for one another. The shadows lengthened, waiting for them to speak. Ma Ganga's gentle waves were playing beautiful wedding music, crashing against the banks.

After a long time, our champion spoke.

'I have something to tell you,' he murmured. I held my breath in anticipation, praying to Narada and Pradyumna that he would not tell her about his upset stomach or sore shoulder.

'Today I need to tell you something,' he continued.

Silence reigned, and Lady Mera's eyes shone bright as she waited. Then she lowered her eyes bashfully, understanding his missive.

'Oh! Please do not do that,' he said.

Her sudden coyness unmanned our hero. He spoke without thinking. She looked up with a fierce stare. Asvathhamma's lifelong luck or lack of it with ladies is a curse inherited by the students, it seems.

'Your beautiful eyes are preventing me from saying what I want to say,' he entreated. Nice save, buddy!

'I hope I can control my beating heart for a few moments to say what I really mean!'

'I have something to tell you!' he finished.

'Maybe what you want to say is what my heart also wants to hear. Maybe we have a common destination for our dreams,' she finally spoke, her smile lighting up the darkness.

'No! The boat is not moving at all. Oh, dreams...,' replied the semantically challenged hero, biting his tongue. 'I am afraid to put it into words. I do not have the right words at all. I might lose these little moments I have found with you.' He again tried to recover.

'I have been waiting to hear these words from you since I saw you last night. My eyes were unable to keep away from the road, waiting for you to come today. Go ahead and say what you want to say. I hope I know what you want to say,' she replied.

'If your heart has already understood the language of my heart, what else is there to say? If not today, I will say it another day,' Kaundinya said, feeling relieved, and he let out a breath through his mouth.

'Speak! Say what you want to say,' she smiled with her eyes.

'Leave it. Now no need to say anymore!' finished our hero.

'Abe khacchar, bol bhi de,'[16] thundered the *Akashvani* (sound from sky).

Startled, the couple looked up at the longan tree where Tarkshya Arishtanemi sat perched comfortably. To my right, Kutsa stood up and hurled choice imprecations at the *Uparicharira18* eavesdropper. The moonlight caught me also, as Lady Mera covered her face with her hands and bashfully ran away from the scene.

Our hero stood open-mouthed looking at us, standing in that static boat.

The father of the nation!

Epilogue

A Quiet Afternoon in Vyadhpura

Elaputra *uvacha*

My great-grandson was in a tearing hurry to get on the road. He wanted to get to the market and try sweetmeats. My tired old bones do not lend themselves to quick movements now.

'Wait up, Kaundinya,' I shouted after him. Soma, my granddaughter, found my turban and adjusted it on my head. I picked up my walking cane. Kaundinya rushed back, picked up the other end and started dragging me to the road and the market.

I was proud of the solid cobblestones of the main road we had constructed, Ulupi Marg, heading eastwards across the rivers and forests to the city of Champa. In the distance, just out of sight, was the bridge over the river Bassak, right next to a beautiful temple built by Visvakarma himself. We had performed all the correct rituals to ensure that this temple would last forever as the beacon for the location of our original meeting and the extended family that has since sprung up.

My descendant pulled me eastwards towards the market town with the impatience of youth. Kavi Shanti stood outside his house and hailed me as we passed by, so familiar was he with my routine.

'Kaka, I have the new play ready for the theatre for our original journey! Adventures of Naunetra Jaimini T. Kutsa! Come see it on *Shanivar*,' he waved.

The Adventures of Captain Jaimini T. Kutsa, indeed! Well! I should not complain. His shana seeds and Jangida plant medicine has kept the deleterious effect of my madhumeha at bay. I would have been as blind as Dhrtrashtra but for them. All around us on the sides of the road, you can see the Jangida plants cared for by the vaidyas.

A father and son (it appeared) and a huge Brahma bull interrupted our journey.

'Lord Elaputra, we need your advice,' petitioned the duo.

I asked my great-grandson to stop, which he did—although not exactly, as his circumambulations around me and the duo continued.

'Why, what has happened?' I enquired.

'Sir, in the morning, my son and I decided to head out for the market with our bull. We want to sell it to buy a few donkeys. Everything was fine till we met an acquaintance who observed that, as we have the bull with us, we did not both need to walk. I put my son up on the bull and continued the journey. In the colony of the dyers, the women working on the dye pots and clotheslines looked at us and shouted at me that they had seen a monkey on a bull for the first time! My son was hurt by their comments, and he got off the bull and asked me to get on it, which I did. We proceeded further past the pig farmers cleaning and smoking their meat. One of them quipped, 'Look at the ungrateful father. He is sitting pretty on the bull, making the poor son walk all the way!' Hearing that, I asked my son to get on the bull as well, and we proceeded apace. After a few moments, we met another group of monks moving towards the temple we had worked on in honour of the first landing. The priests observed that we are torturing the poor bull by overloading it. I answered that we had always taken care of this bull, this Nandivishaal. We would never torture it. First, we had walked alongside the bull, but people advised us to use it as a conveyance. Second, when my son rode on it, the women made fun of him. Third, when I rode on it, I was a bad father, and the fourth time, when we both rode on it, we were guilty of cruelty. What are we going to do? How are we ever going to get to the market? I have half a mind to break all the legs of the bull,' complained the father.

The bull ceased its examination of the quality of the Kambujya roadworks and looked up, alarmed!

They were simple village folk, giving credence and respect to each opinion they heard.

'He Shankar, please do not do that. If you rely solely on the opinions of other people, then you will never get anywhere in life. I left with august company from faraway Bharatavarsha and have found a home here in Suvarnabhumi, in this city Vyadhpura that we built from scratch. Please give the bull to me. Kaundinya, run home quickly and get some *kashaparna* from your mother to pay for the bull. You, gentlemen, can then proceed to the market and buy donkeys to your heart's content,' I rendered judgement.

Later, much later, while returning home, I saw the father and his son with a few donkeys standing by the side of the road.

They waved me over.

'Elaputra, it's an old problem with you. You can't say no to anyone who asks for help,' Yudhamanyu quipped.

End of the story!

Glossary

Aatma: Soul
Apsara: Angel/demi-goddess
Ayushamaan Bhava: May you live a long and healthy life
Balidaan: Sacrifice
Beti bachao: Save the daughter
Beti padhao: Educate the daughter
Bhakti: Faith and devotion towards God
Brahmachari: Bachelor
Brahmahutanirmoksha: Xenia violation fine or guest hospitality debt. Jatasura, father of Alambusha, violated it, thus suspending his rebirth cycle
Chakravyuha: A circular formation with several defence points at each location leaving no weakness for the defending side
Dashi: Arabs
Day of the Great Oath: The 14th day of War when Arjuna took the oath. For details, read *Unsung Valour: Forgotten Warriors of Kurukshetra* by Indica.
Digvijay Rajasuya War expeditions. North under Arjun, East under Bhima, South under Sahadeva and West under Nakula

Fulin: Byzantine

Gurudeva: teacher, here used sarcastically among friends for a boring raconteur

Indu-vamsis: Indians. One of the sources of name India comes from ruled by Indu or Moon dynasty for the longest time

Jangida: Jangida is a potent healing herb used to treat diabetes in *Atharva Veda*. Modern medicine has not completely identified it yet

Kadigai tavalam: City market

Kailasa: Lord Shiva and Goddess Uma (Parvati)'s abode

Karmaphala: Fruits of karma in the same life; means of Moksha

Kasha parna: Copper coins

Khichdi: Rice dish with pulses

Krishna-Paksha: Children of Krishna

Maa: Mother

Madhumeha: Diabetes.

Mahanubhav: Respected leader

Maharathi: Higher Chariot Officer (one who can lead a chariot battalion into battle)

Makhanchor: The name Krishna earned as mischievous child

Makara: Animal with body of crocodile, head of antelope and is the steed for Varuna the ocean god

Mamaji: Maternal uncle

Meri: Mine

Nausarathi: A naval pilot on a ship next to naunetra (captain) responsible for the ship. In those days, ships mostly kept to coastline, so it was a nausarathi who was responsible for making sure the shallows don't wreck the ship like charioteer or sarathi takes care of the chariot

Om Namah Shivaya: Salutations to Lord Shiva (a common prayer in Hinduism)

Pairogava: A chef in the Pandava household, whose persona Bhima used in Agyatvasa

Pattanam: Port cities

Phenapa rishis: A community of fisherman on the coast was called Phenapa Rishis, implying that the original Indian settler was a rishi

Ploy, angkouch, sneng, and krapeau: Cambodian musical instruments. Ploy is a wind instrument with gourd body and several bamboo tubes, angkouch can be described as a jaw harp, sneng is an aerophone made of water buffalo horn, krapeau is a three-stringed boxed zither

Potha: Trunks bound in cloth

Pothi: Books of shastras bound in cloth

Prahar: A quarter of the night or day (3 hours length)

Prahok: A Cambodian fermented fish paste used in cooking a variety of dishes to add extra flavour

Purushartha: Aims to better life

Sadgati: Salvation

Sambhavami yuge yuge: In every age we find people rising to the occasion

Sandhya: A polite term for toilet

Satyanaash: Exclamation for someone ruining the occasion

Savdhani hati to durghatna ghati: Lack of focus leads to disaster

Shakata Vyuha: A cart formation

Shana: Flax seeds used in Ayurveda

Shanivar: Saturday

Sinistral: The left hand of Arjuna

Suchimukha: A needle formation

Tapasya: Rigorous spiritual practice that requires self-discipline performed to seek self-realisation

Teri: Yours

Veerasan: A yoga pose to hold bow and arrow ready, invented by the prince of Ayodhaya Lakshaman

Vela: Spear

Velapuram: Harbour

Vidaai: A bride's farewell

Yawadwipa: Modern-day Java

Yugadharma: The tradition that implies that in Hinduism nothing is set in stone

Yuvaraj: An heir to the king. In the context of Bhima, Lord Protector

Notes

Curator's Note

1 https://bharatkambuja.org/no-55-prah-ko-inscription-of-indravarman/

Chapter 1: Strei

1 Woman
2 Krama is a versatile Cambodian garment used as a scarf or bandanna.
3 Dhovati or Dhoti is a long garment wrapped around the waist, passed between the legs, and tugged into the waistline. It is worn by Hindu men.
4 Teacher
5 https://www.khmertimeskh.com/501410374/malraux-arrest-centenary-marked/
https://www.khmertimeskh.com/50758913/andre-malraux-big-hero-or-little-thief/
https://thediplomat.com/2015/06/thief-or-anti-colonial-agitator-who-is-andre-malraux/
https://angkordatabase.asia/publications/about-andr%C3%A9-malrauxs-infamous-expedition-to-banteay-srei
https://thesiamsociety.org/activity/romance-crime-and-political-awakening-uncovering-hidden-narratives-a-century-after-andre-malraux-plundered-banteay-srei/

6 https://www.khmertimeskh.com/50758913/andre-malraux-big-hero-or-little-thief/
https://thediplomat.com/2015/06/thief-or-anti-colonial-agitator-who-is-andre-malraux/
https://angkordatabase.asia/publications/about-andr%C3%A9-malrauxs-infamous-expedition-to-banteay-srei
https://www.khmertimeskh.com/501410374/malraux-arrest-centenary-marked/

Chapter 2: A Siem Reap Saunter

1 The Bodhi tree is the sacred fig tree seated under which the Buddha attained enlightenment.
2 A statue of a Hindu deity that has been sacralised via rituals and prayers
3 A sacred dot adorning the Hindu forehead to denote the circle of life and divinity within.
4 The churning of the ocean of milk by Vasuki, the celestial snake, with the devatas on one side and asuras on the other.
5 A sacred bath or pouring of water over the deities
6 A thousand Shiva lingas or representations of Shiva
7 Temporary heaven in Hindu cosmology
8 Dharmaraja is the lord of dharma, embodied as Yamaraja, the lord of death. It is also another name for Yudhishthira in the Mahabharata.
9 A morning or evening snack.
10 Hindi phrase that means a petty squabble

Chapter 3: Mekong to Kaveri

1 Banteay Srei today is a very famous tourist spot of archaeological importance near Angkor. It was built as the temple of Tribhuvaneswara in 967 CE by Yajnavaraha, who was a priest and a doctor at the court of Rajendravarman II (944–968 CE) and the guru of Jayavarman V (968–1001 CE), along with his younger brother Visnukumara. The temple houses many inscriptions in Sanskrit and Khmer, and one of them, IC. 147, dated 968 CE records this event. The

inscription, beginning with an invocation to Shiva and Sakti, followed by a eulogy of Jayavarman V, refers to the installation. One of the other inscriptions records Jahnavi's (Yajnavaraha's sister's) installation of a linga in the southern tower. Pratipa is a fictional son of Jahnavi who takes us along a journey from Mekong to Kaveri.

As in the case of most Hindu temples, a great variety of scenes and persons from the Ramayaṇa, the Mahabharata, and the Puranas are depicted in the bas-reliefs at Banteay Srei. A sculpture of particular interest is that of Karaikkalammaiyar, one of the sixty-three Nayanmars. Highly revered in Tamiḻ traditions but nearly unknown in the rest of the country (even in neighbouring states like Andhra Pradesh), we find her depiction in this far-off land. This is the oldest known depiction of Karaikkalammaiyar in stone. Sculptures of her can also be found in later temples of the Khmer Empire in other parts of Cambodia and northeastern Thailand. How and when Karaikkalammaiyar became known to the people of Kamboja is not known, but it indicates the strong religious and cultural influence of the Choḻas.

2 The flourishing trade network of India and the Southeast Asian islands was a part of what today many scholars call the maritime silk road—from China, through the Malacca Strait and Indonesian water, and then towards western India. Srivijaya emerged as a thalassocratic empire and was a significant transitory trading destination for merchants and a well-known maritime kingdom among the Chinese, Persian, Arabian, and Indian kingdoms. Towards the 10th and 11th centuries, Srivijaya sought to establish hegemony over the Strait of Malacca, which was the gate to China for the east. According to the *Zhufan Zhi* (a Chinese chronicle), Srivijayans forced foreign ships to stop at their ports, and failure to do so resulted in being raided and attacked by the Srivijayan navy and pirates.

This period also saw the evolution of trade with commercial institutions and the emergence of powerful and international merchant guilds from South India. Ainurruvar, also known as the Five Hundred Lords of Ayyavole, was among the most prominent guilds. Their activities were spread throughout the Indian peninsula and Southeast Asia. They were prosperous, performed charity, supported *pandita*s, and built temples. They had their own flag, armies to escort their caravans and merchant ships, and colonies in foreign countries. Their eulogies claim they were born to wander in many countries by land and water routes, penetrating the regions of the six continents to fill up the emperor's treasury!

3 The science of dialectics, logic and reasoning, and art of debate that analyzes the nature and source of knowledge and its validity.

4 The king's highway made by Raja Raja Chola.

5 https://ignca.gov.in/Asi_data/87893.pdf

Chapter 4: The Magic of the Dragons

1 The gateway in the body that connects individual energy with cosmic energy.

2 Geometric design that centres universal energy.

Chapter 7: The Search for Iravan

1 Going one place, ending up at another

2 Dimension of nagas

3 Narrators of the Mahabharata

4 Xenia violation fine, or guest-hospitality debt. Jatasura, father of Alambusha, violated it, thus suspending his rebirth cycle.

5 Kumbhayana Kaundinya Kamboja

6 In the company of ghosts, the stings of mosquitos are like a mother's caresses.

7 As my grandpa always says

8 The seed determines the crop

9 The kidnapping of Mayadevi from Sambara by the kidnapped prince Pradyumna!

10 Bhimasena, the second Pandava

11 Ilu, the oil from sesame seeds, is source for the word *Oil.*

12 Yoga pose to hold bow and arrow ready

13 Kavi Pradip
14 Professional storytellers
15 The great lover, ancestor to Kaundinya and son of the nymph Ghrtachi
16 Idiot, speak now!
17 One at a height

About the Curator and Contributors

Ratul Chakraborty

Ratul is one of the most accomplished video-game makers in India. After more than a decade of procrastination and other assorted excuses, he finally gathered enough courage to take a break from the corporate world in late 2019 and complete writing his highly regarded collection of short stories, *Sutradhar*. He is fascinated by history and people, the two lenses that form the foundation of his creative perspective. He loves to travel across India doing street portraiture photography and is also a lifelong follower of Juventus FC. Ratul is currently juggling his corporate leadership responsibilities along with other creative pursuits interspersed with periods of high-quality laziness. He is based out of Kolkata, where he lives with his parents, his wife, Surela, and three daughters—a Labrador, Gogo, and two rescued Indies, Truffles and Mowgli.

Srivalli Rekha

An MBA graduate, Srivalli also has an MA in English literature. Nature is her greatest inspiration. Books and music are her favourite companions. Srivalli calls herself a proud pagan and believes in the beauty of nature worship. She loves to learn the secrets of the universe the Indic way. She is a budding tarot reader and is fascinated by the intricacies of astrology. A freelance content writer during the day, she devours books at night and loves to review them on her blog and Goodreads.

Srivalli is a co-founder and managing partner of The Hive Publishers, an indie publishing collective. Her works have been a part of several Indian and international anthologies (e-books and paperback publications). *Violets in Hand*, *The House of Justice*, and *Pebbles in the Grass* are her self-published e-books.

Kavita Krishna Meegama

Kavita is a student of Pujya Swami Dayananda Saraswati ji of Arsha Vidya Gurukulam, and she is continuing her Vedanta studies with the same paramparaa. She enjoys writing on Indic language, culture, and thought. Kavita has degrees in philosophy and engineering, and a postgraduate degree in international education, along with graduate certificates in public policy and filmmaking. She has contributed to a few anthologies for IndicA (*Aryaa*, *Flight of Deities*, etc.) and is currently the director of university relations at Brhat.in.

Srinidhi Balasubramanian

Srinidhi is a student of engineering and design at IIITDM, Kancheepuram. Beyond her academic pursuits and a passion for Indology, she immerses herself in the captivating tapestry of Indian history, culture, and traditions. A lifelong devotee of Carnatic music, Indian history, and Sanskrit, she actively volunteers with SPIC MACAY (Society for the Promotion of Indian Classical Music and Culture amongst Youth), sharing her love for the arts and heritage.

Eager to explore niche interdisciplinary fields, Srinidhi currently delves into histoinformatics and computational archaeology. Her project on conservation and accessibility of Indian epigraphical heritage using artificial intelligence (AI) has received recognition on the national platform.

At the core of Srinidhi's beliefs is a harmonious pursuit of knowledge and artistic expression, aiming to serve society and safeguard our civilisation's legacy.

Dr Swetha Prakash

Swetha holds a doctorial fellowship in positive psychology and storytelling from the National School of Leadership, Pune. She has completed her MA in writing from the University of Warwick. She has been a recipient of the Charles Wallace India Trust Award for studying creative writing at the University of Edinburgh's Scottish Union's International Summer School. She has received the Times and Scottish Book

Trust Jura New Writer Award. She is the author of Indic books such as *Mahishasur Mardini: Eyes of Durga*, *Indian Storytelling Traditions*, and *Indian Cultural Traditions and Stories from the Jaina Culture*. She has also authored the children's books *Padma Goes to Space* and *Butterfish and Gheefish* and has written nonsense stories such as 'How the Eland Twisted Its Horns', 'Pi Chart', 'Monster Book of Limericks', 'Why Birds Live in the Sky', and 'Winkle Twinkle'. Her book *Padma Goes to Space* has often been listed in the media as one of the best Indian children's books. She is the founder of Touchstone Alice, a literary nonsense initiative for children. She hopes to initiate more such initiatives for children and is currently working on School Story Curriculum India.

Vaishali S.

Vaishali loves reading and discussing the Valmiki Ramayana and various other popular versions of the Ramayana. She inherited her love for the Ramayana from members of her family. Vaishali's grandmother, a devout Lord Rama bhakt, was the first person to narrate to her the story of the Ramayana at a tender age. Vaishali's father has been religiously reading the Sundara Kanda every day for the past twenty-seven years.

Vaishali is an MBA graduate and an aspiring company secretary. She has completed a course on elements of literature and creative communication through the National Programme on Technology Enhanced Learning (NPTEL) initiated by the Indian Institute of Technology,

Kharagpur. She holds a certificate on the Mahabharata and the Ramayana from the Oxford Centre for Hindu Studies. She also holds a certificate on Ramayana Sopanam conducted by Amrita School of Spiritual and Cultural Studies, Amrita Vishwa Vidyapeetham. She is currently pursuing a course, Valmiki Ramayana with the Fragrance of Kamban and Kalidasan, conducted by Chinmaya International Foundation.

Vaishali picked the habit of reading from her mother. Her husband and mother are her best book buddies. She loves to read and review various books on her blog and Goodreads. Other than reading, her hobbies include writing, acting, photography, public speaking, travelling, cooking, and gardening. Vaishali is also a good Carnatic singer.

Sunil Kumar

Sunil has a versatile and multifaceted personality. He has a postgraduate degree from the University of Westminster, London. In creative terms, his achievements span multiple fields. His book *Existential Angst* (1999), an anthology of poetry, is catalogued in the British Council Sussex and the US South Asian Literature List and is available on Amazon. The noted poet Nissim Ezekiel made him a member of PEN (India chapter). He has also written *Surreal City* (2012), a novel spanning multiple generations that takes readers on a journey through time and space.

Sunil has written research papers for the world's leading body in engineering and computer science the IEEE USA. He has also presented a paper recently in the Indica Vaishnavism Conference at Srirangam on the Gaudiya tradition. His startup, Aglaia Interactive, has been the recipient of several prestigious awards, including the Microsoft Bizspark Award for Technology, AC Nielsen Top 10, and World Marketing Congress Awards for Digital Marketing.

Liberal agnosticism and curiosity are Sunil's mantra in life. He feels a deep connection to his cultural roots, and his true passion lies in the study of the limitless ocean of Indic traditions.

Pranshu B. Saxena

Pranshu is a computer scientist. He fell into the habit of recording life around him in his frayed notebooks that acted as fuel for his imagination, which sometimes leak onto the keyboard.

His love for world history and the Mahabharata found an auspicious marriage in this anthology on the shared roots of the stem India and the flower Indosphere through the happy bumblebee. Some of the other black bees are available in Puranas and the Vedas. This is his fourth anthology with Gurumata IndicA.